2000 MOST COMMON KOREAN WORDS IN CONTEXT

Get Fluent & Increase Your Korean
Vocabulary with 2000 Korean Phrases

Korean Language Lessons

www.LingoMastery.com

Free Book Reveals The 6 Step Blueprint That Took Students **From Language Learners To Fluent In 3 Months**

- **6 Unbelievable Hacks** that will accelerate your learning curve
- **Mind Training:** why memorizing vocabulary is easy
- **One Hack To Rule Them All:** This secret nugget will blow you away...

Head over to **LingoMastery.com/hacks**
and claim your free book now!

INTRODUCTION

These days, many people all over the world are fascinated by the Korean culture, with global interest growing in Korean cultural exports such as K-dramas, K-pop music, TV shows and K-beauty. Furthermore, smartphones and home appliances made in South Korea have spread across the globe, reaching more audiences and helping technological markets evolve. Therefore, with this development of Korean cultural influence, the number of people visiting South Korea is increasing, and many college students spend time in South Korea for studying and travel.

Most people who are interested in South Korea try to study the Korean language and become very surprised when they discover that Hangul (or Hangeul), the alphabet of the Korean language, is very logical and easy to learn because it is an alphabet based on sound. Hangul is a phonetic alphabet, and it has the advantage of allowing you to write in your native language in a Romanized fashion. Those who have studied Hangul before may have already experienced this charm.

If you study Hangul and the Korean language in general, you will not just enjoy studying, but also understand more about K-pop, K-drama, and K-beauty, among other incredible aspects of the Korean culture. Besides, you will be able to enjoy various types of content even more, engage in fun conversations in many online communities, and quickly increase your learning in the latest and advanced technologies. If you learn Korean, there will be many benefits to your life.

If you've picked this book up, you've already made good progress in learning the Korean language. This book can give you an incredible tool in learning the Korean language: vocabulary. Now you've just got to learn how to use it.

What this book is about and how to use it:

There are shortcuts to learning every language, but learning the vocabulary is a surefire way of speeding up your learning of a new tongue. Just look at these three amazing stats found in a study done in 1964:

1. *Learning the first thousand (1000) most frequently used words of a language will allow you to understand 76.0% of all non-fiction writing, 79.6% of all fiction writing, and an astounding 87.8% of all oral speech.*
2. *Learning the top two thousand (2000) most frequently used words will get you to 84% for non-fiction, 86.1% for fiction, and 92.7% for oral speech.*
3. *Learning the top three thousand (3000) most frequently used words will get you to 88.2% for non-fiction, 89.6% for fiction, and 94.0% for oral speech.*

Just look at those statistics and imagine what you could do with this book once you've thoroughly read and practiced what it contains? We're providing you with two thousand of the most frequently used words — equivalent to an understanding of 92.7% of oral speech!

We achieve this not only by giving you a long list of words; there must be context to allow the words to sink in, and we provide that. Each of the terms will be listed with its revised romanization (how to pronounce), translation in English, and example sentence with translation, allowing you to study the use of each word in a common, accessible manner. We have ordered the terms in their largest number of occurrences in mass media, allowing you to begin with the simplest and most regularly used words first before moving on to the less used ones.

So now, do you need anything else while reading this book? Yes, you may, as always. There are hundreds of thousands of more words out there, but these will certainly give you a head-start on learning the language and getting closer to mastering it.

Recommendations for readers of *2000 Most Common Words in Korean*:

Although we'd love to begin right away with helping you learn the vocabulary we've provided in this book, we've got a few tips and recommendations for getting the most out of this book:

1. Repetition: The more times you see, hear, say, write a word, the more likely you are to remember it.
2. Concentration: Staying alert when you memorize is vitally important.
3. Application: A word that you find a chance to use in a conversation is more likely to stay with you than the ones you only learn from a book.
4. Movement: Physical movement helps you remember words better. Sway your arms, rock your head, pace the room, do whatever you need to when you attempt to memorize.
5. Associations: Associate a word with something memorable, funny, shocking, etc. It may help to associate the Korean word with some word in your language that the Korean word sounds like – the more absurd, the better.

IMPORTANT NOTE:

Korean has a completely different word order compared to English. For example, the sentence "I have a phone (저는 휴대폰를 가지고 있습니다)" is used in English in the order of subject, verb, and object, but in Korean it is in the order of subject, object, and verb. Those who are familiar with the word order of English should try to get used to the order in which words are placed when learning Korean.

Also, in the case of English, subjects and object are usually written or spoken without omission. For example, when Koreans say, "I like your song (저는 당신의 노래가 좋아요)." in Korean, they usually speak without the subject ("당신의 노래가 좋아요."). Furthermore, when Koreans say, "I like it" (Here, "it" is a placeholder), both subject and object are not used in many cases ("좋아요.").

Another point to keep in mind: in Korean, nouns and pronouns are generally followed by a postposition. The differences of the postposition determine whether a noun or pronoun is the subject or the object. But, the form of the postposition depends on the noun's pronunciation and the context of the entire sentence. For example, when Koreans say, "Mary likes John (메리는 존을 좋아해요)." in Korean, there are two postpositions after "메리 (Mary)", and "존 (John)". The postposition for 메리 is "는" (neun) and the postposition for 존 is "을" (eul). The two postpositions allow us to know that Mary is the subject and John is the object in the given sentence.

You'll find that a lot of example sentences use different forms, or conjugations, of a word. Word conjugation depends on tense, tone, mood, social relation, and other factors. All verbs and adjectives consist of 2 parts: a word stem and a word ending. The word stem remains consistent and the word ending gets conjugated. Here are

4

examples.

먹다/ eat
먹(stem) + 다(word ending)
: The dictionary form of the verb

먹을 거예요 / I'm going to eat
먹 + ㄹ거예요
: Future tense in informal honorific

먹을 수 있어요/ I can eat it
먹 + ㄹ 수 있어요.
: Modal verb 'can' in informal honorific

Also, this book includes not only formal or honorific ways but also casual impolite ways which is called 'banmal(반말)*'. Make sure not to use them to strangers or people who are older than you unless they allow you to. *Banmal is casually impolite and it's used between friends (the same age with you), or people who are younger than you while Jondaemal(존댓말) is a formal way of speaking. Let's see examples of Banmal and Jondaemal below:

Honorific speech (Jondaemal): 안녕**하세요**. 저는 철수**입니다**.
Casual speech (Banmal) : 안녕? 나는 철수야.

Lastly, it is important to note that since Korean is written phonetically, we highly recommend learning to pronounce the Korean characters directly like learning ABC in English. Below are the basics of how a Korean character is put together:

Let take the Korean word for *country*, "나라" (pronounced as nara). It is really ㄴ(=n), ㅏ(=a), ㄹ(=l), ㅏ(=a) bonded to form two characters, 나 & 라. Western languages are not bonded to form a syllabic character like Korean. Through this bonding, we know it is a two-syllable word because each character always equals one syllable.

In Korean, each character is a combination of (1) vowel, (2) consonant & vowel, or (3) consonant & vowel & consonant. An example of (1) is "A" which is written as 아. (Since it is really a *zero* consonant, we add "o" before the vowel.) An example of (2) is "na" which is written as "나". An example of (3) is "Nam", which is written as "남". There is the consonant of ㅁ (m") below 나.

These peculiarities of Korean language can be daunting, especially for the beginners. Learning a new language is like venturing into a new world and it comes with challenges. With diligent effort and willingness to learn, you should soon find yourself mastering the Korean language. We hope, through learning the Korean language, that you will enrich your understanding of the world and broaden your worldview. Enjoy your journey!

Parts of Speech

Here is a short introduction on the parts of speech used for each word on this list. Parts of speech means what *kind* of word it is, whether it is a verb or noun or adjective etc.

[n] – noun; names of things or objects (*i.e.* book, Korea)
[num.] – number (*i.e.* one, twenty)
[pron.] – pronoun; words that refer to a noun (*i.e.* this, it)
[v] – verb; words that express actions (*i.e.* eat, read)
[assistant v.] – assistant verb; verbs that are added to other verbs (*i.e.* do, can)
[a.] – adjective; words that describe nouns (*i.e.* quiet, beautiful)
[adv.] – adverb; words that describe verbs (*i.e.* quickly, slowly)
[determiner] – a word that is used before a noun to show which particular example of the noun you are referring to (*i.e.* my, this)
[interjection] – a word for a sudden expression of emotion (*i.e.* ah, hey)

Knowing the parts of speech can be useful when you are learning new words because you can take an existing sentence like the ones we provided here, and replace a single word to get an entirely new sentence with minimal effort! Here is an example of how we do it:

그는 지금 **집**에 있다.

He is at **home** now.

Now we replace **그 (he)** with 그녀(she) and **집(home)** with 회의(meeting), we get a brand-new expression.

그녀는 지금 **회의 중**에 있다.

She is at **meeting** now.

This process of mixing and matching can increase your language skills. So, once you master 2000 words and sample expressions, do not forget to experiment by replacing words in the sentence with another word you learned.

THE 2000 MOST COMMON WORDS IN KOREAN

Hello again, reader. As we previously stated in the Introduction, the words are arranged by their frequency of use in common media, such as films, series, and books. Feel free to rearrange them during your practice to make things interesting.

You will be provided with a **word, its revised romanization** (how to pronounce), **the meaning of the word and a translation** of the term given. It's as easy as that.

Let's begin:

1- 것**/geot** [n.] *a thing, an object*

이**것**은 내 휴대폰이야.
This **thing** is my mobile phone.

2- 하다**/hada** [v.] *to do, to make*

제가 **하는** 일은 학생들을 가르치는 일 입니다.
What I **do** is teaching students.

3- 있다**/itda** [v.] *to be (in a place), exist, have*

그는 지금 집에 **있다**.
He **is** at home now.

4- 있다**/itda** [assistant v.] *to be (in a state)*

그녀는 버스를 기다리며 그곳에 서 **있다**.
She **is** standing there, waiting for the bus.

5- 되다/doeda [v.] *to become*

그는 그가 원했던 대로 교사가 **되었다**.
He **became** a teacher as he wanted.

6- 수/su [n.] *way, means, possibility*

그 일이 그렇게 될 **수**는 없습니다.
There is no **possibility** that the work would be done like that.

7- 같다/gatda [a.] *(to be) the same, (to be) like or similar, (to be) probably so*

오늘의 날씨는 어제와 **같다**.
The weather today is the **same as** yesterday.

8- 나/na [n.] **I**

나는 어제 여기에 도착했어.
I arrived here yesterday.

9- 그/geu [pron.] *he*

그가 저를 도와줬던 사람이에요.
He is the one who helped me.

10- 아니다/anida [a.] *not be*

이것은 제가 주문했던 것이 **아니에요**.
This **is not** what I ordered.

11- 보다/boda [v.] *to see, look at, watch, read*

나는 어제 그 영화를 **봤다**.
I **watched** the movie yesterday.

12- 등/deung [n.] *back*

그는 바로 내 **등** 뒤에 서 있었다.
He stood right behind my **back**.

13- 때/ttae [n.] *time, an occasion, the time when*

내가 어렸을 **때** 이 마을로 이사를 왔다.
When I was young, I moved to this town.

14- 거/geo [n.] *thing, that which, what*

그 일은 그녀가 한 **거**예요.
That is **what** she did.

15- 가다/gada [v.] *to go*

(넌) 지난 주말에 어디에 **갔었니**?
Where did you **go** last weekend?

16- 주다/juda [v.] *to give*

저 책 좀 저에게 **줄래요**?
Would you **give** that book to me, please?

17- 대하다/daehada [v.] *to respond to*

그가 나를 **대하는** 태도가 마음에 들지 않는다.
I do not like his **responding** attitude towards me.

18- 년/nyeon [n.] *year*

(당신은) 몇 **년**도에 한국에 왔어요?
What **year** did you come to Korea?

19- 한/han [n.] *one, (before a numeral) about, around*

너는 여기에 올 때 딱 **한** 개만 가지고 오면 돼.
You can bring just **one** when you come.

20- 말/mal [n.] *word, speech*

그의 말을 잘 들어 봐.
Please, listen to his **word**.

21- 일/il [n.] *work, job, business, matter*

그녀가 하고 있는 **일**은 무엇이죠?
What is her **job**?

22- 이/i [pron.] *this*

이 책이 당신에게 많은 도움이 될 것입니다.
This book will be helpful for you.

23- 때문에/ttaemune [n.] *Because of, Because*

그 소음 **때문에** 잠을 잘 수가 없었다.
I could not sleep **because of** the noise.

24- 말하다/malhada [v.] *to speak, to talk, to say*

그가 **말하기** 전에 빨리 여기를 떠나자.
Let's leave here before he **speaks**.

25- 위하다/wihada [v.] *to help or benefit, to do for the sake of, for the purpose of*

군인들은 자신들의 나라를 **위해** 그 일을 한다.
The soldiers do it **for (the sake of)** their country.

26- 그러나/geureona [adv.] *but, however*

그는 7시까지 여기에 오기로 약속을 했다. **그러나** 그는 오지 않았다.
He promised to come here by seven, **but** he didn't.

27- 오다/oda [v.] *to come*

너는 내일 몇 시에 **올** 수 있어?
What time can you **come** tomorrow?

28- 알다/alda [v.] *to know, understand*

오늘 제 생일이라는 것을 그들도 **아나요**?
Do they also **know** that today is my birthday?

29- 씨/ssi [n.] *sir or madam, Mr. or Ms.*

민호 **씨**는 어디 출신이에요?
Mr. Minho, where are you from?

30- 그렇다/geureota [a.] *to be correct, to be really so*

선생님이 너 오늘 학교에 안 왔다고 하셨는데 정말 **그랬니**?
Your teacher told me that you didn't come to your school. **Is this correct?**

31- 크다/keuda [a.] *big, large, great, tall*

그 케이크는 정말 **크다**.
The cake is very **big**

32- 또/tto [adv.] *also, again*

그는 **또** 지각을 했다.
He was late **again**.

33- 사회/sahoe [n.] *society*

그는 이 **사회**에서 아주 중요한 역할을 맡고 있어요.
He takes an important role in this **society**.

34- 많은/maneun [a.] *many, much, a lot of, plentiful*

이번 행사에 **많은** 사람들이 모여 들었다.
Many people gathered for this event.

35- 안/an [adv.] *not*

그녀는 오늘 숙제를 **안** 했다.
She did **not** do her homework today.

36- 좋다/jota [a.] *good, great, excellent, nice*

오늘 날씨가 정말 **좋다**.
The weather is really **good** today.

37- 더/deo [adv.] *more*

음식 좀 **더** 드릴까요?
Do you want **more** food?

38- 받다/batda [v.] *to receive, take, obtain*

너 어제 내가 보낸 메시지 **받았니**?
Did you **receive** my message yesterday?

39- 그것/geugeot [pron.] *that*

그것은 제 것이 아닙니다.
That is not mine.

40- 집/jip [n.] *house, home*

이 **집**의 가격은 너무 비쌉니다.
This **house** is so expensive.

41- 나오다/naoda [v.] *to come out*

그는 별을 보기 위해 밖으로 **나왔다**.
He **came out** to see stars.

42- 따르다/ttareuda [v.] *to follow*

여러분들은 선생님의 지시사항을 잘 **따라야** 합니다.
You need to **follow** the instructions of your teacher.

43- 그리고/geurigo [adv.] *and, also, in addition*

이것은 제가 그린 것입니다. **그리고** 저것은 지수가 그린 것입니다.
This is what I drew **and** that is what Jisoo drew.

44- 문제/munje [n.] *problem, question*

우리는 해결해야 할 많은 **문제들**을 가지고 있습니다.
We have a lot of **problems** to be solved.

45- 그런/**geureon** [determiner] *like that, such*

나는 **그런** 경험이 별로 없다.

I do not have any experience **like that.**

46- 살다/**salda** [v.] *to live, to be alive, to dwell*

저는 서울에서 **살아요**.

I **live** in Seoul.

47- 저/**jeo** [pron.] *(humble, formal, polite) the first person deferential singular pronoun, I*

저는 이제 곧 19살이 됩니다.

I will be 19 years old soon.

48- 척하다/**cheokhada** [v.] *to pretend*

강아지는 무서워서 죽은 **척했어요**.

The dog **pretended** to be dead because it was scared.

49- 생각하다/**saenggakhada** [v.] *to think*

그는 그 문제에 대해 어떻게 **생각하니**?

What does he **think** of the issue?

50- 모르다/**moreuda** [v.] *not to know, to be ignorant of*

나는 그의 전화번호를 **모른다**.

I do **not know** his phone number.

51- 속/**sok** [n.] *the inside*

그 상자 **속**에 찾고 있는 게 있어요.

What you are looking for is in **the inside** of the box.

52- 만들다/**mandeulda** [v.] *to make, establish*

저는 친구에게 주려고 종이 비행기를 **만들었어요**.

I **made** a paper airplane for my friend.

53- 곳/kot [n.] *place*

저는 컴퓨터를 둘 **곳**을 찾고 있어요.
I am looking for a **place** to put a computer.

54- 두/du [num.] *two*

오늘은 **두** 사람만 이곳을 방문했어요.
Only **two** people came here today.

55- 앞/ap [n.] *fore, former, front*

앞으로 나오세요.
Please come to the **front**.

56- 경우/gyeongu [n.] *conditions, circumstances, case, event*

그럴 **경우**에는 게임이 연기될 수 있나요?
In the **case** of it being so, could the game be postponed?

57- 중/jung [n] *amongst, in the course of, during*

그 **중**에서 가장 좋아하는 노래는 뭐에요?
What is your favorite song **amongst** them?

58- 어떤/eotteon [determiner] *which, what kind of, some, any, certain, of a certain kind*

어떤 선택이든 확실한 것은 없다.
Any choice is not certain.

59- 잘/jal [adv.] *be good at, well, often, at a good time*

그는 매운 음식을 **잘** 먹어요..
He's **good at** eating spicy food.

60- 그녀/geunyeo [pron.] *she*

그녀는 저에게 이 선물을 주었어요.
She gave me this present.

61- 먹다/meokda [v.] *to eat, have, grow older*

오늘 아침에 뭐 **먹었어요**?

What did you **eat** for breakfast?

62- 자신/jasin [n.] *one's body, oneself*

피터는 **자신**이 부끄러운 줄 알아야해.

Peter ought to be ashamed of **himself**.

63- 문화/munhwa [n.] *culture, civilization*

저는 이곳의 문화에 익숙하지 않아요.

I am not familiar with the **culture** here.

64- 원/won [n.] *won (the official currency of South Korea), circle*

이 책의 가격은 12,000 **원**입니다.

The price of this book is 12,000 **won**.

65- 생각/saenggak [n.] *idea, thought*

그거 정말 좋은 **생각**이네요.

That is a good **idea**.

66- 어떻다/eotteota [a.] *(to be) in what state, (to be) how*

최근에 구입한 새 핸드폰은 **어때요**?

How is the new mobile phone that you have purchased recently?

67- 명/myeong [n.] *counter for people*

오늘은 10 **명**이 참석할 예정입니다.

Today 10 people are going to participate in the conference.

68- 통하다/tonghada [v.] *to pass through, to communicate, to use as a medium*

저는 그녀와 이야기가 잘 **통해요**.

I can **communicate** with her well.

69- 그러다/**geureoda** [v.] *to do so, do it, say so*

그는 여기에 온다고 **그랬어요**.
He **said** that he would come here.

70- 소리/**sori** [n.] *sound, voice,*

음악 **소리**가 너무 커요.
The **sound** of music is too loud.

71- 다시/**dasi** [adv.] *again, once more*

다시 말해 줄 수 있나요?
Can you please say that **again**?

72- 다른/**dareun** [determiner] *different, other*

다른 것을 볼 수 있을까요?
Can I see a **different** thing?

73- 이런/**ireon** [determiner] *like this, such*

이런 물건을 또 사오지 마세요.
Please, do not buy stuff **like this** again.

74- 여자/**yeoja** [n.] *woman, girl, lady, female*

저희 가족 중에 **여자**는 세 명 있습니다.
Among my family members, there are three **women**.

75- 개/**gae** [n.] *dog*

너는 **개**를 좋아하니?
Do you like **dogs**?

76- 정도/**jeongdo** [n.] *degree, extent, an approximate*

amount

이 아파트의 임대료는 어느 **정도**의 금액인가요?

What is **an approximate amount** of the rent for this apartment?

77- 뒤/dwi [n.] *back, latter, rear, afterward, behind*

열쇠는 바로 네 **뒤**에 있어.

The key is right **behind** you.

78- 듣다/deutda [v.] *to listen, hear, take a course*

지금 제 말 잘 **들리나요**?

Can you **hear** me now?

79- 다/da [adv.] *all, completely*

이거 네가 **다** 먹었니?

Did you eat **all** of these?

80- 좀/jom [adv.] *a little, somewhat, a little while, a short time*

좀 있다가 제가 다시 전화 드리겠습니다.

I'll call you back **a little** later.

81- 들다/deulda [v.] *to cost, be spent, hold, carry*

제가 여기에 오는 데 이천 원이 **들었어요**.

It **cost** me 2,000 won to be here.

82- 싶다/sipda [a.] *to desire, want*

저는 정말 설악산에 가 보고 **싶어요**.

I really **want** to go to Mt. Seorak.

83- 보이다/boida [v.] *to be seen, be shown, show, be visible*

너는 저기 있는 간판이 **보이니**?

Is that sign **visible** to you?

84- 가지다**/gajida** [v.] *to have, possess*

너는 차를 **가지고** 있니?
Do you **have** a car?

85- 함께**/hamkke** [adv.] *together*

저희와 **함께** 영화보러 갈래요?
Would you go to a movie **together** with us?

86- 아이**/ai** [n.] *child*

이 **아이**는 엄마를 기다리고 있어요.
This **child** is waiting for his mom.

87- 지나다**/jinada** [v.] *to pass*

도로가 너무 좁아서 차들이 **지나가지**를 못했다.
The road was so narrow that cars were unable to **pass**.

88- 많이**/mani** [adv.] *a lot, in abundance*

나는 그 노래를 **많이** 들었다.
I have listened to that song **a lot**.

89- 시간**/sigan** [n.] *time, hour*

이번 주말에 **시간** 좀 내서 제 방을 청소해야 겠어요.
I should spend some **time** cleaning my room this weekend.

90- 너**/neo** [pron.] *you (informal)*

너는 언제부터 요리하는 법을 배우기 시작했니?
When did **you** start learning how to cook?

91- 인간**/ingan** [n.] *people, humanity, person, mankind, human*

모든 **인간**은 불완전하다.
All **humans** are fallible.

92- 사실/sasil [n.] *fact, reality, truth*

거짓말하지 마. 나는 그 **사실**을 알고 싶어.
Please, don't lie to me. I want to know the **truth**.

93- 나다/nada [v.] *to be born, appear, arise, occur, break out, come out*

결과가 잘 안 **나왔어요**.
The result did not **come out** well.

94- 이렇다/ireota [a.] *(to be) like this, in this way*

이렇게 하면 사람들이 담배를 덜 피울 것입니다.
In this way, there will be less people smoking.

95- 어머니/eomeoni [n.] *mom, mother*

저희 **어머니**께서 차를 파시려고 하는데요.
My **mother** wants to sell her car.

96- 눈/nun [n.] *eye, vision, snow*

나는 **눈**에 안약을 한 방울 넣었다.
I put a drop of medicine in my **eye**.

97- 뭐/mwo [pron.] *what*

이게 **뭐**예요?
What is this?

98- 점/jeom [n.] *a point, spot, aspect*

그 **점**을 반드시 기억해야 합니다.
You have to remember that **point**.

99- 의하다/uihada [v.] *to be due to, to accord with, to be pursuant to*

유효하지 않은 문자에 **의해서** 이러한 문제가 발생할 수도 있습니다.
This may **be due to** invalid characters.

100- 시대/**sidae** [n.] *historical age or period*

이 풍습은 조선 **시대**부터 시작된 것입니다.
The practice dates from the Joseon Dynasty **period**.

101- 다음/**daeum** [n.] *the next, the following*

저희는 **다음** 업무일 정오까지 납품을 보증하겠습니다.
We guarantee delivery by noon on **the next** business day.

102- 이러하다/**ireohada** [a.] *to be like this*

저는 사람들이 **이러한** 책상을 갖고 싶어 한다고 생각해요.
I think people dream about having a desk **like this**.

103- 누구/**nugu** [pron.] *who, someone*

그는 **누구**예요?
Who is he?

104- 전/**jeon** [n.] *front, (time) before, previous, ex-,*

2019 년도의 판매액과 **전**년도의 판매액을 비교해 보면 어떠한가요?
How do sales in 2019 compare to those for the **previous** year?

105- 부탁/**butak** [n.] *request, favor*

부탁이 있는데요.
I have a **favor** to ask.

106- 여러/**yeoreo** [determine] *several, various*

저는 그 프로그램을 이전에 **여러** 번 봤어요.
I watched the show **several** times before.

107- 뻔하다/**ppeonhada** [a.] *clear, obvious, evident*

네가 공부를 안했는데 결과야 **뻔하지**.
Since you didn't study, it's pretty **obvious** what the result will be.

108- 하나/hana [n.] *one*

이 방에는 침대 **하나**와 의자 두개가 있어요.

There are **one** bed and two chairs in this room.

109- 세계/segye [n.] *the world*

세계의 많은 사람들이 복지 혜택을 필요로 합니다.

There are a lot of people in **the world** who need welfare.

110- 버리다/beorida [v.] *to throw away*

여기에 쓰레기를 **버리지** 마세요.

Don't **throw away** trash here.

111- 위/wi [n.] *above, upper, upside, top*

얼굴 **윗**부분을 만져 주세요.

Please, touch the **upper** part of the face.

112- 운동/undong [n.] *exercise, physical activity, sport, movement in general*

저는 일주일에 4 일 **운동**해요.

I **exercise** four days a week.

113- 퍼센트/peosenteu [n.] *percent (a part or other object per hundred)*

오늘 우리은행 주식이 5 **퍼센트** 올랐어요.

Woori Bank's stock gained five **percent** today.

114- 학교/hakgyo [n.] *school*

그는 **학교**에서 저보다 한 학년 위였어요.

He was a year ahead of me in **school**.

115- 자기/jagi [n.] *oneself, the self, the ego*

그 여성은 **자기** 자신에 대해서 무엇이라고 말하고 있나요?

What does the woman say about **herself**?

116- 가장/gajang [adv.] *most, the most, the best*

저는 이 책을 **가장** 좋아해요.

I like this book **the most.**

117- 대통령/daetongnyeong [n.] *president of a country*

대통령은 국민들에 의해 선출된 한 국가의 수장입니다.

The **president** is the head of a country elected by the people.

118- 가지/gaji [n.] *kinds, types*

그 문제를 해결하기 위한 여러 **가지** 방법이 있다.

There are various **kinds** of ways to solve the problem.

119- 어색하다/eosaekhada [a.] *to be awkward, to be odd*

뭐라고 꼭 집어서 말할 수는 없지만, 뭔가 **어색해요**.

I can't quite put a finger on it, but something is **awkward.**

120- 시작하다/sijakhada [v.] *to begin, to start*

도로 공사는 언제 **시작되나요?**

When will the road works **begin?**

121- 바로/baro [adv.] *straight, right (now)*

지금 **바로** 시작합니다.

It will start **right** now.

122- 어느/eoneu [determiner] *which, some*

어느 음료를 좋아하나요?

Which drink do you like?

123- 그래서/geuraeseo [adv.] *so, therefore, accordingly, because of that*

그래서 나는 그에게 이렇게 말했다.

Therefore, I spoke to him like this.

124- 무엇/mueot [pron.] *what, something, anything*

무엇이라고 말했어요?
What did you say?

125- 정부/jeongbu [n.] *national government, particularly the executive branch*

정부는 휴대폰 요금의 인하를 추진하고 있습니다.
The **government** is pushing to lower mobile phone charges.

126- 모든/modeun [determiner] *all, every, each*

모든 사람들이 일어서서 크게 환호성을 지릅니다.
All the people stand and cheer loudly.

127- 번/beon [counter] *times*

저는 1 년에 두 **번** 미국에 방문해요.
I visit the U.S. two **times** a year.

128- 그거/geugeo [pron.] *it, that thing*

그거 무슨 문제 있어요?
What is the problem with **that thing**?

129- 돈/don [n.] *money*

그는 **돈**이 많은 영화 배우예요.
He is a film star with a lot of **money**.

130- 국가/gukga [n.] *political state, nation, country, polity, national anthem*

인근 **국가**에서 많은 사람들이 탈출했습니다.
A lot of people escaped from a nearby **country**.

131- 그런데/geureonde [adv.] *but, however, on the other*

hand

그런데 사실 극히 소수의 사람들이 그것을 좋아해요.
But the truth is, very few people like it.

132- 날/nal [n.] *day, time*

오늘은 일 년 중에 가장 짧은 **날**입니다.
Today is the shortest **day** of the year.

133- 여기/yeogi [pron.] *here*

저 **여기** 있어요.
I am **here**.

134- 모두/modu [adv.] *all, wholly, altogether, entirely*

저희 가족 구성원들 **모두** 이 보험에 적용이 되나요?
Are **all** the members of my family covered under this policy?

135- 여성/yeoseong [n.] *woman, women in general, femininity, womanhood*

저는 석사 학위를 가지고 있는 29 살의 **여성**입니다.
I am a 29-year-old **woman** with a master's degree.

136- 친구/chingu [n.] *friend*

그는 제 **친구**예요.
He is my **friend**.

137- 마음/maeum [n.] *personality, heart, mind*

저는 그 색상을 좋아하지 않아서 **마음**을 바꾸었어요.
I changed my **mind** because I do not like the color.

138- 후/hu [n.] *after*

그는 시간을 본 **후** 급하게 떠났다.
After looking at the time, he left in a hurry.

139- 가다/gada [v.] *go*

그들은 개관식에 참석하러 서울로 **갔어요**.
They **went** to Seoul for the opening.

140- 놓다/nota [v.] *to lay, put, let go*

그녀는 주전자를 불 위에 **놓았어요**.
She **put** a kettle over the fire.

141- 관계/gwangye [n.] *connection, relationship*

사랑은 굳건한 토대 위에 세워진 **관계**입니다.
Love is a **relationship** built on a firm foundation.

142- 아버지/abeoji [n.] *father, dad*

아버지는 올해 환갑을 맞이하셨다.
My **father** reached the age of sixty this year.

143- 남자/namja [n.] *man, boy, male*

이 **남자**는 미국인인가요?
Is this **man** American?

144- 어디/eodi [pron.] *where, somewhere*

혹시 지하철 역이 **어디** 있는지 아세요?
Do you know **where** the subway station is by any chance?

145- 몸/mom [n.] *body, health, shape*

그는 멋진 **몸**을 가지고 있어요.
He has a nice **body**.

146- 얼굴/eolgul [n.] *face, visage*

그녀의 **얼굴**은 창백하고 말라 보여요.
She looks pale and thin in the **face**.

147- 들어가다/deureogada [v.] *to go into, enter, attend (a school, institution, etc.), begin*

저는 내년에 대학교에 **들어가요**.
I will **attend** university next year.

148- 왜/wae [adv.] *why*

너는 이 가수를 **왜** 좋아해?
Why do you like this singer?

149- 나타나다/natanada [v.] *to appear, become manifest*

그것은 다음 순간에 **나타날** 것입니다.
It will **appear** in another moment.

150- 말다/malda [v.] *(used to negate imperatives), to not do something, to stop doing*

잔디에 앉지 **마세요**.
Please, **do not** sit on the lawn.

151- 지역/jiyeok [n.] *area, district, particular geographic region*

이곳이 이 **지역**에서 가장 고급스러운 식당이에요.
This place is the most exclusive restaurant in this **area**.

152- 다르다/dareuda [a.] *(to be) different*

우리 아이들은 서로 매우 **다르다**.
Our children are very **different** from each other.

153- 모습/moseup [n.] *the appearance of a person, surface appearance in general, aspect of a matter*

제 **모습**이 어떤가요?
What do you think of my **appearance**?

154- 물/mul [n.] *water, a liquid widely distributed in the natural world in the form of rivers, lakes, oceans, and groundwater*

물의 순환은 매일 일어납니다.

The cycle of **water** happens every day.

155- 만나다/mannada [v.] *to meet, see, become acquainted with, to encounter*

그를 또 언제 **만나게** 될 지 몰라요.

I do not know when I will **see** him again.

156- 내다/naeda [v.] *to bring about, pull forth, put out, issue, pay, submit*

제품의 품질이 좋으면 제가 돈을 더 **낼게요**.

I will **pay** more for a high-quality product.

157- 보이다/boida [v.] *to be seen, be shown, cause to see, show*

그 배가 강한 북서풍에 시달리고 있는 것이 **보였다**.

The ship **was seen** baffling with a strong northwestern wind.

158- 쓰다/sseuda [v.] *to write, use*

당신은 편지를 잘 **쓰네요**.

You are good at **writing** a letter.

159- 이것/igeot [pron.] *this*

이것은 제 차가 아니에요.

This is not my car.

160- 없이/eopsi [adv.] *without, lacking*

어떤 가족도 가족 간의 화합 **없이**는 행복할 수 없습니다.

No family can be happy **without** harmony among its members.

161- 이번/ibeon [n.] *this time, this occasion*

이번에는 봐주겠지만 다음 달에는 절대 안 됩니다.

I will let you off the hook **this time**, but no mercy next month.

162- 길/gil [n.] *road, path, street, means, course, conduct, moral*

사람들이 **길**을 건너고 있습니다.

There are people crossing the **street**.

163- 생활/saenghwal [n.] *lifestyle, way of life, daily living, living*

저는 **생활**비를 벌기 위해 영화관에서 일하고 있어요.

I work at a movie theater to make a **living**

164- 지금/jigeum [n.] *now, the current time*

지금은 기분이 어때?

How do you feel **now**?

165- 뿐/ppun [p.] *only, nothing more than, just*

주차장에는 차량이 두 대 **뿐**이다.

There are **only** two cars in the parking lot.

166- 사이/sai [n.] *relationship, space between*

저희 가게는 학교와 공원 **사이**에 있어요.

My store is **between** the school and the park.

167- 방법/bangbeop [n.] *method, procedure*

당신의 **방법**은 좋지 않아요.

Your **method** is not good.

168- 새롭다/saeropda [a.] *to be new*

혹시 **새로운** 직원을 채용하고 있나요?

Are you by any chance looking for a **new** staff member?

169- 우리나라/urinara [n.] *My country (that is used when Koreans indicate South Korea)*

저는 **우리나라**에 돌아가게 되어 기쁩니다.

I am glad to be returning to **my country**.

170- 앉다/anda [v.] *to sit, squat,*

우리는 **앉아서** 휴식을 취했다.

We **sat** and took a rest.

171- 처음/cheoeum [n.] *the first time, the beginning*

우리는 2년 전에 **처음** 만났어.

We met for **the first time** two years ago.

172- 손/son [n.] *hand*

그 소녀들은 **손**에 **손**을 잡고 춤을 췄어요.

The girls danced **hand** in **hand**.

173- 몇/myeot [determiner] *how many, which number, some*

몇 개 좀 주세요.

Please, give me **some**.

174- 그때/geuttae [n.] *that time, the given time*

그때 저는 점심 식사하러 나갔어요.

I was out for lunch at **that time**.

175- 과정/gwajeong [n.] *process, a course of events*

그것은 단지 시행착오의 **과정**일 뿐입니다.

It is just a **process** of trial and error.

176- 삶/sam [n.] *life, living*

그는 뛰어난 재능을 가지고 있던 예술가였지만, 힘든 **삶**을
살았습니다.

He was a gifted artist but he lived a hard **life**.

177- 갖다/gatda [v.] *to have, to take*

그는 책임감을 **갖고 있는** 교사입니다.

He is a teacher who **has** responsibility.

178- 찾다/chatda [v.] *to search, look for, find*

그녀가 강아지를 애타게 **찾는** 것을 보게 되었을 때 제 눈에 눈물이
고였습니다.

Tears welled up in my eyes when I saw her anxiously **searching
for** her dog.

179- 특히/teukhi [adv.] **especially,** *in particular, notably*

특히 한 젊은 남자가 그녀의 눈길을 사로잡았다.

One young man **in particular** caught her eye.

180- 시/si [n.] *time, hour*

은행은 오늘 몇 **시**에 문 닫죠?

What **time** does the bank close today?

181- 이상/isang [n.] *strange, abnormal, odd, weird, bizarre*

이것만 빼고 다른 것은 다 맞아서 **이상**하다.

It is **strange** because everything else is right except for this one.

182- 나가다/nagada [v.] *to go out, to leave*

그는 방을 **나갔습니다**.

He **left** the room.

183- 이야기/iyagi [n.] *story, talk, tale*

그는 항상 **이야기**를 지어내요.

He fabricates **stories** all the time.

184- 교육/gyoyuk [n.] *education*

당신은 그곳에서 하는 **교육**의 질에 만족하나요?

Are you content with the quality of **education** there?

185- 사다/sada [v.] *to buy*

뭐 좀 **사야** 해서 시장에 가고 있어요.

I need to **buy** something, so I am going to the market.

186- 경제/gyeongje [n.] *economy*

한국 **경제**는 요즘 튼튼합니다.

The Korean **economy** is strong these days.

187- 아직/ajik [adv.] *still, yet*

버스 운전 기사가 **아직** 안 왔어요.

The bus driver is not here **yet**.

188- 잡다/japda [v.] *to take, hold, grab, seize, arrest, catch*

그는 그녀의 팔을 **잡았습니다**.

He **caught** her by the arm.

189- 같이/gachi [adv.] *with, together*

우리는 선생님과 **같이** 기념 사진을 찍었다.

We took a commemorative photo **with** our teacher.

190- 선생님/seonsaengnim [n.] *teacher, (polite term of address for an elder male or female: sir, mister, miss)*

저는 **선생님**의 도움으로 시험에 합격했어요.
I passed the exam with the help of my **teacher**.

191- 예술/yesul [n.] *art, fine art*

그 화살에는 많은 **예술** 작품들이 있습니다.
The gallery has many pieces of **art**.

192- 서다/seoda [v.] *to stand, stop, halt, hold*

그 버스가 신호등에 **섰다**.
The bus **stopped** at the traffic rights.

193- 못/mot [adv.] *cannot, not to be able to*

저는 한숨도 **못** 잤어요.
I have **not been able to** sleep even a wink.

194- 역사/yeoksa [n.] *history*

우리 학교는 20년의 **역사**를 가지고 있습니다.
My school has a **history** of twenty years.

195- 읽다/ikda [v.] *to read*

저는 모든 신문기사를 **읽었어요**.
I **read** all the news articles.

196- 이제/ije [n.] *now*

이제 점심 시간입니다.
Now it is lunchtime.

197- 결과/gyeolgwa [n.] *result, outcome*

그의 사업에서의 성공은 그의 노력의 **결과**입니다.
His success in business is a **result** of his hard work.

198- 내용/naeyong [n.] *content, that which is contained in a container*

내용을 전체로서 이해하려고 해 보세요.
Try to understand the **content** as a body.

199- 물론/mullon [adv.] *of course, certainly, naturally*

그리고 **물론** 저희 모두 정말 기쁩니다.
And, **of course**, we are all happy.

200- 동안/dongan [n.] *interval, period of time*

많은 학생들이 짧은 시간 **동안**에 영어를 전부 완전히 익히기를 원하고 있습니다.
Many students want to master English in a short **period**.

201- 책/chaek [n.] *book*

그는 그 **책**의 8쪽을 펴서 큰 소리로 읽기 시작했습니다.
He opened the **book** at page eight and began to read aloud.

202- 일어나다/ireonada [v.] *to get up, wake up*

그녀는 아이들의 비명소리에 **일어났습니다**.
She **woke up** to the sound of kids screaming.

203- 당신/dangsin [pron.] *you*

저는 **당신**을 재촉하고 싶지 않습니다.
I do not want to rush **you**.

204- 시장/sijang [n.] *market*

오는 길에 **시장**에 잠깐 들렀어요.
I stopped off at the **market** on my way over.

205- 넣다/neota [v.] *to put in, include, insert*

저는 편지 안에 명함을 **넣었습니다**.

I **included** a business card in the letter.

206- 중요하다/jungyohada [a.] *to be important*

당신의 딸이 경험을 통해 배울 수 있도록 딸의 삶에 독립성을 부여하는 것은 매우 **중요합니다**.

It is very **important** to give your daughter independence in her life so she learns from experience.

207- 무슨/museun [determiner] *what, what kind of, some kind*

무슨 일을 하세요?

What kind of work do you do?

208- 느끼다/neukkida [v.] *to feel*

이렇게 늦은 밤이면, 저는 너무나도 혼자 된 기분을 **느낍니다**.

At this time of night, I **feel** so alone.

209- 어렵다/eoryeopda [a.] *difficult, hard*

시험이 **어려웠니**?

Was the exam **difficult**?

210- 힘/him [n.] *strength, power, force*

무대 위에서 강력한 **힘**을 느낍니다.

On stage, I feel very intense **power**.

211- 너무/neomu [adv.] *too, excessively, so, very, extremely*

그는 일을 **너무** 잘해서 제 도움이 필요 없었어요.

He worked **so** well that my help was superfluous.

212- 나라/nara [n.] *country, nation, kingdom*

월드컵은 온 **나라**에 사람들을 즐겁게 했어요.
The World Cup entertained the people across the **country**.

213- 부르다/bureuda [v.] *to call, name*

그들을 **불러서** 다시 이것을 하라고 해 주세요.
Please **call** them up and do this again.

214- 의미/uimi [n.] *meaning*

당신은 문맥을 통해서 단어의 **의미**를 파악할 수 있을 거예요.
You can use context to figure out the word's **meaning**.

215- 자리/jari [n.] *place occupied by something or someone, seat*

우리 **자리**는 다섯 번째 줄에 있습니다.
Our **seats** are on the fifth row.

216- 밝히다/balkida [v.] *make clear, reveal, disclose*

그는 그 기사의 출처를 **밝히지** 않았습니다.
He did not **disclose** the source of the article.

217- 죽다/jukda [v.] *to die*

나는 그가 **죽지** 않기를 바란다.
I hope he does not **die**.

218- 이미/imi [adv.] *already*

저는 **이미** 몇천 번을 해 봤어요.
I've **already** done it a few thousand times.

219- 쪽/jjok [n.] side

저희 딸은 자기 아버지 **쪽**의 가족분들을 닮았어요.
Our daughter favors her father's **side** of the family.

220- 정치/jeongchi [n.] politics, governmental affairs

저는 **정치**에 큰 관심을 두지 않아요.
I don't concern myself with **politics**.

221- 국민/gungmin [n.] people of a nation

왕은 자신의 **국민들**에 대해 통치권을 갖고 있습니다.
The King holds dominion over the **people of his nation**.

222- 생명/saengmyeong [n.] life

저희는 모든 **생명**이 소중하다는 것을 깨달아야 합니다.
We need to realize that every **life** matters.

223- 얘기/yaegi [n.] talk, story

그는 그것에 대해서 **얘기**하는 것도 귀찮아 합니다.
He doesn't even bother to **talk** about it.

224- 학생/haksaeng [n.] student, school pupil

저는 학교에서 항상 다른 **학생들**보다 뒤처져 있었습니다.
I was behind the other **students** at school all the time.

225- 연구/yeongu [n.] research

저는 백신 **연구** 팀을 운영하고 있습니다.
I run the **research** team working on vaccines.

226- 엄마/omma [n.] mom

엄마와 저는 교외에서 즐거운 시간을 보냈어요.
My **mom** and I had a lovely time in the countryside.

227- 이름/ireum [n.] *name, given name, full name,*

저는 그의 **이름**을 알아요.
I know his **name**.

228- 내리다/naerida [v.] *to come down*

저는 올해 기름값이 **내릴** 것 같지 않습니다.
I don't think gasoline prices will **go down** this year.

229- 사건/sageon [n.] *incident, event, case, affair*

경찰이 그 **사건**에 대해 조사하기를 회피하는 것 같았습니다.
The police seemed to avoid looking into the **case**.

230- 및/mit [adv.] *and, additionally*

사운드 옵션 **및** 스피커 설정을 변경할 수 있습니다.
You can change sound options **and** speaker setup.

231- 쉽다/swipda [adj.] *(to be) easy*

저희는 아직 그 일을 하고 있어요. 그 일이 **쉬운** 일은 아니잖아요.
We're still working on it. It's not an **easy** task.

232- 짓다/jitda [v.] *to make something (food, a house, etc.), to build*

찬호는 자기 집을 **짓다가** 팔이 부러졌어요.
Chan-ho broke his arm while he was **building** his house.

233- 또한/ttohan [adv.] *also, too, furthermore*

당신은 **또한** 야채와 과일을 많이 먹어야 해요.
You **also** need to eat a lot of vegetables and fruit.

234- 이유/iyu [n.] *reason, cause*

이것이 제가 여기에 온 **이유**입니다.
This is the **reason** why I'm here.

235- 또는/ttoneun [adv.] *if not, alternatively, or*

계정 이름 **또는** 비밀번호가 올바르지 않습니다.

The account name **or** password is incorrect.

236- 필요하다/piryohada [a.] *to have a need, be necessary, need*

지금은 말이 아니라 행동이 **필요합니다**.

Now actions **are necessary**, not words.

237- 글/geul [n.] *writing*

저는 제 **글**에 매우 예민합니다.

I'm really neurotic about my **writing**.

238- 생기다/saenggida [v.] *to emerge, have (for something to appear where it had been absent)*

지금 제가 다니는 회사에 큰 문제가 **생겼어요**.

I **have** a big problem with my company right now.

239- 사용하다/sayonghada [v.] *to use*

그는 많은 컴퓨터 프로그램 **사용** 방법을 알고 있어요.

He knows how to **use** many computer programs.

240- 남편/nampyeon [n.] *husband*

제 **남편**은 매일 늦게 퇴근해요.

My **husband** leaves work late every day.

241- 들어오다/deureooda [v.] *to enter, to come in*

백화점 문을 열자마자 사람들이 바로 **들어왔습니다**.

As soon as the department store opened, people **came in** right away.

242- 밖/bak [n.] *outside*

그녀는 **밖**으로 나갔어요.
She went **outside**.

243- 세상/sesang [n.] *world*

좁은 **세상**이에요. 그렇지 않나요?
It's a small **world**, isn't it?

244- 작다/jakda [a.] *(to be) small*

그는 키가 **작아요**.
He is **short**.

245- 타다/tada [v.] *ride, get on*

그들은 하루 종일 걷거나 자전거를 **타요**.
They walk or **ride** a bicycle for a day.

246- 대학/daehak [n.] *college, university*

그는 내년에 **대학**으로 다시 돌아갈 계획입니다.
He is planning to return to **college** next year.

247- 작품/jakpum [n.] *a creative work or product, piece*

그들의 춤은 하나의 예술 **작품**이었어요.
Their dancing was a **work** of art.

248- 상황/sanghwang [n.] *conditions, the situation*

당신은 아주 힘든 **상황**에 놓여 있는 것 같네요.
It looks like you're in a very tough **situation**.

249- 가운데/gaunde [n.] *center, the middle, among, amid, of*

희생자 **가운데**에는 두 명의 경찰관이 있었습니다.
Two policemen were **among** the victims.

250- 보내다/bonaeda [v.] *to send, dispatch*

저희가 얼마나 많은 사본들을 **보내야** 할까요?

How many copies do we need to **send**?

251- 두다/duda [v.] *to put, leave (behind), let there be, preserve*

그것들을 그냥 당신과 함께 **두도록** 할까요?

Should I just **leave** them with you?

252- 즉/jeuk [adv.] *namely, i.e., in other words*

저희는 목표가 되는 독자, **즉** 스무 살과 서른 살 사이에 있는 여성들에게 집중할 필요가 있습니다.

We need to concentrate on our target audience, **namely** women aged between twenty and thirty.

253- 따라서/ttaraseo [adv.] *in accordance with, along*

차들이 길가를 **따라서** 주차가 되어 있습니다.

Cars are parked **along** the edges of the street.

254- 상태/sangtae [n.] *condition, status, state*

제 자동차 **상태**가 좋지 않은 것 같습니다.

I don't think my car is in good **condition**.

255- 이후/ihu [n.] *from now on, after this, henceforth, in the future, after*

오후 2시 **이후**면 아무 때나 괜찮습니다.

Any time **after** two in the afternoon is fine.

256- 당시/dangsi [n.] *then, in those days, at the time of*

사망 **당시** 그는 혼자였나요?

Was he alone **at the time of** his death?

257- 문학/munhak [n.] *literature, the study of literature*

그녀는 **문학** 석사 학위를 가지고 있습니다.
Her master's degree is in **literature**.

258- 더욱/deouk [adv.] *more, even more*

그의 어머니는 그가 **더욱** 성숙되게 행동하기를 원합니다.
His mom wants him to act **more** mature.

259- 아주/aju [adv.] *very*

그들은 **아주** 비싸다고 말하네요.
They say it's **very** expensive.

260- 지방/jibang [n.] *rural areas, region, the country*

그 **지방**에서는 사과가 많이 생산됩니다.
The **country** produces a lot of apples.

261- 밤/bam [n.] *night, evening*

어제 **밤**에 저는 겨우 두 시간만 잤어요.
I slept only for two hours last **night**.

262- 높다/nopda [a.] *to be high, tall, lofty*

그들이 가격을 너무 **높이** 잡았다.
They have pitched their prices too **high**.

263- 최근/choegeun [n., adv., a.] *recent time, recently, recent*

그가 쓴 소설책은 **최근** 몇 년 동안 인기를 얻고 있습니다.
His novels have gained popularity over **recent** years.

264- 채/chae [adv.] *not yet, still... not*

그는 자신의 프로젝트를 **채** 마치지 못했다.
He has **not yet** finished his project.

265- 현실/hyeonsil [n.] *reality, the actual case*

그의 막연한 두려움이 확실히 **현실**화되었습니다.

His vague fear crystallized into a **reality**.

266- 환경/hwangyeong [n.] *environment, the natural environment, conditions*

저 학생은 열악한 **환경**에서 성장하고 있습니다.

That student is growing up in a bad **environment**.

267- 컴퓨터/keompyuteo [n.] *computer*

저는 당신이 구입했던 컴퓨터와 같은 **컴퓨터**를 샀어요.

I bought the same **computer** as you did.

268- 먼저/meonjeo [adv.] *first*

저도 컴퓨터를 사용해야 하지만, 당신 **먼저** 사용해도 됩니다.

I also need to use the computer, but you can use it **first**.

269- 다니다/danida [v.] *to attend, commute*

그는 아직 대학에 **다니고** 있어요.

He is still **attending** the college.

270- 얼마나/eolmana [adv.] *how long, how much, how many*

한국에 사신지 **얼마나** 되셨어요?

How long have you lived in Korea?

271- 자체/jache [n.] *the thing itself, something's/someone's own*

그 주는 **자체** 법에 의해 통치가 이루어집니다.

The state is ruled by **its own** law.

272- 열다/yeolda [v.] *to open, hold (an event)*

저희는 도시 중심 지역 근처에 새로운 사무실을 **열** 계획을 하고 있어요.

We plan to **open** a new office near the downtown area.

273- 머리/meori [n.] *head, hair*

제가 어렸을 때, 저의 **머리**는 곱슬머리였습니다.

When I was young, my **hair** was curly.

274- 묻다/mutda [v.] *to ask, inquire, charge (a person with)*

더 자세한 정보를 알기 원하시면, 관리자에게 **물어보시길** 바랍니다.

For further information, please **ask** the administrator.

275- 남다/namda [v.] *to remain, be left over, profit*

바구니 안에는 아직 쿠키가 조금 **남아 있습니다**.

There **are** still some cookies **left over** in the basket.

276- 부분/bubun [n.] *portion, section, part*

이 부분이 이 영화에서 가장 흥미로운 **부분**입니다.

This is the most interesting **part** of this movie.

277- 기업/gieop [n.] *a business, company, corporation, enterprise*

그들은 아시아에서 다국적 **기업**을 운영하고 있습니다.

They operate a multinational **company** in Asia.

278- 거기/geogi [pron.] *there*

내가 당신을 필요로 할 때 당신은 **거기** 없었습니다.

You weren't **there** when I needed you.

279- 변화/byeonhwa [n.] *change, variation, alteration*

온도계는 기온의 **변화**를 측정합니다.

The thermometer measures **changes** of temperature.

280- 아들/adeul [n.] *son*

그녀는 자신의 **아들**을 돕는 일에 자신의 인생을 바쳤습니다.

She devoted her life to helping her **son**.

281- 뜻/tteut [n.] *meaning, sense, mind, aim, goal, will*

이 단어는 **뜻**이 뭐예요?

What's the **meaning** of this word?

282- 아/a [interjection] *ah, oh*

아! 당신을 다시 만나게 되어서 너무나도 좋네요.

Ah! It's wonderful to see you again.

283- 기다리다/gidarida [v.] *to wait for, await*

왜 그들은 우리를 **기다리지** 않았죠?

Why didn't they **wait for** us?

284- 떨어지다/tteoreojida [v.] *to fall, tumble, drop*

접시가 식탁에서 **떨어졌어요**.

A dish **fell** off of the table.

285- 선거/seongeo [n.] *election*

우리는 **선거**에서 공명정대하게 행동해야 합니다.

It is imperative that we play fair in the **election**.

286- 관하다/gwanhada [v.] *about, concerning, to be in relation to, with regard to*

이 문제에 **관해서는** 저희가 나중에 당신과 이야기를 하도록 할게요.

Concerning this matter, we will talk with you later.

287- 그냥/geunyang [adv.] *simply, just, for free, for no particular reason*

저는 **그냥** 그것을 하고 싶지 않아요.
I **just** don't want to do it.

288- 나누다/nanuda [v.] *to divide (into pieces), split up, share*

이 케이크를 세 개로 **나누어서** 각 사람이 한 조각씩 먹기로 해요.
Let's **divide** this cake into three and each take one piece.

289- 이용하다/iyonghada [v.] *to use, utilize*

모든 회원은 독서실을 무료로 **이용할** 수 있습니다.
All members are free to **use** the reading room.

290- 거의/geoui [adv.] *almost, nearly*

지금은 **거의** 여덟 시입니다.
It's **almost** eight o'clock now.

291- 곧/got [adv.] *soon, immediately, shortly*

야구 경기가 **곧** 시작될 거예요.
The baseball match will begin **shortly**.

292- 중심/jungsim [n.] *center, core, heart*

그의 집은 그 도시의 **중심**에 위치하고 있습니다.
His house is located in the **center** of the city.

293- 활동/hwaldong [n.] *activity, action*

당신은 어떤 종류의 클럽 **활동**을 좋아하나요?
What kind of club **activity** do you like?

294- 오늘/oneul [n.] *today, this day*

오늘은 그녀의 생일이에요.

Today is her birthday.

295- 서로/seoro [pron.] *each other, one another*

저는 제 아이들이 **서로** 도울 때가 너무 좋아요.
I love it when my kids help **each other**.

296- 관심/gwansim [n.] *interest, inclination to, attention, concern*

요리는 그녀의 **관심**사입니다.
Cooking is her matter of **interest**.

297- 역시/yeoksi [adv.] *too, also, just as expected, the same as before*

기후 **역시** 중요한 역할을 합니다.
Climate **also** plays an important role.

298- 이거/igeo [pron.] *this, this thing, this matter*

이거 얼마예요?
How much is **this**?

299- 애/ae [n.] *child, kid*

그 **애**가 당신의 아들인가요?
Is that **kid** your son?

300- 광고/gwanggo [n.] *an advertisement, advertising, commercial*

우리는 우리 **광고**를 하루에 몇 번 방송으로 보내야 할까요?
How many times a day should we air our **advertisement**?

301- 방/bang [n.] *a room*

저는 옆 **방**에 있는 사람들의 목소리를 들을 수 있습니다.
I can hear the voice of people in the next **room**.

302- 정신/jeongsin [n.] *spirit, mind, consciousness, psyche*

초심으로 돌아가서 다시 새로워진 **정신**으로 시작합시다.
Let's go back to the basics and start work with a renewed **mind**.

303- 이르다/ireuda [a.] *to be early, premature*

그는 **이른** 아침부터 자신의 일을 시작합니다.
He starts his work in the **early** morning.

304- 땅/ttang [n.] *earth, land, ground, soil, territory*

강이 제 **땅**을 그의 땅과 갈라놓고 있습니다.
The river divides my **land** from his.

305- 이루다/iruda [v.] *to achieve, accomplish, fulfill*

열심히 일을 한다면 당신이 원하는 모든 것을 **이룰** 것입니다.
You will **achieve** everything you want if you work hard.

306- 아침/achim [n.] *morning, breakfast*

(당신은) 내일 **아침** 몇 시에 떠날 예정인가요?
What time are you leaving tomorrow **morning**?

307- 웃다/utda [v.] *to laugh, grin*

학생들이 당신을 보고 **웃었나요**?
Did your students **laugh** at you?

308- 현상/hyeonsang [n.] *phenomenon, the evident condition or state*

무지개는 자연 **현상**입니다.
A rainbow is a natural **phenomenon**.

309- 떠나다/tteonada [v.] *to leave*

(나는) 일찍 **떠나고** 싶지 않지만, 어쩔 수가 없네.

I don't want to **leave** early, but it can't be helped.

310- 기술/gisul [n.] *technology, technique, skill*

이 칩은 컴퓨터 **기술**에서 가장 최신의 것에 해당합니다.
This chip is the latest **technology** in computer industry.

311- 전체/jeonche [n.] *the whole*

감독은 팀 **전체**를 다 불렀습니다.
The coach called **the whole** team over.

312- 그래/geurae [interjection] *yeah, yes, really?*

그래? 난 정말 그것에 대해 생각하지 못했어.
Really? I didn't really think about that.

313- 얻다/eotda [v.] *to get, receive, obtain, have, win, gain*

최근 몇 년 동안 그의 소설은 인기를 **얻고 있습니다**.
His novels have **gained** popularity over recent years.

314- 분/bun [n.] *(time) minute*

제가 5**분** 뒤에 다시 전화할게요.
I will call you back in five **minutes**.

315- 아름답다/areumdapda [a.] *to be beautiful*

저 호수는 정말 **아름다워요**.
The lake **is** really **beautiful**.

316- 끝/kkeut [n.] *end, conclusion, point*

저는 문장 **끝**에 마침표를 빠뜨렸어요.
I left out a period at the **end** of the sentence.

317- 민족/minjok [n.] *people, nation, ethnicity, race, tribe*

두 **민족**은 전쟁이 시작된 이후로 서로를 미워했다.

The two **peoples** have hated each other since the war began.

318- 간/gan [s.] *(time) for, (place) between*

그녀는 이틀**간** 병가 중입니다.

She is on sick leave **for** two days.

319- 조사/josa [n.] *investigation, examination*

다른 회사들은 아직도 **조사**를 받고 있습니다.

Other companies are still under **investigation**.

320- 듯/deut [n.] *as if, in a manner suggesting that...*

당신은 밤새 못 잔 **듯**하네요.

You look **as if** you haven't slept all night.

321- 입/ip [n.] *mouth, lips, (figuratively) the number of people who eat food*

그 소문은 **입**에서 **입**으로 전해졌습니다.

The rumor traveled from **mouth** to **mouth**.

322- 그대로/geudaero [adv.] *just, exactly, just the way something is, without change*

당신이 말하는 **그대로**입니다.

It is **just** as you say.

323- 영화/yeonghwa [n.] *movie*

그 **영화**는 삼 개월 동안 상영을 하고 있습니다.

The **movie** has been showing for three months.

324- 필요/piryo [n.] *need, necessity*

그는 분명히 휴식이 **필요**하다.

He must be in **need** of rest.

325- 줄/jul [n.] *string, rope, line, strip, row*

그들은 표 판매소에서 **줄**을 서서 기다리고 있습니다.
They're waiting in **line** at the ticket office.

326- 하늘/haneul [n.] *sky, heaven*

무지개가 **하늘**에 걸려 있습니다.
A rainbow hangs in the **sky**.

327- 년대/nyeondae [n.] *a period of years such as decade or century*

그 사건은 1990 **년대**에 일어났습니다.
The incident happened in the decade of 1990.

328- 과학/gwahak [n.] *science*

저는 **과학**을 공부하는 것에 흥미를 느꼈어요.
I felt interested in studying **science**.

329- 듯하다/deuthada [a.] *to be regarded as, to appear to be*

당신은 로그인이 되지 않은 **듯합니다**.
You do **not appear to be** logged in.

330- 자연/jayeon [n.] *nature*

자연은 모든 규칙에 예외를 두고 있습니다.
Nature provides exceptions to every rule.

331- 정말/jeongmal [adv.] *really, truly*

새로운 기계가 **정말** 작동이 잘 됩니다.
The new machine works **really** well.

332- 구조/gujo [n.] *structure*

시간이 흐르면서 가족 **구조**도 변하고 있습니다.
As time goes on, the family **structure** is also changing.

333- 결국/gyeolguk [adv.] *in the end, ultimately, eventually, at last, finally, after all*

저희의 이윤은 **결국** 심각하게 감소할 것입니다.
Our profits will **eventually** be severely reduced.

334- 밥/bap [n.] *cooked rice, food, meal*

매일 아침마다 **밥**을 준비하는 것은 정말 귀찮은 일이에요.
It's a real drag to prepare a **meal** every morning.

335- 입다/ipda [v.] *to wear, put on (clothes)*

그 학생은 파란색 티셔츠를 **입고** 있었습니다.
The student was **wearing** a blue T-shirt.

336- 오히려/ohiryeo [adv.] *on the contrary, unexpectedly, rather*

그 실적은 **오히려** 실패 쪽이었다.
The performance was **rather** a failure.

337- 프로그램/peurogeuraem [n.] *computer program, television program, show*

그녀는 매일 자신의 아침 **프로그램**을 진행해요.
Every day she does her morning **show**.

338- 네/ne [interjection] *yes*

네, 저는 한국어를 공부하고 있어요.
Yes, I am studying the Korean language.

339- 이루어지다/irueojida [v.] *to be attained, fulfilled, be* *made up of*

제 꿈이 **이루어졌어요**.

My dream has been **fulfilled**.

340- 남/nam [n.] *somebody other than myself, other person, other people*

남들이 뭐라고 하든지 상관없이 계속해서 당신의 길을 가세요.

No matter what **others** say, keep going your way.

341- 하루/haru [n.] *a day, 24 hours, daytime*

(당신은) **하루**에 6시간 이상 자나요?

Do you sleep more than six hours **a day**?

342- 그림/geurim [n.] *picture, drawing, painting, sketch*

몇 개의 **그림**이 거실 벽에 걸려 있었습니다.

Some **pictures** were hanging on the wall in the living room.

343- 적/jeok [n.] *enemy, time, occurrence, experience*

저의 가장 친한 친구는 한때 저의 **적**이었습니다.

My best friend was once my **enemy**.

344- 터/teo [n.] *place, space, lot, site, foundation, groundwork*

사업이 잘 되려면 **터**가 중요합니다.

The **location** is important for a business to go well.

345- 마시다/masida [v.] *to drink*

저는 방금 와인 한 잔을 **마셨어요**.

I just **drank** a glass of wine.

346- 치다/chida [v.] *to hit, play*

그는 매일 이른 아침에 테니스를 **칩니다**.

He **plays** tennis every early morning.

347- 혼자/honja [n.] *being alone, by oneself*

혼자 있어야 할 시간이 모든 사람들에게 있다.
There are times when everyone needs **to be alone**.

348- 교수/gyosu [n.] *professor, teaching*

저희 경제학 **교수**님은 저희 집 맞은편에 살고 계십니다.
Our economics **professor** lives just across from my house.

349- 술/sul [n.] *liquor, alcohol*

서로 다른 종류의 **술**을 섞는 것은 좋지 않습니다.
It's not good to mix different kinds of **liquor**.

350- 사랑/sarang [n.] *love, affection*

그는 어린시절 친구와 **사랑**에 빠졌습니다.
He fell in **love** with his childhood friend.

351- 의식/uisik [n.] *consciousness, awareness*

그는 며칠 동안 **의식**을 회복하지 못했습니다.
He did not regain **consciousness** for several days.

352- 전화/jeonhwa [n.] *telephone*

저는 그녀가 일하는 곳의 **전화**번호를 모릅니다.
I do not know the **telephone** number of her workplace.

353- 끝나다/kkeunnada [v.] *to come to an end, become finished, end, finish*

그의 데뷔 경기는 무승부로 **끝났습니다**.
His debut match **ended** in a draw.

354- 돌아오다/doraoda [v.] *to return, to come back*

혈압과 맥박이 정상으로 **돌아왔습니다**.
Blood pressure and pulse **returned** to normal.

355- 맞다/matda [v.] *suit (one's taste)*

이 음식은 제 입맛에 **맞지** 않습니다.
This food doesn't **suit** my taste.

356- 아빠/appa [n.] *dad, father, papa*

당신은 엄마를 더 닮았나요, **아빠**를 더 닮았나요?
Are you more like your mother or your **father**?

357- 걸리다/geollida [v.] *take (time)*

차로 두 시간 정도 **걸립니다**.
It **takes** about two hours by car.

358- 지키다/jikida [v.] *to protect, defend, watch over, keep to, abide by*

저는 당신을 **지키기** 위해 최선을 다할 것입니다.
I will do all my best to **protect** you.

359- 한번/hanbeon [n.] *once, at a time, sometime (when there is a change)*

다시 **한번** 시도해 보는 건 어떨까요?
Why don't you try it **once** again?

360- 커피/keopi [n.] *coffee*

졸리면 **커피** 좀 마셔 보는 건 어때요?
How about drinking some **coffee** if you feel sleepy?

361- 가슴/gaseum [n.] *chest, breast, bosom, heart, mind*

기뻐서 제 **가슴**이 터질 지경이에요.

My **heart** will burst with joy.

362- 길다/**gilda** [a.] *to be long*

여름에는 낮 시간이 **길어요**.

In summer the days **are long**.

363- 바라보다/**baraboda** [v.] *to observe, stare, look forward to, gaze*

밤하늘을 **바라볼** 때 당신은 무엇을 찾나요?

What do you look for when you **gaze** into the night sky?

364- 알아보다/**araboda** [v.] *to recognize, examine, check*

그녀는 목소리를 듣고 자신의 어머니를 **알아보았다**.

She **recognized** her mother by her voice.

365- 회사/**hoesa** [n.] *company, corporation*

그 **회사**는 일 년에 백만 달러어치의 운동화를 판매합니다.

The **company** sells one million dollars of sneakers a year.

366- 맛/**mat** [n.] *taste, flavor*

겉보기로 그것의 **맛**을 판단하지 마세요.

Don't judge its **taste** by how it looks.

367- 대부분/**daebubun** [n.] *the majority, the better part*

그것에 제 월급의 **대부분**이 들어갔어요.

It cost **the better part** of my pay.

368- 산업/**saneop** [n.] *industry*

할리우드는 세계 영화 **산업**의 중심지입니다.

Hollywood is the heart of the world movie **industry**.

369- 매우/maeu [adv.] *very, extremely*

그는 **매우** 키가 큽니다.
He is **very** tall.

370- 오르다/oreuda [v.] *to go up*

이 산은 가파르기 때문에 저는 더 이상 **오를** 수가 없어요.
This mountain is steep, so I can't **go up** any farther.

371- 음식/eumsik [n.] *food*

저는 매운 **음식**에 익숙합니다.
I'm used to eating spicy **food**.

372- 표정/pyojeong [n.] *look, face, an expression of feeling, especially a facial expression*

그가 그 슬픈 소식을 들었을 때 그의 **표정**은 어두워졌다.
His **face** clouded over when he heard the sad news.

373- 꼭/kkok [adv.] *grasping tightly, firmly, absolutely*

서로의 눈을 보면서 손을 **꼭** 잡아주세요.
Please, hold each other's hand **firmly** while looking at their eyes.

374- 일부/ilbu [n.] *part of a whole, portion, some*

일부 주차장이 공사에 들어갈 것입니다.
Some of the parking lots will be under construction.

375- 요즘/yojeum [n.] *recent times, recently, these days, nowadays*

그는 **요즘** 저랑 같이 시간을 보내고 싶어 하지 않아요.
He doesn't want to spend time with me **these days**.

376- 계획/gyehoek [n.] *plan*

당신은 이 **계획**에 대해서 어떻게 생각하나요?

What do you think of this **plan**?

377- 느낌/neukkim [n.] *feeling, sense, touch*

앞을 볼 수 없는 장애를 가진 사람들은 **느낌**에 많이 의존을 합니다.
Blind people rely a lot on **touch**.

378- 얼마/eolma [n.] *how much, how many, some amount or quantity*

이건 **얼마**예요?
How much is this?

379- 고개/gogae [n.] *nape of the neck, head*

그 여성은 **고개**를 갸우뚱하고 있습니다.
The woman is tilting her **head**.

380- 성격/seonggyeok [n.] *character, temperament, personality, nature*

그들은 **성격** 면에서 아주 비슷합니다.
They are much alike in **character**.

381- 계속/gyesok [adv.] *continuously, consecutively, unceasingly*

그는 두 시간 동안 **계속** 피아노를 쳤습니다.
He played the piano **continuously** for two hours.

382- 세기/segi [n.] *century (100 years)*

그것은 19 **세기** 중반에 지어졌습니다.
It was built in the middle of the nineteenth **century**.

383- 세우다/seuda [v.] *to cause to stand, set up, erect, put up*

그는 상체를 똑바로 **세웠다**.

He **erected** his upper body.

384- 아내/anae [n.] *wife*

그의 **아내**는 매우 친절합니다.
His **wife** is so kind.

385- 가족/gajok [n.] *household, family*

제 **가족**을 소개해 드리겠습니다.
I will introduce my **family**.

386- 현재/hyeonjae [n.] *the present, now, currently*

노조는 **현재** 회사와 협상 중입니다.
The labor union is **currently** negotiating with the company.

387- 세/se [determiner] *three (of something)*

교실에는 **세** 명의 학생이 있습니다.
There are **three** students in the classroom.

388- 발전/baljeon [n.] *development, growth, progress*

저희는 회사 **발전**에 있어서 중요한 기로를 맞이했습니다.
We faced a critical crossroad in our corporate **development**.

389- 차/cha [n.] *tea*

저는 커피보다 **차**를 선호해요.
I would rather have **tea** rather than coffee.

390- 놀다/nolda [v.] *to play, frolic, enjoy oneself, idle away, hang out*

저는 어젯밤에 친구들과 **놀았어요**.
I **hung out** with friends last night.

391- 향하다/hyanghada [v.] *to go towards, face, look,*

head

그는 독일을 떠나 고국으로 **향했습니다**.

He departed from Germany to **head** home.

392- 관련/**gwallyeon** [n.] *connection, relation*

한 남자가 그 강도 사건과 **관련**해서 체포되었습니다.

A man has been arrested in **connection** with the robbery.

393- 형태/**hyeongtae** [n.] *shape, form, type*

물, 눈, 수증기는 물의 다른 **형태들**입니다.

Ice, snow, and steam are different **forms** of water.

394- 각/**gak** [determiner] *each*

그는 **각** 사람에게 할 일을 부여했습니다.

He assigned **each** person a job to do.

395- 도시/**dosi** [n.] *city*

그는 **도시**에서 떨어져 있는 시골에서 살고 있습니다.

He lives in the country remote from the **city**.

396- 작업/**jageop** [n.] *work, working, job, operation*

제가 하고 있는 **작업**은 이번 주말까지 계속됩니다.

My **work** continues until this weekend.

397- 분위기/**bunwigi** [n.] *atmosphere, environment, mood*

회의의 **분위기**는 희망적이었습니다.

The **mood** of the meeting was hopeful.

398- 그러하다/**geureohada** [a.] *to be like that*

나는 그가 **그랬는지(그러했는지)** 몰랐어.

I didn't know he **was like that**.

399- 나이/nai [n.] *age of a person or other living thing*

그는 자신의 **나이**에 비해 늙어 보입니다.

He looks old for his **age**.

400- 우선/useon [adv.] *first, foremost, above all, for now*

이후에 무슨 일이 일어나더라도 **우선** 먹도록 합시다.

Let's eat **first**, whatever else may happen afterward.

401- 믿다/mitda [v.] *to believe in something, trust someone*

낯선 사람을 너무 쉽게 **믿으려고** 하지 마세요.

Don't be too ready to **trust** a stranger.

402- 바꾸다/bakkuda [v.] *to change, replace, exchange, modify*

그녀는 자신의 이름을 지은에서 지선으로 **바꾸었습니다**.

She **changed** her name from Jieun to Ji-sun.

403- 낳다/nata [v.] *to lay (an egg), to give birth, spawn*

연어는 물길을 거슬러 올라가서 알을 **낳는다**.

The salmon swims upstream to **lay** eggs.

404- 바/ba [counter] *thing, what, way, method, how to do, extent*

이것이 저희가 반대하는 **바**입니다.

This is **what** we oppose.

405- 정보/jeongbo [n.] *information*

그 책은 유익한 **정보**를 많이 담고 있습니다.

The book contains a lot of useful **information**.

406- 열리다/yeollida [v.] *to be opened, be held, take place*

그 행사는 공원에서 **열릴** 것입니다.

The event will **be held** at a park.

407- 좋아하다/joahada [v.] *to like, prefer, love*

저는 단것들을 **좋아합니다**.

I **like** sweet things.

408- 그리다/geurida [v.] *to draw, paint, sketch, depict*

그녀는 그림 **그리는** 것을 잘 합니다.

She is good at **drawing** a picture.

409- 만큼/mankeum [p.] *the degree or extent to which, as much as*

당신이 원하는 **만큼** 마실 수 있습니다.

You can have **as much as** you'd like.

410- 배우다/baeuda [v.] *to learn, study*

저는 매일 새로운 기술에 대해 더 많이 **배우고** 있습니다.

I **learn** more about new technology every day.

411- 역할/yeokhal [n.] *role, part*

당신이 떠나기 전에 당신의 **역할**에 관해 브리핑을 하도록 하겠습니다.

I will give you a briefing about your **role** before you leave.

412- 옆/yeop [n.] *side, flank, vicinity, next*

당신 **옆**에 앉아도 될까요?

Do you mind if I sit **next** to you?

413- 행동/**haengdong** [n.] *action, behavior, conduct*

그의 **행동들**은 그의 약속과 대비된다.
His **actions** contrast with his promise.

414- 어/**eo** [interjection] *ah! oh! uh-huh, huh?*

어, 그것은 나에게 확실히 효과가 있었어.
Uh-huh, it certainly worked for me.

415- 국내/**gungnae** [n.] *that which is within a country, domestic*

국내 시장에서는 경쟁이 아주 치열합니다.
There is a lot of competition in the **domestic** market.

416- 비하다/**bihada** [v.] *to compare*

올해 매출은 전년도의 매출에 **비해** 어떠한가요?
How do sales in this year **compare** to those for the previous year?

417- 기관/**gigwan** [n.] *engine, machine, agency, organization*

이 **기관**은 증기로 움직입니다.
This **engine** is driven by steam.

418- 입장/**ipjang** [n.] *standpoint, perspective, position*

관점이라는 것은 어떤 것을 바라보게 되는 **입장**을 말한다.
A point of view means a **position** from which something is seen.

419- 만하다/**manhada** [a.] *sufficient, suitable, worth, deserve*

그는 일을 너무나도 잘해서 휴가를 받을 **만합니다**.
He did such good work that he **deserves** a vacation.

420- 예/ye [interjection] *yes*

예, 그것은 제가 한 것입니다.
Yes, that is what I did.

421- 아래/arae [n.] *below, bottom, lower, underneath*

관심이 있는 당사자들은 **아래** 주소로 연락을 하시면 됩니다.
If you are interested, you should contact the address **below**.

422- 방식/bangsik [n.] *method, form, way, means*

저는 매일 똑같은 **방식**으로 화장을 합니다.
I put my makeup on the same **way** every day.

423- 영향/yeonghyang [n.] *influence, effect, impact*

그 법은 어떤 **영향**을 미쳤나요?
What **effect** has the law had?

424- 그럼/geureom [interjection] *of course, sure, absolutely*

그럼, 내가 널 도와줄게.
Of course, I will help you.

425- 나서다/naseoda [v.] *to go forth, present oneself*

저는 많은 사람들 앞에 **나서는** 것을 원하지 않습니다.
I do not want to **present myself** in front of many people.

426- 흐르다/heureuda [v.] *to flow, pass by, run*

강은 그 마을 옆으로 **흐른다**.
The river **runs** beside the village.

427- 깊다/gipda [a.] *to be deep*

그 산의 골짜기는 아주 **깊습니다**.
The mountain valley is very **deep**.

428- 배/bae [n.] *ship, boat, vessel*

사람들은 **배** 안에서 점심을 먹고 있습니다.
People are having lunch in a **boat**.

429- 내/nae [n.] *I (a form of the first-person pronoun),*
my

바로 오늘이 **내** 생일이다.
This very day is **my** birthday.

430- 모양/moyang [n.] *shape, appearance, condition,*
situation, form

다양한 **모양**의 그림이 벽에 그려져 있었다.
Various **shapes** were painted on the wall.

431- 산/san [n.] *mountain, tall hill*

사람들은 **산** 정상에 있습니다.
The people are on top of a **mountain**.

432- 새/sae [n., determinder] *new*

(당신은) **새** 집으로 벌써 이사왔나요?
Did you already move into your **new** house?

433- 하지만/hajiman [adv.] *but, however*

그것은 멋져 보이네요. **하지만**, 저는 그것을 가지고 싶지 않아요.
It looks nice, **but** I do not want to have it.

434- 조건/jogeon [n.] *precondition(s), terms,*
qualification

계약상의 **조건**을 정확하게 설명해 주세요.
Please define the **terms** of the agreement.

435- 문/mun [n.] *door*

그 자동차 **문**은 차의 나머지 부분과 색이 다릅니다.

The **door** is a different color from the rest of the car.

436- 꽃/kkot [n.] *flower, flowering plant, bloom*

그 여성이 그 **꽃**의 향기를 맡고 있습니다.

The woman is smelling the **flower**.

437- 단계/dangye [n.] *stage of progress, step, phase*

우리는 이 문제를 **단계**별로 해결해야 합니다.

We must solve this problem **stage** by **stage**.

438- 올리다/ollida [v.] *to raise, increase*

저의 월급을 **올려주세요**. 그러면 제가 훨씬 더 열심히 일을 할게요.

Please **raise** my salary, and I will work even harder.

439- 그동안/geudongan [adv.] *since the last meeting or conversation, the period of time just mentioned, meantime, meanwhile*

저는 **그동안** 즐거운 시간을 가졌습니다.

I have had a great time in the **meantime**.

440- 교사/gyosa [n.] *teacher, tutor*

저는 **교사**가 된 것을 후회해 본 적이 없습니다.

I have never regretted being a **teacher**.

441- 갑자기/gapjagi [adv.] *suddenly, all of a sudden, unexpectedly*

그 남자가 **갑자기** 제 팔을 꽉 잡았습니다.

The man **suddenly** clenched my arm.

442- 넘다/neomda [v.] *to surpass, go beyond, conquer,*

jump, cross, exceed

당신의 차는 제한 속도를 **넘었습니다**.
Your car **exceeded** the speed limit.

443- 지니다/**jinida** [v.] *to keep, preserve, carry, retain, have*

그 나라는 풍부한 역사적, 그리고 문화적 유산을 **지니고 있습니다**.
The country **has** a rich historical and cultural heritage.

444- 바람/**baram** [n.] *wind, air, draft*

바람이 세게 불고 있습니다.
The **wind** is blowing hard.

445- 잘하다/**jalhada** [v.] *to do something well, be good at*

그녀는 공부를 **잘해요**.
She **is good at** studying.

446- 마을/**maeul** [n.] *village, hamlet, town*

저희 **마을**은 약 서른 채의 집으로 이루어져 있습니다.
Our **village** consists of about thirty houses.

447- 어리다/**eorida** [a.] *to be young, infantile, juvenile, immature, childish*

아이들 중 일부는 여덟 살에 불과할 정도로 **어립니다**.
Some of these children are as **young** as 8 years old.

448- 대표/**daepyo** [n.] *representative, delegate*

각 나라는 대회에 두 명의 **대표**를 보냅니다.
Each country sends two **delegates** to the rally.

449- 가능성/**ganeungseong** [n.] *possibility, probability,*

likelihood, chance

그가 승리할 **가능성**이 있습니다.

There is a **chance** that he will win.

450- 방향/banghyang [n.] *direction, orientation, course, way*

그들은 같은 **방향**을 바라보고 있었습니다.

They were looking in the same **direction**.

451- 대회/daehoe [n.] *conference, convention, competition, rally*

어떻게 해서든지 이 **대회**에서 반드시 우승해야 합니다.

We must win the **competition** at any cost.

452- 목소리/moksori [n.] *voice, tone*

그녀는 아름다운 **목소리**로 교회 사람들을 놀라게 했습니다.

She surprised the church members with her beautiful **voice**.

453- 노래/norae [n.] *song, music*

그녀의 첫 번째 **노래**는 인기있는 뮤지컬에 나오는 **노래**였습니다.

Her first song was a **song** from a popular musical.

454- 바다/bada [n.] *sea, ocean*

그들은 배를 저어 **바다**를 건너고 있습니다.

They are rowing a boat across the **sea**.

455- 힘들다/himdeulda [a.] *difficult, tired, hard, go to trouble*

그 언덕은 오르기 **힘듭니다**.

The hill is **hard** to climb.

456- 공부/gongbu [n.] *learning, studying, study*

밤새도록 **공부**했더니 피곤하네요.

I am tired from **studying** all night.

457- 움직이다/umjigida [v.] *to move, take action*

오른쪽으로 조금만 **움직여** 주세요.

Please, **move** a little to the right.

458- 의원/uiwon [n.] *member of a parliament or assembly*

그는 한때 국회**의원**이었습니다.

He was once a **member** of the National Assembly.

459- 노력/noryeok [n.] *striving, effort, endeavor, exertion, hard work*

사업의 성공은 그의 **노력**의 결과입니다.

His success in business is a result of his **hard work**.

460- 전혀/jeonhyeo [adv.] *(not) at all, absolutely, completely, utterly, totally*

저는 그것을 **전혀** 좋아하지 않습니다.

I do not like it **at all**.

461- 언니/onni [n.] *elder sister of a female, often used as a polite replacement for a second person singular pronoun*

언니는 삼 년 전에 피아노 치는 것을 그만두었어요.

My **sister** stopped playing the piano three years ago.

462- 단체/danche [n.] *group or organization of people*

열다섯 명 이상이 되는 **단체**는 십 퍼센트의 할인을 받습니다.

Groups of fifteen or more receive a ten percent discount.

463- 알려지다/**allyeojida** [v.] *to be made known, become known, be known*

그의 아버지는 대중에게 **알려져 있습니다**.
His father **is known** to the public.

464- 가능하다/**ganeunghada** [a.] *to be possible, able, feasible*

우리가 그렇게 하는 것은 **가능하다**.
It **is possible** for us to do so.

465- 능력/**neungnyeok** [n.] *capacity, ability (especially of a person), competence*

죄송하지만 이 일은 제 **능력** 밖의 일입니다.
I'm sorry, but this work is beyond my **capability**.

466- 주장하다/**jujanghada** [v.] *to make a claim or assertion, claim, insist, maintain*

그는 자신의 말이 사실이라고 **주장했습니다**.
He **asserted** that his saying were true.

467- 자식/**jasik** [n.] *a child or children*

아버지는 자신의 **자식들**을 키울 책임이 있습니다.
A father is bound by duty to raise his **children**.

468- 돌리다/**dollida** [v.] *to turn something, spin, circulate*

그 공을 몇 번만 **돌려** 보세요.
Please, **spin** the ball around a few times.

469- 불/**bul** [n.] *fire, flame, light, furnace, fireplace*

집에 **불**이 나서 벽과 가구가 새까맣게 타버렸습니다.
The **fire** in the house charred the walls and the furniture.

470- 주민/**jumin** [n.] *residents in a place, legal residency,*

inhabitant

그 마을에는 삼만 명의 **주민들**이 있습니다.
The town numbers thirty thousand **inhabitants**.

471- 모으다/moeuda [v.] *to gather, collect*

저는 불을 피우기 위해 마른 나뭇가지들을 **모았습니다**.
I **gathered** dry sticks for the fire.

472- 자료/jaryo [n.] *data, documentation, materials*

그 학생은 **자료**에 대해 무엇을 물어봤나요?
What did the student ask about the **data**?

473- 존재/jonjae [n.] *existence, (philosophy) being*

UFO 의 **존재**를 알 수 있는 방법이 없습니다.
There is no way to know the **existence** of UFOs.

474- 학년/hangnyeon [n.] *school year, grade*

오늘 새 **학년**이 시작되었습니다.
A new **school year** began today.

475- 신문/sinmun [n.] *newspaper*

저는 오늘 **신문**의 모든 기사를 읽었습니다.
I read all the articles in today's **newspapers**.

476- 이해하다/ihaehada [v.] *to understand, comprehend*

저는 그의 뜻을 **이해하지** 못하고 있어요.
I do not **understand** what he means.

477- 제품/jepum [n.] *product, manufacture, goods*

저희 **제품들**은 크기에 따라 다르게 디자인됩니다.
Our **products** are designed differently according to size.

478- 분야/bunya [n.] *sector, field of business or study, area, field*

토목 공학은 공학 **분야**에서 가장 오래된 것입니다.
Civil engineering is the oldest in the **field** of engineering.

479- 선생님/seonsaengnim [n.] *teacher, often used to address a person whose professional status is unknown*

선생님의 말씀대로 하세요.
Please, do as your **teacher** tells you.

480- 돌아가다/doragada [v.] *to return, go back*

그는 내년에 고국으로 **돌아갈** 계획을 가지고 있어요.
He is planning to **return** to his country next year.

481- 사업/saeop [n.] *business, project*

저는 더 나은 실적을 위해 **사업** 투자에 대해 이야기하고 싶습니다.
I would like to talk about the **business** investment for better performance.

482- 행위/haengwi [n.] *act, action, behavior, deed*

그와 같은 **행위**는 당신에게 맞지 않아요.
Such **actions** do not befit you.

483- 수준/sujun [n.] *standard, criterion level*

그는 중학교 **수준**의 독해 능력을 가지고 있습니다.
He reads at a junior high school **level**.

484- 지난해/jinanhae [n.] *the previous year, last year*

그는 **지난해**를 뒤돌아보고 새로운 해를 바라보고 있습니다.
He looked back to the **last year** and forward to the new one.

485- 표현/pyohyeon [n.] *expression*

이러한 **표현**은 주로 문어체가 아닌 구어체에서 쓰입니다.

Expressions like these are used mainly in speech, not in writing.

486- 기분/gibun [n.] *feeling, mood*

그녀는 오늘 정말 **기분이** 좋지 않습니다.

She is really in a bad **mood** today.

487- 젊다/jeomda [a.] *to be young, youthful*

그는 나이는 많지만 힘은 **젊은** 사람 못지 않습니다.

He is old in years, but **young** in vigor.

488- 동시/dongsi [n.] *the same time, concurrently*

동시에 많은 사람들과 대화를 나눌 수 있습니다.

You can communicate with many people at **the same time**.

489- 옷/ot [n.] *clothing, clothes, dress*

그 새 **옷**을 입으니까 정말 멋져 보여요.

You look great in that new **clothes**.

490- 기능/gineung [n.] *capacity, ability, function, functionality, feature*

열은 우리의 일상 생활에서 많은 중요한 **기능**을 담당합니다.

Heat serves many important **functions** in our daily lives.

491- 순간/sungan [n.] *instant, moment*

저는 여행의 모든 **순간**을 즐겼습니다.

I enjoyed every **moment** of the trip.

492- 전쟁/jeonjaeng [n.] *war*

항상 **전쟁**에 대해 대비를 하는 것이 전쟁을 피할 수 있는 가장 확실한 방법이다.
To be always ready for **war** is the surest way to avoid it

493- 꿈/kkum [n.] *dream*

꿈이야, 아니면 진짜야?
Is it a **dream**, or is it real?

494- 할머니/halmeoni [n.] *grandmother, elderly female*

저는 저희 **할머니**의 오랜 요리법을 그대로 사용해요.
I just use my **grandmother's** old recipe the same way.

495- 회의/hoeui [n.] *meeting, conference, council, convention*

위원회 의원들은 두 시에 **회의**를 소집했습니다.
The committee members convened for a **meeting** at two.

496- 방송/bangsong [n.] *broadcasting, a radio or television program*

그 **방송**은 생방송이 아니라 녹화된 것이었습니다.
The **broadcast** was recorded, not live.

497- 이야기하다/iyagihada [v.] *to talk, tell, speak*

그 남자가 제 동생에게 **이야기하고** 있어요.
The man is **talking** to my brother.

498- 나무/namu [n.] *tree, wood*

나무는 종이를 만들 때 사용되는 재료입니다.
Wood is the material used to make paper.

499- 자다/jada [v.] *to sleep*

대부분의 사람들은 밤에 **자고** 아침에 일어납니다.
Most people **sleep** at night and wake up in the morning.

500- 연극/**yeongeuk** [n.] *a public show or performance, play, drama, act*

저희는 특별히 **연극**의 세 번째 막을 즐겁게 관람했습니다.
We especially enjoyed the third act of the **play**.

501- 마찬가지/**machangaji** [n.] *being exactly the same, identical, likewise*

그것은 누구에게나 **마찬가지**예요.
That is **the same** for anyone.

502- 걷다/**geotda** [v.] *to walk*

하루에 삼십 분씩 **걷는** 것은 건강에 좋습니다.
Walking thirty minutes a day is good for your health.

503- 노동/**nodong** [n.] *labor, work, working*

나는 네가 **노동**의 중요성을 배웠으면 해.
I want you to learn the importance of **working**.

504- 이때/**ittae** [n.] *now, at this time, right now*

항상 일 년 중 **이때** 눈이 내리기 시작합니다.
It always begins to snow **at this time** of year.

505- 과거/**gwageo** [n.] *the past*

고고학을 통해 사람들은 **과거**의 삶을 추측할 수 있습니다.
Through archaeology, people can guess the life of **the past**.

506- 가치/**gachi** [n.] *value, worth*

사람들은 건강을 잃어버리기 전까지는 그 **가치**를 모릅니다.
People do not know the **value** of health till they lose it.

507- 집단/**jipdan** [n.] *a group of people, body*

학생들은 전형적으로 자신들의 또래 **집단**을 매우 중요하게 여긴다.

The students typically place great importance on their peer **group**.

508- 현대/hyeondae [n.] *contemporary (times), modern age, modern times*

현대 사람들은 휴대폰 없는 삶을 상상할 수 없다.

People in **modern times** cannot imagine life without a cell phone.

509- 살펴보다/salpyeoboda [v.] *to observe, watch attentively, examine, search, check*

그 남자가 카펫을 **살펴보고** 있습니다.

The man is **examining** the carpets.

510- 장관/janggwan [n.] *a minister, a member of cabinet, secretary*

그 기사는 새로운 재무**장관**에 대한 것입니다.

The article is about the new finance **minister**.

511- 차이/chai [n.] *distinction, difference, gap, disparity*

일등석과 이코노미석의 **차이**는 무엇인가요?

What is the **difference** between first class and economy?

512- 풀다/pulda [v.] *to untie, loosen up, solve, unwind, untangle*

그녀는 그 매듭을 **풀려고** 했습니다.

She tried to **untie** the knot.

513- 시절/sijeol [n.] *a period of time, a time of life, a season, days, years*

저는 학창 **시절**에 축구를 잘했습니다.

I was good at playing soccer in my school **years**.

514- 물건/mulgeon [n.] *item, article, thing, stuff, object,*

product

해변에 **물건**을 파는 사람들이 많이 있습니다.

There are a lot of people selling **things** on the beach.

515- 직접/jikjeop [adv.] *directly, on one's own, by oneself, personally, in person*

저는 정말로 그녀와 **직접** 이야기하고 싶습니다.

I really want to speak to her **directly**.

516- 개인/gaein [n.] *an individual, individuals, personal*

목표는 **개인**이 고통에서 벗어날 수 있도록 돕는 것입니다.

The goal is to help the **individual** become free of suffering.

517- 근데/geunde [adv.] *however, nonetheless, by the way*

근데 내일 저녁에 식사를 할 시간이 있나요?

By the way, are you free for dinner tomorrow evening?

518- 발/bal [n.] *foot, feet*

저는 **발**을 다쳐서 걷기가 힘들어요.

I hurt my **foot** and it's difficult to walk.

519- 작가/jakga [n.] *writer, author, poet, novelist*

그 **작가**는 주요 줄거리를 머릿속에 구상했습니다.

The **writer** formed an idea of the main plot.

520- 효과/hyogwa [n.] *result, effect, effectiveness, impact*

그것은 특수 **효과**가 아니었습니다.

That was not a special **effect**.

521- 끌다/kkeulda [v.] *to pull, draw out*

그의 연설은 사람들의 관심을 **끌었습니다**.

His speech **drew** people's attention.

522- 대로/daero [n.] *(in) the same way as, the manner of, as*

선생님의 말씀**대로** 하세요.

Please, do **as** your teacher tells you.

523- 빨리/ppalli [adv.] *quickly, without delay, fast, early*

가능한 한 **빨리** 여기로 오세요.

Please, come here as **quickly** as possible.

524- 시작되다/sijakdoeda [v.] *to start, begin*

오늘 새 학년이 **시작되었습니다**.

A new school year **began** today.

525- 생산/saengsan [n.] *production, manufacture*

새로운 기술은 **생산** 비용을 낮출 것입니다.

The new technique will lower the cost of **production**.

526- 설명하다/seolmyeonghada [v.] *to explain*

새 제품에 대해 제가 간단하게 **설명하도록** 하겠습니다.

I will **explain** briefly about the new product.

527- 우주/uju [n.] *space, outer space, the universe, the cosmos*

지구는 **우주**에서 볼 때 너무나도 아름답게 보였습니다.

The earth looked so beautiful from **space**.

528- 시기/sigi [n.] *a time, a period of time*

그 **시기**는 삼 년 동안 지속되었습니다.

The **period of time** lasted for three years.

529- 마치/machi [adv.] *exactly the same, as if, just like*

저는 **마치** 공중에 떠 있었던 것처럼 느꼈습니다.

I felt **as if** I were floating in the air.

530- 살/sal [n.] *flesh, skin*

탄환이 **살** 속에 박혀 있습니다.

A bullet is embedded in the **flesh**.

531- 바라다/barada [v.] *to wish, hope, desire, long for, want*

당신과 제가 영원히 좋은 친구가 될 수 있기를 **바랍니다**.

I **hope** you and I can be good friends forever.

532- 강하다/ganghada [a.] *strong, powerful, mighty*

강한 바람은 홍수로 인한 피해를 가중시켰습니다.

A **strong** wind increased the damage caused by the flooding.

533- 경험/gyeongheom [n.] *experience*

저는 판매원으로서 사 년 이상의 **경험**이 있습니다.

I have over four years of **experience** as a sales clerk.

534- 음악/eumak [n.] *music*

저는 그들과 소통하기 위해 **음악**을 사용합니다.

I use **music** to communicate with them.

535- 최고/choego [n.] *the peak, the pinnacle, the topmost point, the best, the most*

그녀는 **최고**는 아니었지만, 우수한 편이였습니다.

She was not **the best**, but she also was good.

536- 나타내다/natanaeda [v.] *to indicate, represent,*

show, appear, express

일반적으로 따뜻함을 **나타내는** 색은 무엇인가요?
What color typically **represents** warmth?

537- 아프다/apeuda [a.] *to be painful, ache, hurt*

저는 머리가 아파요.
My head **hurts**.

538- 적다/jeokda [a.] *to be little, few, small*

저희는 **적은** 성공 가능성을 가지고 있었습니다.
We had **little** chance of success.

539- 비/bi [n.] *rain*

비가 쏟아져 내리고 있습니다.
The **rain** is pouring down.

540- 고향/gohyang [n.] *hometown, birthplace, home*

그의 부모님은 아직 그의 **고향**에서 살고 계십니다.
His parents still live in his **hometown**.

541- 놀라다/nollada [v.] *to be surprised, be astonished, be amazed*

그는 그 소식을 듣고 깜짝 **놀랐습니다**.
He **was astonished** at the news.

542- 다양하다/dayanghada [a.] *to be diverse, various, varied*

그 회사의 문화는 매우 **다양합니다**.
The culture of the company is very **diverse**.

543- 울다/**ulda** [v.] *to cry, weep*

많은 아기들이 시끄러운 소리를 듣고 **울기** 시작했습니다.

When the babies heard a loud noise, many began to **cry**.

544- 농민/**nongmin** [n.] *farmers, peasantry*

폭풍은 **농민들**에게 재난을 가져다 주었습니다.

The storm brought disaster to the **farmers**.

545- 드러나다/**deureonada** [v.] *to appear, become manifest, be exposed, come out, turn out, be revealed*

부정부패 사건들이 **드러났다**.

Corruption cases **were revealed**.

546- 은행/**eunhaeng** [n.] *a bank (financial institution)*

오늘 **은행**은 몇 시에 문을 닫나요?

What time does the **bank** close today?

547- 지내다/**jinaeda** [v.] *to spend (one's time), live, get along*

그는 하루의 일부를 바닷가에서 **지냅니다**.

He **spends** a part of each day at the beach.

548- 결혼/**gyeolhon** [n.] *marriage*

결혼은 인생의 두 번째 시작입니다.

Marriage is the second beginning of life.

549- 동생/**dongsaeng** [n.] *younger sibling, younger sister or brother*

그는 제 **동생**이에요.

He is my **younger brother**.

550- 법/beop [n.] *law*

많은 사람들이 동의할 경우, 투표를 통해 **법**은 개정될 수 있습니다.
The **law** can be amended through voting if many people agree.

551- 소설/soseol [n.] *novel, fiction*

그는 아직 그의 **소설**을 완성하지 못했습니다.
He has not yet finished his **novel**.

552- 오후/ohu [n.] *afternoon, p.m.*

날이 추워지기 시작했지만, **오후**에는 조금 따뜻해졌어요.
The day began cold, but warmed up a little in the **afternoon**.

553- 질서/jilseo [n.] *order, good order, public order, appropriate behavior*

경찰이 나서서 평화와 **질서**를 유지하기 위해 힘을 쓸 것입니다.
The police will be out in force to maintain peace and **order**.

554- 담다/damda [v.] *to put into (a container)*

그녀는 김치를 만들어서 통에 담았습니다.
She made kimchi and **put** it **into** a container.

555- 모이다/moida [v.] *to be gathered, be collected together, gather, assemble*

그들은 서울에서 **모일** 것입니다.
They will **gather** in Seoul.

556- 시민/simin [n.] *citizen(s), citizenry, the people of a city*

시민들은 자신들의 의무를 다해야 할 필요가 있습니다.
Citizens need to meet their obligations.

557- 회장/hoejang [n.] *chairman, president*

민수는 **회장**의 대리인 역할을 하고 있습니다.

Min-soo is acting as the **chairman**'s deputy.

558- 빠르다/ppareuda [a.] *(to be) fast, quick, soon, early, rapid, speedy*

박 선생님은 걸음이 **빠릅니다**.

Mr. Park is a **quick** walker.

559- 스스로/seuseuro [adv.] *by oneself, on one's own, without assistance, for oneself*

저는 그 문제를 **스스로** 해결해 냈습니다.

I managed to fix the problem **on my own**.

560- 아기/agi [n.] *baby, infant, child*

그 **아기**는 매일 밤마다 몇 번이고 일어나 젖을 달라고 보챘다.

The **baby** woke up crying several times every night to be fed.

561- 아저씨/ajeossi [n.] *middle-aged elder male, uncle, mister, gentleman*

저는 어젯밤에 **아저씨** 댁에서 머물렀습니다.

Last night I stayed at my **uncle**'s.

562- 옛날/yennal [n.] *(in) the past, long ago, once upon a time, the old days*

옛날에 그곳에 학교가 있었다고 합니다.

They say that a school stood there in **the old days**.

563- 이날/inal [n.] *that day, this day, the very day*

저희는 일 년에 한 번 **이날**을 기념합니다.

We celebrate **this day** once a year.

564- 제대로/jedaero [adv.] *properly, in the appropriate manner, according to one's standards*

그 기계는 **제대로** 작동하고 있나요?
Does the machine work **properly**?

565- 달/dal [n.] *month*

저희 어머니는 이번 **달**에 일흔 살이 되십니다.
My mother turns seventy years old this **month**.

566- 던지다/deonjida [v.] *to throw, cast, toss, pitch*

그 아이는 연못에 그물을 **던졌습니다**.
The child **cast** the net into the pond.

567- 참/cham [adv.] *truly, really, indeed*

그녀는 **참** 친절합니다.
She is **really** kind.

568- 공간/gonggan [n.] *(empty) space, room*

그 도서관에는 사람들이 이용할 수 있는 더 많은 **공간**이 필요합니다.
The library needs more **space** for people to use.

569- 이곳/igot [pron.] *here, this place*

이곳이 이 지역에서 가장 특별한 식당입니다.
This place is the most unique restaurant in this area.

570- 딸/ttal [n.] *daughter*

그녀에게는 아들 셋과 **딸** 하나가 있습니다.
She has three sons and one **daughter**.

571- 마지막/majimak [n.] *the end, the last thing*

마지막 공연이 몇 시인가요?
What time is **the last** show?

572- 벌이다/beorida [v.] *to start, begin, stage*

그들은 행진을 **벌였다**.
They **staged** a march.

573- 병원/byeongwon [n.] *hospital, clinic*

그들은 부상을 당한 사람들을 **병원**으로 이송해 주었습니다.
They drove the injured people to the **hospital**.

574- 자세/jase [n.] *posture, carriage, attitude, pose*

그녀는 일에 대해 훌륭한 **자세**를 가지고 있습니다.
She has a good **attitude** toward work.

575- 강조하다/gangjohada [v.] *to emphasize, highlight*

어떤 사람들은 자신들의 주장을 **강조하기** 위해 감정적인 호소를 사용한다.
Some people use emotional appeals to **emphasize** their points.

576- 경찰/gyeongchal [n.] *police*

경찰은 그 남자를 감옥으로 보냈습니다.
The **police** sent the man to jail.

577- 맡다/matda [v.] *to take on a task or job, take charge of, manage*

누가 너의 수업을 **맡게** 되니?
Who is going to **take charge of** your class?

578- 저녁/jeonyeok [n.] *evening, evening meal, supper, dinner*

저희가 금요일 **저녁**에 떠나면, 일요일 **저녁**에 돌아올 수 있을 것입니다.
If we leave Friday **evening**, we can come back Sunday **evening**.

579- 한편/hanpyeon [adv.] *on the other hand, while, meanwhile*

한편, 소년들의 경우 긴 머리를 갖는 것이 허락되지 않았습니다.
Boys, **meanwhile**, were not allowed to have long hair.

580- 그러면/geureomyeon [adv.] *if so, in that case, then*

그러면 그 가격에 대해 저에게 말해주실 수 있나요?
Then can you tell me about the price?

581- 기자/gija [n.] *reporter, journalist, newsman, correspondent*

기자가 한 학생을 인터뷰하고 있습니다.
A **reporter** is interviewing a student.

582- 넓다/neolda [a.] *wide, large, broad, extensive, spacious, roomy*

이 규제의 범위는 매우 **넓습니다**.
The scope of this regulation is very **broad**.

583- 시험/siheom [n.] *test, exam, experimentation*

저는 취직 필기 **시험**을 치르는 것이 걱정입니다.
I am worried about taking a written **test** for a job.

584- 잠/jam [n.] *sleep, nap*

당신은 **잠**을 더 자야할 것 같아요.
I think you need more **sleep**.

585- 주로/juro [adv.] *chiefly, principally, mostly, mainly*

이 방송국은 **주로** 팝 명곡을 틉니다.
This radio station plays **mainly** classic pop.

586- 훨씬/hwolssin [adv.] *much (more or less), a lot*

그것은 이전 것보다 **훨씬** 더 큽니다.
It is **much** larger than the previous one.

587- 들어서다/deureoseoda [v.] *to enter*

사람들이 막 건물 안으로 **들어서려고** 합니다.
People are about to **enter** the building.

588- 건강/geongang [n.] *health*

저는 당신의 **건강**이 가장 중요하다고 생각해요.
I think the most important thing is your **health**.

589- 가깝다/gakkapda [a.] *to be close, near*

학교는 저희 집에서 **가깝습니다**.
The school **is close** to my house.

590- 건물/geonmul [n.] *building, construction, edifice*

그 **건물**은 수리가 심각하게 필요한 상태입니다.
The **building** is badly in need of repair.

591- 시설/siseol [n.] *facilities, establishment*

건물 안에 있는 **시설**을 이용해도 좋습니다.
You can use the **facilities** in the building.

592- 외국/oeguk [n.] *a foreign country*

저는 내년에 **외국**으로 여행을 갈 것입니다.
I will travel to **a foreign country** next year.

593- 밑/mit [n.] *below, bottom, lower, underneath*

밑에 서명해주세요.
Please sign at the **bottom**.

594- 어른/eoreun [n.] *grownup, adult, elder, senior*

어른들은 어린 사람이 말참견하는 것을 좋아하지 않습니다.
Adults do not like youngsters putting in a word.

595- 주변/jubyeon [n.] *the vicinity, the periphery*

상처 **주변**에 이도와 삼도의 화상이 있습니다.
On the **periphery** of the wound, there are second and third-degree burns.

596- 대신/daesin [n.] *substitution, replacement, instead of*

그들은 현금 대신 신용카드를 사용합니다.
They use credit cards **instead of** cash.

597- 원인/wonin [n.] *cause*

화재의 **원인**은 알려지지 않았습니다.
The **cause** of the fire is unknown.

598- 팔다/palda [v.] *to sell*

오늘날 사람들은 인터넷에서 물건들을 사고 **팝니다**.
Today people buy and **sell** the things on the Internet.

599- 차례/charye [n.] *sequence, times*

그는 오늘 오후에 여러 **차례** 전화했습니다.
He called several **times** this afternoon.

600- 열심히/yeolsimhi [adv.] *enthusiastically, fervently, with dedication, hard*

그는 농장에서 **열심히** 일했습니다.
He worked **hard** on his farm.

601- 일하다/ilhada [v.] *to work, do one's job, labor, serve*

저희는 주야 교대로 **일합니다**.

We **work** in shifts day and night.

602- 재산/jaesan [n.] *public or private property, monetary assets, treasure, possessions, fortune*

그는 자신의 딸에게 **재산**을 양도하는 서명을 했습니다.

He signed his **property** over to his daughter.

603- 조금/jogeum [adv.] *a little, a bit*

저는 요즘 **조금** 바빠요.

I am **a little** busy these days.

604- 팀/tim [n.] *team*

당시에 저희 **팀**이 앞서고 있었어요.

Our **team** was ahead at that time.

605- 부모/bumo [n.] *parents*

당신은 **부모**님과 함께 살고 있나요?

Are you living with your **parents**?

606- 약간/yakgan [adv.] *a little, a bit, somewhat*

국이 **약간** 짜네요.

The soup is **a little** salty.

607- 언어/eoneo [n.] *language*

몇 가지 **언어**를 할 수 있나요?

How many **languages** do you speak?

608- 요구하다/yoguhada [v.] *to demand, require, request, claim*

그는 돈을 갚으라고 **요구했다**.

He **requested** the return of the money.

609- 올라가다/ollagada [v.] *to go up, ascend, rise, increase*

위로 **올라가자** 공기가 차가워졌다.
The air became colder as I **ascended.**

610- 첫/cheot [n.] *first, initial*

부산으로 가는 **첫** 기차는 몇 시죠?
What time is the **first** train to Busan?

611- 감독/gamdok [n.] *direction, supervision, the director of a cinematic or theatrical production, supervisor, coach*

감독이 신호를 주자 배우들이 연기를 시작했습니다.
The actors started acting on cue from the **director.**

612- 그날/geunal [n.] *that day, the day, the very day*

그날 매출은 총 오만 원이었습니다.
The sales for **the day** totaled fifty thousand won.

613- 자주/jaju [adv.] *often, frequently*

매주 얼마나 **자주** 운동을 하나요?
How **often** do you exercise each week?

614- 할아버지/harabeoji [n.] *grandfather, elderly male*

저희 **할아버지**는 지금도 자신의 땅에서 농사를 짓고 계세요.
My **grandfather** still farms on his own land.

615- 삼다/samda [v.] *to take as, forge a relationship, adopt*

그는 그 젊은 남자를 자신의 후계자로 **삼았습니다.**

90

He **adopted** the young man as his heir.

616- 약/yak [adv.] *approximately, about, roughly*

저는 거기서 **약** 삼 년 동안 일했습니다.
I worked there for **about** three years.

617- 기간/gigan [n.] *a set interval or period of time, term*

새로운 계약 **기간**은 2 년입니다.
The new contract **period** is two years.

618- 담배/dambae [n.] *tobacco, cigarette*

하루에 **담배**를 얼마나 많이 피우세요?
How many **cigarettes** do you smoke a day?

619- 일으키다/ireukida [v.] *to rouse, cause, trigger, raise, kindle, stir up*

스트레스는 심장에 문제를 **일으킬** 수 있습니다.
Stress can **cause** heart problems.

620- 일단/ildan [adv.] *first and foremost, first, for a moment, just for starters, for now, once*

일단 그것을 시작하게 되면, 넌 멈출 수 없을 거야.
If you start to do it **once**, you will not be able to stop it.

621- 조직/jojik [n.] *organization, group*

그 **조직**은 평판이 좋습니다.
The **organization** is in high repute.

622- 태어나다/taeeonada [v.] *to be born*

그는 그의 아버지가 중국으로 떠난 날에 **태어났습니다**.
He **was born** the day that his father left for China.

623- 공장/gongjang [n.] *factory, plant*

그 **공장**은 완전 가동 중입니다.
That **factory** is working at capacity.

624- 벌써/beolsseo [adv.] *already*

저는 **벌써** 당신을 세 번이나 불렀어요.
I have called you three times **already**.

625- 즐기다/jeulgida [v.] *to enjoy, have fun*

함께 열심히 해요. 그러면 모두가 수학 수업을 **즐길** 수 있을 거예요.
Let's work together, and everyone can **enjoy** math class.

626- 환자/hwanja [n.] *a medical patient, the sick*

심장병으로 인해 여기에 있는 **환자**를 만나려고 왔습니다.
I am here to visit a **patient** who is here for a heart problem.

627- 변하다/byeonhada [v.] *to change*

날씨가 하루에도 여러 차례 **변합니다**.
The weather **changes** many times throughout the course of a day.

628- 사고/sago [n.] *accident, trouble*

이 남자가 교통 **사고**를 목격했습니다.
This man witnessed the traffic **accident**.

629- 그래도/geuraedo [adv.] *nevertheless, but, however*

그래도 저는 제가 완료할 수 있을 것이라고 믿고 있어요.
Nevertheless, I do believe I can complete it.

630- 맞추다/matchuda [v.] *to set, adjust, tune, adapt*

당신은 시계를 바른 시간에 **맞출** 필요가 있어요.
You need to **set** the clock to the proper hour of the day.

631- 쌀/ssal [n.] *rice*

쌀 가격은 한 가마에 만오천 원입니다.
The price of **rice** is one hundred fifty thousand won a bag.

632- 일반/ilban [n.] *general, overall*

그들은 **일반** 대중에게 전력을 공급하지 않습니다.
They do not provide power to the **general** public.

633- 재미있다/jaemiitda [a.] *amusing, entertaining, funny, interesting*

제가 읽고 있는 이 책은 **재미있습니다**.
The book that I am reading is **interesting**.

634- 가르치다/gareuchida [v.] *to teach, impart knowledge, instruct, coach*

그에게 휴대폰 사용법을 **가르쳐** 주는 일은 쉽지 않아요.
It is not easy to **teach** him how to use the mobile phone.

635- 대화/daehwa [n.] *dialogue, conversation, talk*

그녀는 사람들과 **대화**를 잘 나누는 기술에 대해 알고 있습니다.
She knows the art of making good **conversation** with people.

636- 막다/makda [v.] *to stop, enclose, fence, hinder, prevent, block, obstruct*

우리는 병의 확산을 **막아야** 합니다.
We have to **prevent** the spread of disease.

637- 올해/olhae [n.] *this year, the current year*

올해 처음으로 눈이 왔던 것이었습니다.
It was the first time it snowed **this year**.

638- 붙이다/buchida [v.] *to affix, attach, stick, glue*

저희는 도시 벽에 영화 포스터를 **붙였습니다**.

We **pasted** up movie posters on the walls of the city.

639- 인물/inmul [n.] *the physical figure of a person, a person of importance, character*

그는 경제개혁 운동의 핵심 **인물**입니다.

He is a central **person** in the economic reform movement.

640- 늘/neul [adv.] *always, forever, all the time, the whole time*

그는 **늘** 담배를 피고 있어요.

He is constantly smoking.

641- 전국/jeonguk [n.] *the whole land making up a country, the whole country*

한파가 **전국**을 덮쳤습니다.

A cold wave hit **the whole country**.

642- 마치다/machida [v.] *to finish, end, complete, close*

저는 오늘 이 일을 **마쳐야** 합니다.

I must **finish** this work today.

643- 도움/doum [n.] *help, assistance, favor*

저는 선생님의 **도움**으로 시험에 합격했습니다.

I passed the exam with the **help** of my teacher.

644- 가정/gajeong [n.] *family, household, supposition, hypothesis*

어떤 **가정**도 가족 구성원 간의 화합 없이는 행복할 수 없습니다.

No **family** can be happy without harmony among its members.

645- 걸다/geolda [v.] *to hang*

저는 벽에 거울을 **걸었습니다**.
I **hung** a mirror on a wall.

646- 빠지다/ppajida [v.] *to fall into, sink*

그는 물에 **빠졌습니다**.
He **fell into** the water.

647- 멀다/meolda [a.] *far*

너희 집에서 학교까지 **멀어**?
Is it **far** from your home to school?

648- 버스/beoseu [n.] *bus*

버스가 오네요.
Here comes the **bus**.

649- 오늘날/oneullal [n.] *today, these days, modern times, present times*

오늘날 가스는 요리를 할 때 널리 쓰입니다.
Today, gas is widely used for cooking.

650- 잠시/jamsi [n.] *a moment, a short time*

잠시 기다려 주세요.
Please, wait **a minute**.

651- 농업/nongeop [n.] *agriculture, farming*

요즘에는 유기 **농업**이 매우 인기가 많습니다.
These days organic **farming** is very popular.

652- 의견/uigyeon [n.] *opinion, view, suggestion*

당신의 **의견**은 저의 의견과 비슷합니다.
Your **opinion** is similar to mine.

653- 무대/mudae [n.] *a performance stage*

사람들이 **무대**에서 춤을 추고 있습니다.

People are dancing on the **stage**.

654- 사진/sajin [n.] *photograph, picture*

그 여성이 **사진**을 찾고 있습니다.

The woman is looking for a **picture**.

655- 주장/jujang [n.] *claim, assertion, opinion, contention*

그 두 사람은 법정에서 서로의 **주장**에 대해 반론을 제기했습니다.

The two people disputed each other's **claims** in court.

656- 표현하다/pyohyeonhada [v.] *to express*

예술가들은 상징주의를 사용하여 깊이 내재된 감정을 **표현합니다**.

Artists use symbolism to **express** deep feelings.

657- 인하다/inhada [v.] *to be due to, be caused by, arise from, result from*

비로 **인해** 게임이 세 차례 중단되었습니다.

The game was halted three times **due to** the rain.

658- 이상하다/isanghada [a.] *to be strange, unusual, weird, odd*

그녀의 옷은 너무 **이상해** 보여요.

Her clothes look so **weird**.

659- 제일/jeil [adv.] *number one, the first, the primary, most*

제가 생각하기에 **제일** 중요한 것은 당신의 사랑입니다.

I think the **most** important thing is your love.

660- 붙다/**butda** [v.] *pass (the exam or test)*

그는 시험에 **붙었나요**?
Did he **pass** the exam?

661- 아마/**ama** [adv.] *perhaps, maybe, probably, possibly*

아마 괜찮을 거예요.
Probably it will be all right.

662- 얘기하다/**yaegihada** [v.] *to talk, have a conversation*

당신과 **얘기하다** 보니까 시간이 가는 줄도 몰랐어요.
I have lost track of the time **talking** with you.

663- 잇다/**itda** [v.] *to join, connect*

유라시아 횡단 여정은 아시아와 유럽을 **이어줍니다**.
A transeurasia journey **connects** Asia with Europe.

664- 경기/**gyoenggi** [n.] *a sporting or athletic competition or match*

축구 **경기**를 친구들과 함께 보는 것은 너무나도 신나는 일입니다.
It is so exciting to watch the soccer **game** with my friends.

665- 목적/**mokjeok** [n.] *goal, objective, purpose*

이 연구의 **목적**은 에너지 사용을 조사하는 것입니다.
The **objective** of this study is to research energy use.

666- 태도/**taedo** [n.] *attitude, manner*

선생님은 저의 **태도**를 문제 삼으셨습니다.
My teacher brought my **attitude** into question.

667- 남성/**namseong** [n.] *male, the masculine gender, man*

연구원들은 11 년 동안 남성들을 연구했습니다.

The researchers have studied the **men** for eleven years.

668- 발생하다/balsaenghada [v.] *to occur, happen*

그런 일들이 가끔씩 **발생합니다**.
Such things **happen** from time to time.

669- 대책/daechaek [n.] *policy with regard to a particular issue, measure*

이 상황은 과감한 **대책**을 필요로 합니다.
This situation calls for drastic **measures**.

670- 그만/geuman [adv.] *this much only, no more*

그만 먹어요.
Please, don't eat **anymore**.

671- 다리/dari [n.] *leg, bridge*

개울이 **다리** 아래를 흐르고 있습니다.
A stream flows under the **bridge**.

672- 아무/amu [determiner] *any*

다음 주 **아무** 때나 편하신 때에 만날 수 있습니다.
We can meet at your convenience **any** time next week.

673- 어쩌다/eojjeoda [adv.] *by chance, somehow, accidentally, by accident*

저는 **어쩌다** 그녀를 또 만났어요.
I met her again **by chance**.

674- 재료/jaeryo [n.] *ingredient, material, raw material*

건축에 사용되는 또 다른 **재료**는 나무였습니다.
Another **material** that was used for building was wood.

675- 각각/gakgak [adv.] *each, every, respectively*

견본이 **각각** 얼마나 많이 필요하신가요?
How many samples of **each** do you need?

676- 결코/gyeolko [adv.] *(not) at all, never*

그들 대부분은 **결코** 거기에 있고 싶어하지 않았습니다.
Most of them did not want to be there **at all**.

677- 옮기다/omgida [v.] *to move, shift, transfer*

저희 엄마는 탁자를 구석에서 방 한 가운데로 **옮겼습니다**.
My mom **moved** a table from a corner to the center of the room.

678- 항상/hangsang [adv.] *always, at all times, all the time*

저는 **항상** 매년 이맘때쯤 일 때문에 너무나도 바쁩니다.
I am **always** too busy with work at that time of year.

679- 해/hae [n.] *sun, sunlight*

해가 지고 나면 날씨가 추워질 것입니다.
The weather will become cold after the **sun** goes down.

680- 잃다/ilta [v.] *to lose*

저희가 건강을 **잃으면** 돈과 성공이 무슨 의미가 있겠어요?
What good are money and success when we **lose** our health?

681- 자유/jayu [n.] *freedom, liberty*

민주 국가의 기본은 **자유**입니다.
The basis of a democratic state is **liberty**.

682- 책임/chaegim [n.] *responsibility, duty*

가족을 부양한다는 것은 엄청난 **책임**입니다.
Supporting a family is a great **responsibility**.

683- 바뀌다/**bakkwuida** [v.] *to be changed, be exchanged, be transformed, turn*

저희의 월례 회의 날짜가 **바뀐다고** 메모에 쓰여 있습니다.
The memo states the date of our monthly meeting is **changing.**

684- 비슷하다/**biseuthada** [a.] *similar, alike*

그들은 성격이 많이 **비슷합니다**.
They are much **alike** in character.

685- 심하다/**simhada** [a.] *severe, extreme*

올해 늦더위가 **심합니다**.
The heat of late summer is **severe** this year.

686- 경쟁/**gyeongjaeng** [n.] *competition*

그러한 직종에 대한 **경쟁**이 심해질 것입니다.
Competition for such jobs will be strong.

687- 달러/**dalleo** [n.] *dollar*

일 **달러**의 사분의 일은 이십 오센트입니다.
A quarter of a **dollar** is twenty-five cents.

688- 사랑하다/**saranghada** [v.] *to love*

저는 죽는 날까지 당신만을 **사랑할** 것입니다.
I will **love** only you until the day I die.

689- 여름/**yeoreum** [n.] *summer, summer time*

여름에는 해가 깁니다.
In **summer**, the days are long.

690- 자라다/**jarada** [v.] *to grow*

녹색 풀이 마당에서 **자라고 있습니다**.
Green grass **grows** in the yard.

691- 구체적/**guchejoek** [determiner] *concrete, not abstract, detailed, specific*

제가 **구체적** 질문 몇 가지를 여쭈어보겠습니다.
Let me ask you some **specific** questions.

692- 기회/**gihoe** [n.] *opportunity, chance*

당신에게 좋은 투자 **기회**에 대해 이야기해 주고 싶었어요.
I wanted to tell you about a great investment **opportunity**.

693- 실시하다/**silsihada** [v.] *to put into practice, implement, carry into effect, carry out, perform*

그 의사는 통상적인 외과 수술을 **실시했습니다**.
The doctor **performed** a routine surgical procedure.

694- 지구/**jigu** [n.] *earth*

달은 **지구**의 위성입니다.
The moon is a satellite of the **Earth**.

695- 소비자/**sobija** [n.] *consumer*

자본주의 사회에서는 **소비자**가 왕입니다.
In capitalist societies, the **consumer** is king.

696- 싫다/**silta** [a.] *to be unpleasant, hate, dislike, not want*

저는 대도시에 사는 것이 **싫어요**.
I **dislike** living in a large city.

697- 규모/**gyumo** [n.] *scale, dimension, framework, size*

저희는 현재 큰 **규모**의 프로젝트를 작업하고 있습니다.
We are currently working on a large-**scale** project.

698- 기준/**gijun** [n.] *standard, criterion*

자신의 **기준**으로 다른 사람을 평가하지 마세요.
Do not measure others by your own **standard**.

699- 반드시/**bandeusi** [adv.] *surely, certainly, without fail, at any cost*

당신은 그것을 **반드시** 찾아내야 합니다.
You must find it out **at any cost**.

700- 갖추다/**gatchuda** [v.] *to make the necessary preparations, prepare or equip oneself, possess a desirable attribute, get ready, have*

그 사무실은 가장 고급의 컴퓨터들을 **갖추고 있습니다**.
The office **is equipped** with the most advanced computers.

701- 그러니까/**geureonikka** [adv.] *therefore, accordingly, so*

저는 그것을 쓸 일이 없어요. **그러니까** 당신이 원하는 만큼 오래 가지고 있으세요.
I never use it, **so** keep it as long as you want.

702- 받아들이다/**badadeurida** [v.] *to accept, adopt, follow, embrace, take*

저는 그의 제안을 **받아들였습니다**.
I **accepted** his offer.

703- 값/**gap** [n.] *price, value*

값이 얼마인가요?
What is the **price**?

704- 현장/**hyeonjang** [n.] *the location of a thing or event, site, scene, field*

범죄 **현장**에는 기자들이 있었습니다.

There were reporters at the **scene** of the crime.

705- 건설/geonseol [n.] *construction, building*

건설 인부들이 벽을 무너뜨리고 있습니다.
Construction workers are knocking down the wall.

706- 꺼내다/kkeonaeda [v.] *to pull something out, take out, bring up*

그는 상자에서 책을 **꺼냈습니다**.
He **took** a book **out** of a box.

707- 노동자/nodongja [n.] *worker, laborer, working people*

그 외국인 **노동자**는 한국에서 영구 거주할 수 있는 자격을 신청했습니다.
The foreign **worker** applied for permanent residence in Korea.

708- 동네/dongne [n.] *neighborhood, village, town*

저희 **동네**는 날마다 더욱 커져가고 있습니다.
Our **neighborhood** is becoming larger day after day.

709- 언제나/eonjena [adv.] *always, all the time, every time*

사랑은 **언제나** 미움을 물리칠 것입니다.
Love will conquer hatred **every time**.

710- 완전히/wanjeonhi [adv.] *completely, totally, absolutely, fully*

수트를 입으니 **완전히** 다른 사람으로 보이네요.
You look like a **totally** different person in that suit.

711- 자동차/jadongcha [n.] *automobile, car*

서울시의 **자동차** 수가 급격하게 증가하고 있습니다.

The number of **cars** in Seoul is increasing rapidly.

712- 전하다/jeonhada [v.] *to pass along, convey, tell, communicate, send*

제가 여기에 있다고 그에게 **전해주세요**.
Please **tell** him I am here.

713- 존재하다/jonjaehada [v.] *to exist*

인류는 수천 년 동안 **존재해** 왔습니다.
Mankind has **existed** for thousands of years.

714- 어린이/eorini [n.] *child, kid*

이 프로그램은 여덟 살 이상의 **어린이들**에게만 허용이 됩니다.
This program is allowed for **children** above eight years old.

715- 정하다/jeonghada [v.] *to designate, specify, decide, determine, choose, fix*

그녀는 그 행사를 위한 적당한 시기와 장소를 **정했습니다**.
She **decided** on a good time and place for that event.

716- 한마디/hanmadi [n.] *a brief statement, a few words, a word*

저는 **한마디**도 하지 않을 것입니다.
I will not utter **a word**.

717- 유지하다/yujihada [v.] *to maintain, continue, keep, retain, preserve*

그 나라는 다른 나라들과 우호 관계를 **유지하고** 있습니다.
The country **maintains** friendly relations with other countries.

718- 이데올로기/ideollogi [n.] *ideology*

양측의 **이데올로기**는 첨예하게 대립하고 있습니다.

The two parties' **ideologies** are opposed sharply.

719- 공부하다/gongbuhada [v.] *to study, learn*

그 커플은 대구에서 **공부하다**가 만났습니다.

The couple met while **studying** in Daegu.

720- 대중/daejung [n.] *crowd, party, the masses, the public*

그녀는 **대중**에게 알려져 있습니다.

She is known to **the public**.

721- 늘어나다/neureonada [v.] *to expand or increase in numbers, stretch*

사망자 수는 계속 **늘어날** 수 있습니다.

The number of deaths could **increase**.

722- 닦다/dakda [v.] *to polish, wipe, clean, mop*

그는 오늘 아침에 창을 **닦았습니다**.

He **cleaned** the window this morning.

723- 만/man [p.] *only*

저는 그 사람들 중에서 한 사람**만** 뽑아야 했습니다.

I had to choose **only** one person among those people.

724- 괜찮다/gwaenchanta [a.] *nice, good, all right, safe, secure, ok, fine*

무리하지 않는 한 음주는 **괜찮습니다**.

Drinking is **all right** as long as you don't do it to excess.

725- 눈물/nunmul [n.] *tear*

그 슬픈 이야기는 우리 가족이 **눈물**을 흘리게 만들었다.

The sad story drew **tears** from my family.

726- 각종/gakjong [n.] *every sort, all kinds, every kind*

병원은 **각종** 병을 치료할 수 있도록 갖추어져 있습니다.

Hospitals are equipped to treat **every kind** of illness.

727- 빛/bit [n.] *light, gleam, glow, gloss, glaze*

이러한 깜빡이는 **빛**은 무엇을 의미하나요?

What does this blinking **light** mean?

728- 피하다/pihada [v.] *to evade, avoid, escape*

가능한 갈등을 **피해야** 합니다.

You need to **avoid** a conflict as far as possible.

729- 거치다/geochida [v.] *to cross through or over, pass through or undergo*

그 관광버스는 판교를 **거쳐** 서울로 갑니다.

The tour bus goes to Seoul by **crossing through** Pan-gyo.

730- 나아가다/naagada [v.] *to go forward, progress, advance, proceed*

그들은 산정상을 향해 **나아가고** 있습니다.

They are **going forward** to the mountain peak.

731- 지식/jisik [n.] *knowledge*

저는 법률에 대한 **지식**이 조금도 없습니다.

I do not have any **knowledge** about law.

732- 여전히/yeojeonhi [adv.] *still, just as before, as ever*

그는 **여전히** 전과 같은 장소에서 살고 있습니다.

He **still** lives in the same place as before.

733- 주인/juin [n.] *master, owner, proprietor, landlord, host*

저는 이 차의 **주인**이 누구였는지 몰랐습니다.

I did not know who the owner of this car was.

734- 발견하다/balgyeonhada [v.] *to discover, find out, detect*

그는 시스템의 결함을 **발견했습니다**.
He **detected** a fault in the system.

735- 선/seon [n.] *line, wire, cable*

제가 다른 **선**으로 연결해 드리겠습니다.
Let me put you through the other **line**.

736- 인류/illyu [n.] *human, mankind, humanity, human beings*

과학은 정말 **인류**에게 많은 것을 제공해 주었습니다.
Science has indeed provided much for **humanity**.

737- 특징/teukjing [n.] *characteristic, feature*

이 제품에는 여러가지 새로운 **특징들**이 있습니다.
There are a number of new **features** in this product.

738- 드리다/deurida [v.] *(humble form of) give, offer, present*

음식 좀 **드려도** 될까요?
Can I **give** you some food?

739- 선수/seonsu [n.] *athlete, sportsman, player*

저는 그 야구 **선수**의 광팬입니다.
I am a huge fan of the baseball **player**.

740- 형식/hyeongsik [n.] *form, template, format*

시간을 24 시간 **형식**으로 입력해 주세요.
Please, enter the time in 24-hour **format**.

741- 마련하다/**maryeonhada** [v.] *to have something ready, prepare, arrange*

그는 긴급 상황에 대비한 통신 수단을 **마련했습니다**.

He **prepared** a means of communication in case of emergency.

742- 반/**ban** [n.] *half, a group of class or of working unit*

그들은 학교에서 같은 **반**에 있습니다.

They are in the same **class** at their school.

743- 발표하다/**balpyohada** [v.] *to give a presentation, announce, publish*

선생님이 시험 결과를 **발표했습니다**.

The teacher **published** the results of the examination.

744- 주제/**juje** [n.] *topic, main idea, subject, theme*

이 책의 **주제**는 십대 흡연입니다.

The **subject** of this book is teenage smoking.

745- 관점/**gwanjeom** [n.] *standpoint, point of view, perspective*

저는 당신의 **관점**을 지지하지 않습니다.

I do not support your **point of view**.

746- 귀/**gwi** [n.] *ear*

그녀는 강아지의 **귀**를 잡았습니다.

She grabbed the dog's **ear**.

747- 기본/**gibon** [n.] *basis, foundation, default, basic*

가정은 사회의 **기본** 단위이다.

The family is the **basic** unit of society.

748- 미터/miteo [n.] *meter*

발전소는 이십만 제곱 **미터**가 될 것입니다.

The power plant will be two hundred thousand square **meters**.

749- 사라지다/sarajida [v.] *to vanish, disappear, vanish, fade away*

그 소년은 흔적도 없이 **사라졌습니다**.

The boy **disappeared** without a trace.

750- 감정/gamjeong [n.] *emotion, feeling*

그 시는 독자들에게 사랑의 **감정**을 불러 일으켰습니다.

The poem evoked a **feeling** of love in the reader.

751- 기억/gieok [n.] *recall, memory, remembrance*

그의 이름은 저희의 **기억**에 남아 있습니다.

His name lives in our **memory**.

752- 인기/ingi [n.] *popularity*

그녀의 **인기**는 현재 절정입니다.

She is now at the peak of her **popularity**.

753- 아파트/apateu [n.] *apartment building, an apartment*

그녀는 최근에 새 **아파트**로 이사를 갔어요.

She moved to a new **apartment** recently.

754- 가끔/gakkeum [adv.] *occasionally, sometimes, once in a while*

가끔 저에게 편지를 써서 안부를 전해줄 수 있나요?

Can you write to me **once in a while** and let me know how you are?

755- 구성/guseong [n.] *configuration, arrangement, composition*

이 공간 **구성**이 마음에 드시나요?

Do you like this spatial **composition**?

756- 실제로/**siljero** [adv.] *in fact, in practice, actually*

그것들은 벽에 **실제로** 새겨져 있습니다.

They are **actually** carved into the walls.

757- 짧다/**jjalda** [a.] *short, brief*

새 바지가 너무 **짧아요**.

The new pants are too **short**.

758- 관리/**gwalli** [n.] *administration, management, supervision, control*

공정 변동이 **관리** 상태에 있습니다.

The process variation is in **control**.

759- 그곳에/**geugose** [adv.] *there, in that place*

저희는 탑승 시간 두 시간 전에 **그곳에** 도착해야 합니다.

We need to be **there** two hours before boarding time.

760- 달다/**dalda** [a.] *sweet, delicious*

케이크가 너무 **달아요**.

The cake is too sweet.

761- 들리다/**deullida** [v.] *to be heard*

옆방에 있는 사람들의 목소리가 **들렸습니다**.

The voices of people in the next room **were heard**.

762- 달리다/**dallida** [v.] *to run, move quickly*

아이는 엄마에게 **달려** 갔다.

The child **ran** to his mother.

763- 바쁘다/bappeuda [a.] *busy*

그녀는 아이들을 돌보느라 **바쁩니다**.

She is **busy** with the care of her children.

764- 인정하다/injeonghada [v.] *to affirm, acknowledge, admit, recognize*

그는 그의 잘못을 **인정했습니다**.

He **admitted** his guilt.

765- 중앙/jungang [n.] *center, middle*

그녀는 방 **중앙**에 탁자를 놓았습니다.

She puts a table in the **middle** of her room.

766- 나쁘다/nappeuda [a.] *bad, inferior, evil, harmful, poor*

흡연은 건강에 **나빠요**.

Smoking is **bad** for your health.

767- 게임/geim [n.] *game, computer game*

우리는 컴퓨터 **게임** 하는 데 너무 많은 시간을 보내고 있어.

We spend too much time on computer **games**.

768- 국제/gukje [n.] *international, internationality*

이 수업의 주제는 **국제** 금융입니다.

The subject matter of this class is **international** banking.

769- 그룹/geurup [n.] *group*

저는 정남이와 함께 스터디 **그룹**을 시작했어요.

I started a study **group** with Jeongnam.

770- 인생/insaeng [n.] *(human) life*

청춘은 **인생**의 꽃입니다.

Youth is the flower of **life**.

771- 전통/jeontong [n.] *tradition*

한국의 대가족 제도는 오랜 **전통**을 가지고 있습니다.
The extended family structure in Korea has a long **tradition**.

772- 기르다/gireuda [v.] *to grow, raise, breed, cultivate, bring up*

저는 강아지 한 마리를 **기르고 있어요**.
I am **raising** a dog.

773- 조사하다/josahada [v.] *to investigate, examine, conduct a survey, probe*

그는 그 사건의 원인을 철저하게 **조사했습니다**.
He thoroughly **investigated** the cause of the accident.

774- 커다랗다/keodarata [a.] *huge, big, large*

강한 바람을 만들기 위해서 **커다란** 선풍기가 사용됩니다.
Huge fans are used to create strong winds.

775- 시인/siin [n.] *poet*

그는 **시인**으로서 높이 인정받고 있습니다.
He is highly regarded as a **poet**.

776- 언제/eonje [pron.] *when*

언제가 네 생일이니?
When is your birthday?

777- 외/oe [n.] *other things, except, the outside, but*

기도 **외**에는 희망이 없습니다.
There is no hope **but** through prayer.

778- 평가/pyeongga [n.] *evaluation, assessment,*

valuation

그 시스템의 **평가**에 대해 어떻게 생각하세요?

What do you think of the system's **evaluation**?

779- 내려오다/naeryeooda [v.] *to come down, descend, get off*

아이가 계단을 **내려오고** 있습니다.

The child is **coming down** the stairs.

780- 위치/wichi [n.] *location, position*

보고서를 저장할 **위치**를 입력해 주세요.

Please, enter a **location** to store the reports.

781- 줄이다/jurida [v.] *to reduce, decrease, lessen, cut back*

재료의 손실을 최소한으로 **줄일** 필요가 있습니다.

You need to **reduce** waste of materials to a minimum.

782- 가격/gagyeok [n.] *price*

그것은 특별 **가격**에 제공됩니다.

It is offered at a special **price**.

783- 달라지다/dallajida [v.] *to become different, change or diverge over time*

이것이 하룻밤 사이에 **달라질** 것이라고 기대하지 마세요.

Do not expect this to **change** overnight.

784- 비다/bida [a.] *empty, hollow, vacant*

저것은 **비어 있는** 집이에요.

That is an **empty** house.

785- 손님/sonmin [n.] *guest, visitor, customer, client*

손님 수는 하루에 평균 열 명입니다.

The number of **guests** is ten a day on average.

786- 원하다/wonhada [v.] *to want, hope, wish*

저는 그를 돕기를 **원합니다**.

I **want** to help him.

787- 통신/tongsin [n.] *communication, telecommunication*

컴퓨터는 **통신** 도구로 널리 사용되고 있습니다.

Computers are widely used as **communication** tools.

788- 확인하다/hwaginhada [v.] *to confirm, verify, check, see, affirm*

당신의 은행 잔고를 **확인해** 주세요.

Please, **check** your bank balance.

789- 모임/moim [n.] *gathering, meeting*

오늘 밤 **모임** 때 그 옷이 필요해요.

I need the clothes for tonight's **meeting**.

790- 웃음/useum [n.] *laughter, smile*

그는 우리에게 항상 **웃음**을 가져다 주었습니다.

He always brought us **laughter**.

791- 기계/gigye [n.] *machinery, heavy equipment, instrument*

그 남자가 **기계**를 고치고 있습니다.

The man is fixing the **machine**.

792- 물질/muljil [n.] *substance, material, wealth, property*

얼음과 물은 똑같은 **물질**입니다.
Ice and water are the same **substance**.

793- 아나운서/anaunseo [n.] *announcer, anchor*

그녀는 KBS TV 방송국의 **아나운서**입니다.
She is an **announcer** for KBS TV station.

794- 뉴스/nyuseu [n.] *news broadcast, important new information*

뉴스에서는 사상자가 없다고 보도했습니다.
The **news** reported there were no injuries.

795- 펴다/pyeoda [v.] *to spread, stretch, expand, unfold, open, straighten*

그는 땅에 지도를 **폈습니다**.
He **spread** a map on the ground.

796- 수업/sueop [n.] *class*

수업이 몇 시에 끝나죠?
What time does the **class** end?

797- 겨울/gyeoul [n.] *winter*

추운 **겨울** 날씨로 인해 철도 운행이 중단되었습니다.
Rail services were shut down due to cold **winter** weather.

798- 종교/jonggyo [n.] *religion*

여러분은 무슨 **종교**를 믿고 있나요?
Which **religion** do you all believe in?

799- 층/cheung [n.] *story, floor, layer, level*

다음 **층**으로 걸어 내려 가세요.

Please, walk down to the next **floor**.

800- 자연스럽다/jayeonseureopda [a.] *natural, unaffected*

그의 연기는 **자연스럽습니다**.

His acting is **natural**.

801- 장/jang [n.] *sauce, head (of an organization), sheet (of paper), chapter*

저는 이 책의 마지막 **장**을 읽고 있어요.

I am reading the final **chapter** of this book.

802- 돌다/dolda [v.] *to revolve, rotate, spin, turn*

길 끝에서 왼쪽으로 **도세요**.

Please, **turn** left at the end of the road.

803- 식사/siksa [n.] *meal*

이렇게 멋진 **식사**를 해서 기분이 좋습니다.

I am glad I had such a wonderful **meal**.

804- 안다/anda [v.] *to embrace, hold a person, embrace, cuddle*

많은 아이들이 잠을 잘 때 인형을 **안고** 잡니다.

Many children **cuddle** a toy when they go to bed.

805- 이해/ihae [n.] *understanding, comprehension*

수업 시간에 들은 내용에 대한 그의 **이해**는 매우 훌륭합니다.

His **comprehension** of what is said in class is good.

806- 잊다/itda [v.] *to forget, leave behind*

안전띠를 매는 것을 **잊지** 마세요.

Do not **forget** to fasten your seatbelt.

807- 제시하다/jesihada [v.] *to present, indicate, provide*

떠날 때 도착 예정 시간을 **제시해** 주세요.

Please, **provide** an estimated time of arrival when leaving.

808- 혹은/hogeun [adv.] *or, or else*

그들은 물을 아주 적은 비용으로 **혹은** 무상으로 제공하고 있습니다.

They provide water at little **or** no cost.

809- 엄청나다/eomcheongnada [a.] *to be amazingly, astonish, huge, great, enormous*

빈부 격차가 **엄청납니다.**

The gulf between rich and poor is **enormous**.

810- 편/pyeon [n.] *side, inclination, tendency, way*

부모님은 항상 제 **편**을 들어주십니다.

My parents always play for my **side**.

811- 텔레비전/tellebijeon [n.] *television, TV*

저는 주말이 되면 **텔레비전**을 보는 것 외에는 다른 것은 안 합니다.

I do nothing but watch **television** on weekends.

812- 파악하다/paakhada [v.] *to understand, grasp thoroughly, grasp, apprehend*

관계 당국은 사망자 수를 **파악하기** 위해 노력하고 있습니다.

Authorities are making an effort to **grasp** the number of deaths.

813- 실천/silcheon [n.] *praxis, practical application, practice, action*

실천이 없는 이론은 아무런 소용이 없습니다.

Theory without **practice** will serve for nothing.

814- 노력하다/noryeokhada [v.] *to strive, exert oneself, make every effort, try, endeavor*

저는 학교 방송반에 들어갈 수 있도록 **노력할** 것입니다.

I will **try** to join the broadcasting club at school.

815- 보호/boho [n.] *protection, preservation*

방화벽 **보호** 서비스가 비활성화되었습니다.

The firewall **protection** service is disabled.

816- 씻다/ssitda [v.] *to wash clean, rinse, clean*

비누로 손을 **씻으세요**.

Please, **wash** your hands with soap.

817- 늦다/neutda [a.] *late, far behind, slow*

다시 시작하기에는 너무 **늦습니다**.

It is too **late** to start again.

818- 이웃/iut [n.] *neighbor, neighborhood*

저는 **이웃**과 몇 마디를 나누었습니다.

I exchanged a few words with my **neighbor**.

819- 편지/pyeonji [n.] *(postal) letter, epistle*

저는 그에게 **편지**를 부쳐달라고 부탁했습니다.

I asked him to mail the **letter**.

820- 공동/gongdong [n.] *commonality, sharedness, joint*

그는 **공동** 기금에 돈을 기부했습니다.

He contributed money to a **common** fund.

821- 까닭/kkadak [n.] *reason, cause*

그 **까닭**은 무엇이죠?

What is the **reason**?

822- 방안/bangan [n.] *plan, way, measure, method*

이것은 도시 한옥의 재생 **방안**에 관한 연구입니다.

This is a study on the renewal **method** of urban traditional housing.

823- 센티미터/sentimiteo [n.] *centimeter*

이 도표의 기본 단위는 **센티미터**입니다.

The basic unit of the chart is **centimeters**.

824- 팔/pal [n.] *arm*

그는 그녀의 **팔**을 잡았습니다.

He caught her by the **arm**.

825- 분명하다/bunmyeonghada [a.] *obvious, clear, without doubt, distinct, plain*

당신은 속은 것이 **분명합니다**.

It is **clear** that you have been cheated.

826- 분석/bunseok [n.] *analysis*

분석 쪽 일을 또 누가 했죠?

Who else worked on the **analysis**?

827- 소녀/sonyeo [n.] *a little girl, girl*

소녀들이 친구들에게 손을 흔들고 있습니다.

The **girls** are waving to their friends.

828- 지나가다/jinagada [v.] *to pass, go past, go by*

지나가게 되면 들러주세요.

If you are **passing by**, please drop in.

829- 상품/sangpum [n.] *merchandise, commodity, goods,*

product

상품 정보가 필요하시면, 숫자 이(2)번을 눌러 주세요.
If you need **product** information, press number two.

830- 설명/seolmyeong [n.] *explanation*

어디서부터 **설명**을 시작해야 할지 모르겠어요.
I do not know where to begin the explanation.

831- 훌륭하다/hullyunghada [a.] *wonderful, amazing, great, excellent*

이 모델은 모든 면에서 **훌륭합니다**.
This model is **great** in every respect.

832- 관계자/gwangyeja [n.] *a concerned, involved or interested party, authorized personnel, official*

그 산의 **관계자**는 작년에 이백만 명의 방문객이 그 산을 방문했었다고 보고했습니다.
The mountain **official** reported that two million visitors visited the mountain last year.

833- 봄/bom [n.] *spring, springtime*

많은 외국인 관광객들은 **봄**이나 가을에 한국에 옵니다.
Most foreign tourists come to Korea in **spring** or fall.

834- 종류/jongnyu [n.] *type, kind*

당신은 어떤 **종류**의 한국 음식을 좋아하나요?
What **kind** of Korean food do you like?

835- 낮다/natda [a.] *low*

시험에 합격할 가능성이 **낮습니다**.
The chance of passing the examination is **low**.

836- 어깨/**eokkae** [n.] *shoulder*

팔을 **어깨** 위로 올려주세요.

Please, raise your arms over your **shoulders**.

837- 지적하다/**jijeokhada** [v.] *to point to, point out, indicate*

그들은 온라인 게임이 위험할 수 있다고 **지적합니다**.

They **point out** that online games can be dangerous.

838- 부부/**bubu** [n.] *couple, husband and wife, marital*

세상에 완벽한 **부부**는 없습니다.

There is no perfect **couple** in the world.

839- 오래/**orae** [adv.] *long, for a long time or while*

얼마나 **오래** 비가 내렸나요?

How **long** has it been raining?

840- 요구/**yogu** [n.] *something required or demanded, claim*

당신의 **요구**는 법적 근거가 없어요.

Your **demand** has no legal basis.

841- 키우다/**kiuda** [v.] *to rear, raise, cultivate, bring up*

그녀는 아이를 모유로 **키운다**.

She **rears** a child at the breast.

842- 눕다/**nupda** [v.] *to lie down, lie*

저는 침대에 **누워** 이불을 덮었습니다.

I **laid** on the bed and covered myself with a blanket.

843- 발달하다/baldalhada [v.] *to develop, improve*

달리기를 열심히 하면, 당신의 폐 기능이 **발달될** 수 있습니다.
If you diligently practice running, then your lung function can
improve.

844- 발전하다/baljeonhada [v.] *to develop, evolve*

각 학교는 자기들만의 운영 방식을 **발전시켜야** 합니다.
Each school must **develop** its own way of working.

845- 여행/yeohaeng [n.] *travel, journey, trip, voyage line*

일행 중 일부는 **여행** 중에 그들의 가방을 잃어버렸습니다.
Some of the members lost their suitcases on the **trip**.

846- 죽음/jugeum [n.] *death, dying*

죽음보다 사는 것을 더 두려워하는 사람들이 있습니다.
There are people who are more afraid of living than **dying**.

847- 고통/gotong [n.] *pain, agony, suffering*

전쟁으로 받은 **고통**을 돌이키는 것은 불가능합니다.
It is impossible to undo the **suffering** caused by war.

848- 등장하다/deungjanghada [v.] *to enter the stage, come into play, appear*

증기 기관차는 십구 세기 초에 처음으로 **등장했습니다**.
Steam locomotives **appeared** for the first time at the beginning of
the nineteenth century.

849- 공/gong [n.] *ball*

그 소년은 **공**을 사고 있습니다.
The boy is buying a **ball**.

850- 어울리다/eoullida [v.] *to suit, fit nicely, match, get along, socialize, associate*

저는 이 셔츠와 **어울리는** 넥타이가 필요합니다.
I need a tie that **matches** with this shirt.

851- 오월/owol [n.] *May*

저희는 오월에 결혼할 예정입니다.
We are to be married in **May**.

852- 쉬다/swida [v.] *to rest, take a break, relax*

쉬도록 해요.
Let's **take a break**.

853- 알리다/allida [v.] *to inform, announce, make known, notify*

왜 저에게 이것을 **알려** 주지 않았어요?
Why didn't you **inform** me of this?

854- 차다/chada [v.] *to fill, become filled*

그 방은 장난감으로 **찼습니다**.
The room **was filled** with toys.

855- 과/gwa [p.] *and, with, together with*

저에게 연필**과** 책을 가져다 주세요.
Please, bring me pencils **and** books.

856- 멀리/meolli [adv.] *afar, at a distance, far*

너무 **멀리** 가지 마세요. 돌아오기 힘들어요.
Do not go too **far**. It is difficult to come back.

857- 빼다/ppeda [v.] *to remove, take out, subtract*

그녀는 그의 이름을 명단에서 **뺐어요**.
She **removed** his name from a list.

858- 즐겁다/jeulgeopda [a.] *pleasant, enjoyable, joyful, pleased, cheerful, glad*

음악은 듣기에 **즐겁습니다**.

Music is **pleasant** to listen to.

859- 한계/hangye [n.] *limit, limitation*

우리가 할 수 있는 것에는 **한계**가 있습니다.

There is a **limit** as to what we can do.

860- 흔히/heunhi [adv.] *frequently, often, commonly, ordinarily*

젓가락은 한국에서 **흔히** 사용됩니다.

Chopsticks are **commonly** used in Korea.

861- 사월/sawol [n.] *April*

첫 학기는 **사월**에 시작됩니다.

The first term commences in **April**.

862- 싸우다/ssauda [v.] *to fight, struggle, battle, argue*

그들은 자유를 되찾기 위해 죽을 때까지 **싸웠습니다**.

They **fought** to the death to regain freedom.

863- 예쁘다/yeppeuda [a.] *pretty, lovely, beautiful, comely, adorable, nice*

그녀는 너무 예쁘기 때문에 모든 사람들이 그녀를 좋아합니다.

She is so **beautiful** that everybody likes her.

864- 갈등/galdeung [n.] *discord, conflict, strife*

그 사건으로 인해 큰 **갈등**이 시작되었습니다.

The incident sparked off a major **conflict**.

865- 느껴지다/**neukkyeojida** [v.] *to be felt, be perceived, feel*

노란색 같은 어떤 색들은 따뜻하게 **느껴집니다**.
Some colors, like yellow, **feel** warm.

866- 의지/**uiji** [n.] *determination to accomplish something, steadfastness, will*

저는 살고자 하는 그의 **의지**를 느꼈습니다.
I sensed his **determination** to live.

867- 전문/**jeonmun** [n.] *expertise, one's field of specialization*

저는 그것이 당신의 **전문** 분야가 아니라는 것을 알고 있어요.
I know that this is not your area of **expertise**.

868- 정확하다/**jeonghwakhada** [a.] *accurate, exact*

사고가 발생했던 **정확한** 지점은 어디인가요?
Where is the **exact** spot the accident happened?

869- 초기/**chogi** [n.] *the initial period, the beginning, the early part, the early days*

병은 **초기**에 치료되어야 합니다.
Disease should be treated at **the beginning**.

870- 맛있다/**masitda** [a.] *delicious, tasty*

모든 사람들이 그곳 음식이 **맛있다**고 말해요.
Everybody says that the food is **delicious** there.

871- 며칠/**myeochil** [n.] *several days, a few of days, what date? how many days?*

그는 **며칠** 전에 여기를 떠났습니다.
He left here **a few days** ago.

872- 신경/singyeong [n.] *nerve*

그것은 **신경** 손상을 입은 사람들에게 도움이 됩니다.
It is helpful for people who have **nerve** damage.

873- 찾아오다/chajaoda [v.] *to come to visit someone, drop by, visit*

제 친구들이 어제 저를 **찾아왔어요**.
My friends **visited** me yesterday.

874- 사용/sayong [n.] *use, usage*

물 **사용**은 지난 백 년 동안 꾸준하게 증가해 왔습니다.
Water **usage** has increased steadily over the past one hundred years.

875- 언론/eollon [n.] *speech, public discourse, the press, the media*

그는 일부러 **언론**에 뉴스를 흘렸습니다.
He intentionally leaked the news to **the press**.

876- 투자/tuja [n.] *investment*

저는 당신에게 굉장한 **투자** 기회에 관해 이야기해 주고 싶었어요.
I wanted to tell you about a great **investment** opportunity.

877- 지원/jiwon [n.] *support, aid*

계속된 **지원**에 감사드립니다.
Thank you for your continued **support**.

878- 결정하다/gyeoljeonghada [v.] *to decide, make a decision, determine*

그녀는 그것을 사기로 **결정했습니다**.
She **decided** to buy it.

879- 경영 / gyeongyeong [n.] *management, administration*

이러한 문제들은 수년간의 부실 **경영**의 결과입니다.

These problems are the result of years of bad **management**.

880- 목표 / mokpyo [n.] *goal, target, objective*

저희 부서는 한 해 동안 판매 **목표**를 달성했습니다.

Our department met its sales **goal** for the year.

881- 성장 / seongjang [n.] *growth, expansion*

햇빛은 식물 **성장**에 필요합니다.

Sunlight is needed for plant **growth**.

882- 숲 / sup [n.] *forest, wood*

많은 사람들이 여름에 **숲**에서 캠프를 합니다.

Many people camp in the **woods** in the summer.

883- 없어지다 / eopseojida [v.] *to disappear, vanish, be lost*

전문가들은 수동 기어 차량들이 곧 **없어질** 것이라고 생각합니다.

Experts think that manual-shift vehicles may soon **disappear**.

884- 작년 / jangnyeon [n.] *last year, the year before*

기름값이 **작년**에 최고치에 이르렀습니다.

Oil prices reached their peak **last year**.

885- 내려가다 / naeryeogada [v.] *to go downwards, descend, decline*

저희는 가격이 **내려가기**를 희망했습니다.

We hoped that prices would **decline**.

886- 떠오르다 / tteooreuda [v.] *to rise, arise*

태양이 산 위로 **떠오르고** 있었습니다.

The sun was **rising** over the hills.

887- 미치다/michida [v.] *to go crazy, be insane*

당신 **미쳤어요**?
Are you insane?

888- 새벽/saebyeok [n.] *dawn, daybreak, early morning*

저는 **새벽** 다섯 시에 일어났어요.
I woke up at five **a.m.**

889- 쓰레기/sseuregi [n.] *trash, garbage, waste*

아이들이 **쓰레기**를 줍고 있습니다.
The children are picking up the **trash**.

890- 임금/imgeum [n.] *wage, pay*

노조는 **임금** 인상을 타결했습니다.
The labor union negotiated a **wage** increase.

891- 피해/pihae [n.] *harm, damage*

태풍이 전국 각 지역에 막대한 **피해**를 주었습니다.
The typhoon caused much **damage** to all parts of the country.

892- 직장/jikjang [n.] *workplace, job, work*

저의 새로운 **직장**은 아주 좋은 의료 보험을 제공해 줍니다.
My new **job** offers a great health insurance policy.

893- 참다/chamda [v.] *to bear, endure, suppress, hold, contain*

그는 웃음을 **참았습니다**.
He **held** his laughter.

894- 크기/keugi [n.] *size*

저희 제품은 **크기**에 따라 다르게 디자인됩니다.
Our products are designed differently according to **size**.

895- 고기/gogi [n.] *meat, fish*

채식을 하는 사람들은 **고기**를 먹지 않습니다.
People who live on vegetables do not eat **meat.**

896- 남기다/namgida [v.] *to leave behind, leave, set aside*

그는 메시지를 **남겼습니다.**
He **left** a message.

897- 가져오다/gajyeooda [v.] *to bring, incur, entail*

그녀는 자신의 모바일 기기를 **가져왔습니다.**
She **brought** her mobile device.

898- 냄새/naemsae [n.] *smell, odor, scent*

나쁜 **냄새**의 원인은 썩은 음식입니다.
The cause of the bad **smell** is the rotten food.

899- 부드럽다/budeureopda [a.] *soft, smooth, gentle, mild, tender*

벨벳의 촉감은 매우 **부드럽습니다.**
The feel of velvet is very **smooth.**

900- 여기다/yeogida [v.] *to consider, regard, think*

그는 그녀가 이룬 바를 가볍게 **여겼어요.**
He **thought** lightly of her achievements.

901- 공연/gongyeon [n.] *a public performance, show, concert*

공연은 몇 시에 시작하죠?
What time does the **show** begin?

902- 속도/sokdo [n.] *speed, velocity, pace*

당신은 **속도** 제한을 어겼습니다.
You violated the **speed** limit.

903- 심각하다/**simgakhada** [a.] *severe, serious, critical*

서울의 대기 오염은 **심각합니다**.

Air pollution in Seoul is **serious**.

904- 준비/**junbi** [n.] *readiness, preparation*

대부분의 경우는 적절한 **준비**를 하지 않아서 발생한 것들입니다.

Most cases resulted from a lack of proper **preparation**.

905- 계속되다/**gyesokdoeda** [v.] *to continue*

두 나라 사이의 전쟁은 **계속되었고** 많은 사람들이 죽었습니다.

Wars between the two countries **continued**, and many people died.

906- 구월/**guwol** [n.] *September*

가을 학기는 **구월**에 시작됩니다.

The fall semester begins in **September**.

907- 맑다/**makda** [a.] *clear, clean, fresh, pure, transparent*

물이 수정처럼 **맑습니다**.

The water is as **clear** as crystal.

908- 소년/**sonyeon** [n.] *boy*

그 **소년**은 강아지를 그리고 있습니다.

The **boy** is drawing a dog.

909- 소식/**sosik** [n.] *news*

그 소식으로 인해 마음이 어수선해졌어요.

My mind was disturbed by the **news**.

910- 유월/yuwol [n.] *June*

여름 방학은 **유월**에 시작됩니다.
Summer vacation begins in **June**.

911- 작용/jagyong [n.] *function, operation, effect, action*

강 바닥에 있는 깊은 골짜기는 이러한 **작용**을 통해 형성됩니다.
A deep valley on the riverbed is formed by such an **action**.

912- 허리/heori [n.] *side of waist or hip, back*

그는 **허리** 주변에 지방이 많이 있습니다.
He has a lot of fat around his **waist**.

913- 공업/gongeop [n.] *heavy industry, manufacturing, industry*

농업에서 **공업**으로 변화가 있었습니다.
There was a change from agriculture to **industry**.

914- 노인/noin [n.] *an old person, the elderly*

의사가 **노인**의 맥박을 측정하고 있습니다.
The doctor is measuring the **old man**'s pulse rate.

915- 영어/yeongeo [n.] *the English language, English*

저는 **영어**를 잘 말하지 못합니다.
I do not speak **English** well.

916- 경향/gyeonghyang [n.] *trend, tendency, inclination*

주가가 갑자기 오르는 경향을 보였습니다.
Stock prices showed a suddenly rising **tendency**.

917- 기록/girok [n.] *record*

당신의 전화 **기록**을 저에게 공유해 줄 수 있나요?
Could you share your phone **record** with me?

918- 대답하다/daedaphada [v.] *to answer, reply, respond*

나는 그녀의 직업을 물어봤지만, 그녀는 **대답하지** 않았다.
I asked her what she does, but she did not **reply.**

919- 썰다/sseolda [v.] *to chop, cut, saw, mince, slice*

그녀는 양배추를 **썰었습니다.**
She **chopped** up a cabbage.

920- 터지다/teojida [v.] *to explode, blow up, burst, pop*

그 장비가 **터졌습니다.**
The device **exploded.**

921- 특성/teukseong [n.] *characteristic, nature, property, trait*

각 도시는 각자의 **특성**을 가지고 있습니다.
Each city has its own **characteristics.**

922- 교장/gyojang [n.] *the principal or head teacher of a school*

교장 선생님이 오늘 아침에 저희에게 말씀하셨어요.
The **principal** spoke to us this morning.

923- 벗다/beotda [v.] *to take off, remove, undress, strip, put off*

신발을 **벗을** 필요가 없습니다.
You do not have to **take** your shoes **off.**

924- 업무/eommu [n.] *business, work, task, duty, service*

그의 비서가 그의 **업무**를 도왔습니다.
His secretary helped him with his **work.**

925- 준비하다/junbihada [v.] *to prepare*

그는 고기잡이를 위해 그물을 **준비했습니다**.

He **prepared** a net for fishing.

926- 돕다/dopda [v.] *to help, contribute*

당신을 **도우려고** 저희가 왔어요.

We are here to **help** you.

927- 이기다/igida [v.] *to win, beat, defeat, gain, overcome*

그 팀이 삼 대 이의 득점으로 **이겼습니다**.

The team **won** by a score of three to two.

928- 다루다/daruda [v.] *to handle, deal with, operate, treat*

그는 그 문제를 모든 면에서 **다루었습니다**.

He **handled** the problem in all its aspects.

929- 삼월/samwol [n.] *March*

봄은 **삼월**에 시작됩니다.

Spring begins in **March**.

930- 구하다/guhada [v.] *to look for, seek, save, acquire something needed*

그녀는 일자리를 **구하고** 있었어요.

She was **looking for** a job.

931- 포함하다/pohamhada [v.] *to include, entail, contain, cover*

이 수치들은 저희의 해외 판매도 **포함하고 있나요**?

Do these figures **include** our overseas sales as well?

932- 걱정/geokjeong [n.] *anxiety, worry, concern*

당신의 **걱정**을 의사에게 말해 보세요.
Please, share your **anxieties** with your doctor.

933- 결혼하다/gyeolhonhada [v.] *to marry, get married*

당신은 **결혼했나요?**
Are you **married**?

934- 만약/manyak [n.] *if, in the event that*

만약 당신이 자신을 믿지 않는다면, 아무도 당신을 믿지 않을 것입니다.
If you don't believe in yourself, nobody will.

935- 바르다/bareuda [v.] *cover, apply, spread, rub*

그녀는 크림을 자신의 얼굴에 **발랐습니다**.
She **applied** the cream to her face.

936- 숨/sum [n.] *breath*

잠시 동안 **숨**을 참아 보세요.
Please, hold your **breath** for a moment.

937- 행사/haengsa [n.] *event, action, occasion, ceremony*

그의 결혼식은 엄청난 **행사**였습니다.
His wedding was a great **occasion**.

938- 깨닫다/kkaedatda [v.] *to apprehend, become aware of, realize*

나는 내가 이용당하고 있었다는 것을 **깨닫지** 못했다.
I did not **realize** I was being manipulated.

939- 질문/jilmun [n.] *question*

질문 있으시면, 저에게 알려 주세요.

If you have any **questions**, please let me know.

940- 해결하다/haegyeolhada [v.] *to resolve, solve, fix*

그 문제를 **해결하는** 데에는 많은 방법이 있습니다.

There are many ways to **fix** the problem.

941- 거리/geori [n.] *distance, range, space, street*

거리에는 주차 장소가 많이 있습니다.

There are a lot of parking sports on the **street**.

942- 계속하다/gyesokhada [v.] *to continue, be continuous, without interruption*

계속하기 전에 작업 내용을 저장하고 모든 응용 프로그램을 닫아주시기 바랍니다.

Please, save your work and then close all applications before **continuing**.

943- 그치다/geuchida [v.] *to stop*

비가 **그쳤어요**.

Rain **stopped**.

944- 근처/geuncheo [n.] *near, neighborhood, vicinity, the nearby area*

여기 **근처**에 슈퍼마켓이 있나요?

Is there a supermarket **near** here?

945- 너무나/neomuna [adv.] *far too much, excessively, so*

이러한 밤 시간이 되면, 저는 **너무나** 외로움을 느껴요.

At this time of night, I feel **so** alone.

946- 부모님/bumonim [n.] *parents*

너의 **부모님**은 지금 무엇을 하고 계시니?
What are your **parents** doing now?

947- 수출/suchul [n.] *export*

그는 **수출** 부서를 담당하고 있습니다.
He is in charge of the **export** department.

948- 자르다/jareuda [v.] *to cut*

언제 머리를 **자를** 거예요?
When will you **cut** your hair?

949- 무척/mucheok [adv.] *very, extremely, extraordinarily, exceedingly*

이것은 **무척** 비싼 집으로 보여요.
This looks like a **very** expensive house.

950- 비용/biyong [n.] *cost, expense*

학생 기숙사 **비용**은 얼마죠?
How much does the student housing **cost**?

951- 비행기/bihaenggi [n.] *airplane, plane, aircraft*

그들이 탄 **비행기**는 아침에 제일 먼저 도착할 것입니다.
Their **plane** will arrive first thing in the morning.

952- 옳다/olta [a.] *right, true, correct*

그녀는 항상 **옳은** 일을 합니다.
She always does the **right** thing.

953- 최초/choecho [n.] *first, earliest*

최초의 기계는 오래 전에 발명되었습니다.
The **first** machine was invented a long time ago.

954- 뜨겁다/tteugeopda [a.] *hot, heated, burning*

태양의 복사열은 극도로 **뜨겁습니다**.
The radiance of the sun is extremely **hot**.

955- 뿌리/ppuri [n.] *root, origin, source*

나무 **뿌리**가 건물에 해를 줄 수 있습니다.
Tree **roots** can cause damage to buildings.

956- 수입/suip [n.] *import, income, revenue*

올해 **수입**은 작년 것의 세 배에 해당합니다.
This year's **revenues** are three times as much as last year's.

957- 초/cho [n.] *second, the early part of a time period*

샘플 간격은 일 **초**와 일 분 사이여야 합니다.
The sample interval must be between one **second** and one minute.

958- 낮/nat [n.] *daytime, noon, day*

지구의 자전이 **낮**과 밤을 생기게 합니다.
The rotation of the earth causes **day** and night.

959- 일찍/iljjik [adv.] *early*

저는 **일찍** 떠나고 싶지 않습니다.
I do not want to leave **early**.

960- 직원/jigwon [n.] *employee, staff*

그는 어떤 **직원**을 원하나요?
What kind of **employees** does he want?

961- 찍다/jjikda [v.] *to stamp or mark, apply cosmetics, take (picture or video)*

그녀는 사진을 **찍었습니다**.
She **took** pictures.

962- 가볍다/gabyeopda [a.] *light*

이 짐은 부피가 크지만 무게는 **가볍습니다**.
This luggage is bulky in size but **light** in weight.

963- 내부/naebu [n.] *the interior or inside*

그 집의 **내부**를 본 적이 있나요?
Have you seen **the interior** of the house?

964- 오전/ojeon [n.] *a.m., forenoon, morning*

첫 번째 공연은 **오전** 열한 시에 시작합니다.
The first show starts at eleven **a.m.**

965- 피부/pibu [n.] *skin*

매일 세수를 하지 않으면, 얼굴 **피부**에 먼지가 달라붙어서 여드름이
생길 수 있습니다.
If you do not wash your face every day, dust will stick to the **skin**
of your face and cause pimples.

966- 가게/gage [n.] *store, shop*

나는 어제 그 가게에 가서 마실 것을 샀다.
I went to that **shop** and bought something to drink yesterday.

967- 벽/byeok [n.] *wall, obstacle, hindrance*

지진 때문에 벽이 무너졌습니다.
The **wall** collapsed due to the earthquake.

968- 무역/muyeok [n.] *trade, commerce*

우리나라 **무역**은 매년 더 크게 성장하고 있습니다.
The **trade** of our country grows larger every year.

969- 부담/budam [n.] *burden, responsibility*

그녀는 자신의 문제로 인한 **부담**을 우리에게 떠넘기고 싶어하지 않았습니다.

She did not want to cast her **burden** on us with her problems.

970- 약속/yaksok [n.] *promise, appointment, engagement*

그의 행동은 그가 **약속**한 것과는 대비되는 모습입니다.

His actions contrast with his **promise**.

971- 쳐다보다/chyeodaboda [v.] *to look at, glance*

저를 **쳐다보지** 마세요.

Please, do not **look** at me.

972- 충분히/chungbunhi [adv.] *sufficiently, enough, fully*

제가 **충분히** 연습을 하지 않는다는 의미인가요?

Do you mean I do not practice **enough**?

973- 신체/sinche [n.] *the human body*

쓸개는 **신체**가 지방을 소화하는 것을 돕습니다.

The gallbladder helps **the body** digest fat.

974- 에너지/eneoji [n.] *energy, power*

그것은 화학 **에너지**를 전기 **에너지**로 바꿔 줍니다.

It changes chemical **energy** into electrical **energy**.

975- 위원/wiwon [n.] *member of a committee*

위원들은 회의에 소집되었습니다.

The **committee members** convened for a meeting.

976- 정리하다/jeongnihada [v.] *to organize, arrange,*

straighten out, put in order

그녀는 물건들을 질서 있게 **정리했습니다**.

She **arranged** things in order.

977- 배경/baegyeong [n.] *background, setting*

저희는 직원을 뽑을 때 **배경** 조사를 실시할 것입니다.

We will conduct **background** checks on potential employees.

978- 죽이다/jugida [v.] *to kill, cause to die, murder*

그는 동물을 **죽였습니다**.

He **killed** an animal.

979- 단순하다/dansunhada [a.] *simple*

그가 인기가 있는 이유는 매우 **단순합니다**.

The reason for his popularity is quite **simple**.

980- 반대/bandae [n.] *oppositeness, opposing, opposition*

정부에 대한 정치적 **반대**가 있었습니다.

There was political **opposition** to the government.

981- 법칙/beopchik [n.] *law, rule*

수요와 공급의 **법칙**에 대해 들어 봤나요?

Have you heard of the **law** of supply and demand?

982- 소금/sogeum [n.] *salt*

소금과 설탕은 물에 녹습니다.

Salt and sugar dissolve in water.

983- 오염/oyeom [n.] *pollution, contamination*

저희는 먼저 **오염** 문제를 극복해야 합니다.

We have to overcome the **pollution** problem first.

984- 자전거/jajeongeo [n.] *bicycle, bike, cycle*

그 남자가 **자전거**를 고치고 있습니다.

The man is fixing the **bike**.

985- 참여하다/chamyeohada [v.] *to participate*

당신은 그 모임에 **참여했나요**?

Did you **participate** in that meeting?

986- 탓/tat [n.] *cause, reason, defect, fault, blame, fault*

그의 친구들은 그 실패를 그의 **탓**으로 돌렸습니다.

His friends put the **blame** for the failure on him.

987- 푸르다/pureuda [a.] *blue, green*

저는 **푸른** 하늘을 너무 좋아해요.

I love the **blue** sky.

988- 목/mok [n.] *neck, throat*

그녀가 두 팔로 제 **목**을 단단히 조였습니다.

She fastened both of her arms around my **neck**.

989- 범죄/beomjoe [n.] *crime, offense*

범죄는 어디에서나 큰 문제입니다.

Crime is a big problem everywhere.

990- 흔들다/heundeulda [v.] *to shake, wave*

그 여성은 그에게 손을 **흔들고** 있습니다.

The woman is **waving** her hand at him.

991- 기초/gicho [n.] *foundation, basis, basics, base*

모든 국가의 **기초**는 그 나라의 젊은이의 교육입니다.

The **foundation** of every country is the education of its youth.

992- 논리/**nolli** [n.] *logic, reasoning*

그의 의견에는 **논리**의 비약이 있습니다.

There is a jump in the **logic** of his opinion.

993- 드라마/**deurama** [n.] *drama, soap opera, television drama*

그 **드라마**는 저녁 뉴스 바로 전에 방송될 것입니다.

The **drama** will be on the air right before the evening news.

994- 뽑다/**ppopda** [v.] *to extract, pull out, pluck, root up, draw, pull up*

그는 나무를 뿌리채 **뽑았습니다**.

He **pulled up** a tree by the roots.

995- 피우다/**piuda** [v.] *to smoke*

그는 화장실에서 담배를 **피우다** 선생님께 걸렸습니다.

He got caught **smoking** in the restroom by the teacher.

996- 감각/**gamgak** [n.] *sensation, sense, feeling*

저는 당신의 유머 **감각**이 너무 좋아요.

I love your **sense** of humor.

997- 미리/**miri** [adv.] *beforehand, in advance*

그만두고 싶을 때는 일주일 전에 **미리** 저에게 알려 주세요.

Let me know a week **in advance** when you want to quit.

998- 부족하다/**bujokhada** [a.] *to be insufficient, not enough, be short of*

우리는 지금 현금이 **부족해요**.

We **are short of** cash at the moment.

999- 인사/insa [n.] *greeting, salutation*

당신 친구 분들에게 제 **인사**를 전해 주세요.

Please, send my **greetings** to your friends.

1000- 진행되다/jinhaengdoeda [v.] *to progress, come to progress, be in progress*

연수 과정이 **진행되고 있습니다**.

A training session **is in progress**.

1001- 교통/gyotong [n.] *transportation, traffic*

이 남자가 **교통** 사고를 목격했습니다.

This man witnessed the **traffic** accident.

1002- 열기구/ yeolgigu [n.] *balloon*

석탄 가스가 열**기구**를 떠오르게 할 것입니다.

Coal gas will float a **balloon**.

1003- 오랜/oraen [determiner] *(of past time) longstanding, of long duration, longtime, old*

다희는 제 **오랜** 친구입니다.

Dahee is an **old** friend of mine.

1004- 젊은이/jeolmeuni [n.] *youth, young person, young adult*

그 도둑은 용감한 **젊은이**에게 붙잡혔습니다.

The thief was caught by the brave **young man**.

1005- 후보/hubo [n.] *candidate, nominee*

대통령 선거에 몇 명의 **후보**가 출마하나요?

How many **candidates** are running for president?

1006- 과제/**gwaje** [n.] *task, (school) assignment, project, homework, problem*

체중 감량은 매우 어려운 **과제**가 될 수 있습니다.

Losing weight can be a very difficult **task**.

1007- 근거/**geungeo** [n.] *base, basis, grounds, reason, foundation*

당신의 요구는 법적 **근거**가 없습니다.

Your demand has no legal **basis**.

1008- 기록하다/**girokhada** [v.] *to record (in a document), to break a record*

지출 보고서에 그 지출 내역을 **기록할까요**?

Do I **record** those expenses on the expense report?

1009- 다가오다/**dagaoda** [v.] *to approach, draw near, come closer*

그 강아지가 저에게 **다가왔을** 때 저는 두려움에 떨었어요.

I was terrified as the puppy **approached** me.

1010- 불다/**bulda** [v.] *to blow, whistle*

바람이 하루 종일 **불었어요**.

The wind **blew** all day long.

1011- 시각/**sigak** [n.] *time, a specific point in time, a moment, a brief time*

모든 사람들이 정해진 **시각**에 모였습니다.

Everyone assembled at the appointed **time**.

1012- 이끌다/**ikkeulda** [v.] *to pull, lead, guide, shepherd*

그녀는 관현악단을 **이끄느라** 바쁩니다.

She is busy **leading** an orchestra.

1013- 한글/hangeul [n.] *Korean letters, the Korean language, Korean native word*

그는 자기의 아이 이름을 **한글** 이름으로 지을 거라고 말했어요.
He said he would create his child's name by using **Korean** native words.

1014- 가을/gaeul [n.] *autumn, fall*

그 산은 **가을**에 정말 아름답습니다.
The mountains are beautiful in the **fall**.

1015- 개발하다/gaebalhada [v.] *to develop, exploit*

과학자들은 연구실에서 신제품을 **개발합니다**.
Scientists **develop** new products in the laboratory.

1016- 내일/naeil [n.] *tomorrow*

내일이 바로 우리가 소풍을 가는 날입니다.
Tomorrow is the day we are going on a picnic.

1017- 떨다/tteolda [v.] *to shake, shiver, tremble, shudder, quiver*

저는 매우 긴장했고 몸을 **떨었어요**.
I was very nervous and **trembled**.

1018- 매일/maeil [adv.] *every day*

그는 **매일** TV 를 봐요.
He watches TV **every day**.

1019- 손가락/songarak [n.] *finger*

그녀는 **손가락**에 큰 다이아몬드 반지를 끼고 있었습니다.
She was wearing a large diamond ring on her **finger**.

1020- 수단/sudan [n.] _means, way, measure, method_

그의 친구들은 그를 돕기 위해 모든 **수단**을 다 썼습니다.
His friends used every **means** to help him.

1021- 자유롭다/jayuropda [a.] _to be free, unfettered_

저는 화요일 오후나 또는 수요일 오전에 **자유롭습니다**.
I **am free** either Tuesday afternoon or Wednesday morning.

1022- 적극적/jeokgeukjeok [a.] _positive, active, enthusiastic, aggressive_

그녀는 지난 캠페인에서 **적극적**이었습니다.
She was **active** in the last campaign.

1023- 판매/panmae [n.] _selling, sale_

저희 부서는 올해 **판매** 목표를 달성했습니다.
Our department met its **sales** goal for the year.

1024- 길이/giri [n.] _length, distance_

두 옷은 형태, **길이**, 색상 면에서 동일한 것으로 보입니다.
The two clothes look alike in shape, **length**, and color.

1025- 장면/jangmyeon [n.] _scene, situation, sight_

사람들은 이 영화가 폭력적인 **장면들**로 가득 차 있다고 말합니다.
People say that this film is full of violent **scenes**.

1026- 점차/jeomcha [adv.] _gradually, incrementally, slowly, steadily, by degrees_

세계는 **점차** 석유가 고갈되고 있습니다.
The world is **gradually** running short of oil.

1027- 톤/ton [n.] _tone (of color, music, etc.)_

많은 사람들이 제 목소리 **톤**이 성숙해졌다고 말했습니다.
Many people have told me that my **tone** of voice has matured.

1028- 관련되다/gwallyeondoeda [v.] *to have a connection, be connected, have to do with, be involved, relate*

두 사건이 어떤 식으로든 **관련되어** 있는 것이 확실합니다.
There is no doubt that the two incidents **are connected** in some way.

1029- 급/geup [n.] *level, grade, class, rank*

그는 레슬링 그레코로만형 60kg **급**에서 금메달을 차지했습니다.
He won the gold medal in the 60kg **class** of Greco-Roman wrestling.

1030- 나머지/nameoji [n.] *the remainder, leftovers, the rest*

그룹의 **나머지** 사람들은 행방불명이 되었습니다.
The remainder of the group was missing.

1031- 날씨/nalssi [n.] *weather*

저희 할머니는 추운 **날씨**를 좋아하지 않으셔요.
My grandmother does not like cold **weather**.

1032- 동물/dongmul [n.] *animal*

이 동물원은 모든 **동물들**에게 충분한 공간을 제공해 주고 있습니다.
This zoo has lots of room for all the **animals**.

1033- 의사/uisa [n.] *doctor*

의사가 노인의 맥박을 측정하고 있습니다.
The **doctor** is measuring the old man's pulse rate.

1034- 개방/gaebang [a.] *opening, liberalization, open*

그 시설은 모든 사람들에게 **개방**될 것입니다.
The facility will be **open** to all people.

1035- 건강하다/**geonganghada** [a.] *to be healthy*

그는 힘이 세고 **건강합니다**.

He is strong and **healthy**.

1036- 미래/**mirae** [n.] *the future*

미래에는 공해가 큰 문제가 될 것입니다.

Pollution will be a very big problem in **the future**.

1037- 앞서/**apseo** [adv.] *previously, foregoing, before, earlier, in advance, ahead of*

관객은 영화에 **앞서** 몇 가지 광고를 보게 될 것입니다.

The audience will see some advertisements **before** the movie.

1038- 인구/**ingu** [n.] *population, people*

이 지역의 **인구**는 매일매일 증가하고 있습니다.

The **population** in this neighborhood increases day by day.

1039- 기대하다/**gidaehada** [v.] *to expect, look forward to, anticipate, count on*

저희는 약 백 명 정도의 사람들을 **기대하고** 있습니다.

We are **expecting** about one hundred people.

1040- 도착하다/**dochakhada** [v.] *to arrive*

당신은 몇 시에 공항에 **도착했나요**?

What time did you **arrive** at the airport?

1041- 병/**byeong** [n.] *bottle*

제가 이 **병**을 어떻게 열어야 하나요?

How do I open this **bottle**?

1042- 소프트웨어/**sopeuteuweeo** [n.] *(computing)*

software (encoded computer instructions)

게임과 엔터테인먼트 **소프트웨어**가 학습에 도움이 될까요?
Do games and entertainment **software** aid in learning?

1043- 흘리다/heullida [v.] *drop (something)*

그는 식당에서 지갑을 **흘렸어요**.
He **dropped** his wallet in the restaurant.

1044- 반응/baneung [n.] *reaction, response*

고양이는 즉각적인 **반응**을 잘 보입니다.
Cats are good at showing immediate **responses**.

1045- 주인공/juingong [n.] *(theater, literature) protagonist, leading character, hero, heroine, main character*

저는 그 책의 **주인공**이 마음에 들지 않아요.
I do not like the **main character** in that book.

1046- 당연하다/dangyeonhada [a.] *to be reasonable, natural, fair*

그들이 자신들의 아이들을 보고 싶어하는 것은 **당연해요**.
It **is natural** that they would miss their children.

1047- 따뜻하다/ttatteuthada [a.] *to be warm*

여기는 일 년 내내 **따뜻해요**.
It **is warm** here all the year round.

1048- 따로/ttaro [adv.] *differently, separately, privately*

이자는 **따로** 지불해도 될까요?
Can I pay the interest **separately**?

1049- 비판/bipan [n.] *criticism, critique*

저는 그의 **비판**이 아닌 그의 지원이 필요합니다.

I need his support, not his **criticism**.

1050- 빌리다/billida [v.] *to borrow, rent, quote, lease*

그는 그녀로부터 돈을 많이 **빌렸어요**.
He **borrowed** a lot of money from her.

1051- 세대/sedae [n.] *age, generation, era*

제주도는 모든 **세대**의 사람들에게 완벽한 휴양지입니다.
Jeju Island is the perfect holiday place for people of all **ages**.

1052- 축구/chukgu [n.] *football, soccer*

친구들과 함께 **축구** 경기를 보는 것은 정말 신나는 일입니다.
It is so exciting to watch the **soccer** game with my friends.

1053- 놓이다/noida [v.] *to be laid, be put, lie*

당신의 옷은 탁자 위에 **놓여 있어요**.
Your clothes **are put** on the table.

1054- 당장/dangjang [adv.] *at once, immediately thereafter, right now*

당신은 그것을 또 잊어버리기 전에 **당장** 기록해 두는 것이 좋을 거예요.
You had better record it **right now** before you forget it again.

1055- 무렵/muryeop [n.] *the time when, around the time of, about the time*

그가 복싱을 전문적으로 시작했을 **무렵** 그는 열다섯 살이었습니다.
He was fifteen years old **when** he began boxing professionally.

1056- 밝다/**bakda** [a.] *to be bright, brilliant, light, clear, keen, acute*

당신 차의 전조등의 불빛은 매우 **밝네요**.
The headlight of your car is very **bright**.

1057- 사물/**samul** [n.] *thing, object, matter*

당신은 항상 자신의 기준으로만 **사물**을 봅니다.
You always see **things** just by your own measure.

1058- 일반적/**ilbanjeok** [determiner] *general, overall, usual, ordinary, common, typical*

일반 감기는 전염병입니다.
The **common** cold is a contagious disease.

1059- 장소/**jangso** [n.] *place, spot, point, scene, location*

저희는 새로운 공장을 위한 적합한 **장소**를 원합니다.
We want a suitable **location** for a new factory.

1060- 곱다/**gopda** [a.] *to be sweet, beautiful, good, kind, pretty*

그녀는 **고운** 얼굴을 가졌을 뿐만 아니라 마음씨도 곱다.
She has not only a **pretty** face but also a warm heart.

1061- 바닥/**badak** [n.] *floor, bottom, base, bed, foundation, ground*

그 아이가 **바닥**에 물을 쏟았습니다.
The child spilled the water on the **floor**.

1062- 새끼/**saekki** [n.] *a young animal, baby*

그가 나타나면 **새끼** 염소들은 비명을 지르며 집안 여기저기에 숨습니다.
The **baby** goats cry out and hide around the house when he appears.

1063- 서비스/**seobiseu** [n.] *service, on the house*

이 가게는 고객에게 배달 **서비스**를 제공합니다.
This shop offers delivery **service** for customers.

1064- 선택하다/**seontaekhada** [v.] *to choose, select, make a choice*

일주일 중에서 요일을 **선택해야** 합니다.
You need to **select** the day of a week.

1065- 심다/**simda** [v.] *to plant, sow, implant, instill, inoculate*

그녀는 자신의 정원에 사과 나무를 **심었어요**.
She **planted** an apple tree in her garden.

1066- 코/**ko** [n.] *nose, nasal fluid, tip*

눈이나 **코**를 비비지 마세요.
Do not rub your eyes or **nose**.

1067- 간단하다/**gandanhada** [a.] *to be simple, straightforward, brief*

이 기계의 조작은 매우 **간단합니다**.
The operation of this machine is quite **simple**.

1068- 고등학교/**godeunghakgyo** [n.] *high school*

고등학교를 졸업하고 나서 십오 년의 시간이 흘렀네요.
It has been fifteen years since we graduated from **high school**.

1069- 교실/**gyosil** [n.] *classroom, class*

선생님은 한 아이가 **교실**에 있는 것을 발견했습니다.
The teacher found a child in a **classroom**.

1070- 견디다/gyeondida [v.] *to endure, bear, tolerate, put up with, stand*

저희 할머니는 삶의 모든 고난을 **견뎠습니다**.
My grandmother **bore** all the troubles of her life.

1071- 기사/gisa [n.] *report, account, article, news*

그 신문은 비난을 받고 정정 **기사**를 개재했습니다.
The newspaper reported corrections of the **article** under fire.

1072- 막히다/makhida [v.] *to become blocked or closed, be obstructed or clogged, be stopped*

도로가 공사로 인해 **막혀** 있습니다.
The road is being **blocked** by construction.

1073- 매체/maeche [n.] *(news) media*

주요 언론 **매체**들은 그의 이름을 공개하지 않았습니다.
The major news **media** did not release his name.

1074- 별/byeol [n.] *star*

우리는 늦게까지 깨어 있다가 하늘에 있는 **별들**을 올려다 보았다.
We stayed up late to look up at the **stars** in the sky.

1075- 복잡하다/bokjaphada [a.] *to be complicated, complex, intricate, crowded, busy, congested*

그 미스터리 소설은 **복잡한** 구성으로 이루어져 있습니다.
The mystery novel has an **intricate** plot.

1076- 뿌리다/ppurida [v.] *to sprinkle, scatter, spray, spread, sow (seeds)*

농부는 땅에 씨를 **뿌렸습니다**.
The farmer **sowed** the seeds in the ground.

1077- 영역/**yeongyeok** [n.] *sphere or field of activity or effect, the territory of a nation, area, domain*

이미지를 보낼 **영역**을 선택하세요.
Select the **area** to send the image.

1078- 체험/**cheheom** [n.] *experience*

그녀는 여행을 하면서 귀중한 **체험**을 했습니다.
She had an invaluable **experience** while traveling.

1079- 때로/**ttaero** [adv.] *on occasion, occasionally, sometimes, from time to time, at times*

비행 시간이 **때로** 열두 시간 또는 열세 시간이 걸립니다.
The flight **occasionally** lasts twelve or thirteen hours.

1080- 극복하다/**geukbokhada** [v.] *to overcome, prevail against adversity*

그것은 그가 슬픔을 **극복하는** 데 도움이 될 것입니다.
It will help him **overcome** his sorrow.

1081- 불법/**bulbeop** [n.] *illegality, the illegal, unlawfulness*

불법과 부패는 뿌리 뽑혀야 합니다.
Illegality and corruption should be eradicated.

1082- 비밀/**bimil** [n.] *secret, confidence*

그녀는 자신의 친구에게 **비밀**을 밝혔습니다.
She disclosed the **secret** to her friend.

1083- 색/**saek** [n.] *color*

어떤 **색**으로 그것을 칠하고 싶나요?
What **color** do you want to paint it?

1084- 쓰이다/sseuida [v.] *to be used, serve*

오늘날 가스는 요리를 할 때 널리 **쓰입니다**.
Today, gas **is** widely **used** for cooking.

1085- 일정하다/iljeonghada [a.] *to be fixed, specified, constant, regular*

그것은 **일정한** 속도로 떨어지나요? 아니면, 가속도가 붙나요?
Does it fall at a **constant** rate, or accelerate?

1086- 밝혀지다/balkyeojida [v.] *to be discovered, be revealed, be known, turn out*

그녀에 대한 소문은 아무 것도 아닌 것으로 **밝혀졌습니다**.
The rumor about her **turned out** to be nothing.

1087- 아까/akka [adv.] *just now, a moment ago, a while ago, earlier, a bit ago*

당신이 **아까** 전화를 하셨던 분인가요?
Are you the one who called **a while ago**?

1088- 알맞다/almatda [a.] *to be just right, suited, appropriate, suitable, proper*

그는 교사가 **알맞습니다**.
He is **suited** to be a teacher.

1089- 이념/inyeom [n.] *ideology, idea, philosophy*

그녀는 **이념**을 그림 속에 구체적으로 나타냈습니다.
She embodied the **idea** in her painting.

1090- 희다/huida [a.] *to be white, light gray*

그녀의 피부는 눈처럼 **흽니다**.
Her skin is as **white** as snow.

1091- 가리키다/garikida [v.] *to point, indicate, show,*

그녀는 지도에서 그 장소를 **가리켰습니다**.
She **indicated** the place on the map.

1092- 모시다/mosida [v.] *to serve or wait on a higher-status person*

그녀는 자신의 부모님을 헌신적으로 **모셨습니다**.
She **served** her parents with devotion.

1093- 발달/baldal [n.] *development, growth, progress*

상상력은 초기 정신 **발달**에 중요합니다.
Imagination is important for early mental **development**.

1094- 수많다/sumanta [a.] *to be many, numerous*

수많은 사람들이 콘서트에 참석했습니다.
Numerous people attended the concert.

1095- 치르다/chireuda [v.] *to pay, hold, have, carry out*

나는 네가 이것에 대한 대가를 **치를** 줄 알았어.
I knew you would **pay** a price for this.

1096- 평화/pyeonghwa [n.] *peace, harmony*

세계 **평화**를 위협하는 문제들이 많이 있습니다.
There are many issues which threaten world **peace**.

1097- 공사/gongsa [n.] *construction*

건물 **공사**가 완료되었습니다.
The **construction** of a building is completed.

1098- 돌/dol [n.] *stone, pebble, rock*

그는 지렛대로 **돌**을 옮겼습니다.

He moved the **rock** with a lever.

1099- 똑같다/ttokgatda [a.] *to be just the same, exactly equal, identical*

규칙은 기본적으로 **똑같습니다**.
The rules **are** basically **the same**.

1100- 박사/baksa [n.] *doctorate, doctor (recipient of a doctorate), expert*

제 오빠는 작년에 **박사** 학위를 취득했습니다.
My older brother obtained a **doctorate** degree last year.

1101- 성/seong [n.] *sex, sexuality, gender*

저희는 **성**차별에 대해서 토론을 해야 합니다.
We have to discuss **gender** discrimination.

1102- 전문가/jeonmunga [n.] *expert, specialist, professional, master*

전문가들은 이 약이 면역 체계를 약화시킬 수도 있다고 말합니다.
Experts say this drug may weaken the immune system.

1103- 단지/danji [adv.] *just, only the designated one*

제가 원했던 모든 것은 **단지** 그녀처럼 되고 싶은 것이었습니다.
All I wanted was to be **just** like her.

1104- 말씀하다/malsseumhada [v.] *(honorific) to speak, say, tell, mention*

선생님은 그에게 뒤로 오라고 **말씀하셨습니다**.
A teacher **told** him to bring up the rear.

1105- 불리다/bullida [v.] *to be called, named*

금성은 저녁 별로 **불립니다**.

Venus **is called** the evening star.

1106- 싸움/ssaum [n.] *fighting, fight, quarrel, battle, contest*

토론 끝에 **싸움**이 시작되었습니다.
A **quarrel** was started at the end of the discussion.

1107- 자꾸/jakku [adv.] *repeatedly, incessantly, again and again*

당신은 왜 **자꾸** 계속해서 똑같은 모퉁이를 도는 것인가요?
Why do you keep turning the same corners **again and again**?

1108- 차리다/charida [v.] *to prepare, equip oneself, set*

그녀는 그의 생일을 맞이해서 식탁을 **차렸어요**.
She **set** a table for his birthday.

1109- 해외/haeoe [n.] *overseas, foreign countries*

그 가족은 **해외** 여행을 계획하고 있습니다.
The family is planning an **overseas** trip.

1110- 뜨다/tteuda [v.] *to float, rise*

수영을 하려면 먼저 물 위에 **뜰** 수 있어야 합니다.
First, you need be able to **float** on the water to swim.

1111- 문화재/munhwajae [n.] *cultural treasure, cultural assets, cultural properties*

우리의 가치 있는 **문화재**를 소중하게 여깁시다.
Let's cherish our valuable **cultural properties**.

1112- 미소/miso [n.] *smile*

그 소녀는 항상 **미소**를 띠고 있습니다.
The girl always wears a **smile**.

1113- 보통/botong [adv.] *usually, normally*

저는 **보통** 책을 읽지만, 다른 경우에는 TV 를 보기도 합니다.
I **usually** read books, but I watch TV at other times.

1114- 식당/sikdang [n.] *a restaurant*

그들은 패스트푸드 **식당**으로 들어갔습니다.
They entered a fast food **restaurant**.

1115- 의미하다/uimihada [v.] *to mean, signify*

친구가 된다는 것은 항상 서로의 의견에 동의를 해야만 한다는 것을 **의미하지** 않습니다.
Being friends does not **mean** that you must always agree with each other.

1116- 체육/cheyuk [n.] *physical education, physical exercise*

저희는 내일 **체육** 시간에 천 미터를 달려야 합니다.
We have to run one thousand meters tomorrow in the **physical education** class.

1117- 구성되다/guseongdoeda [v.] *to be configured or shaped, be plotted, be made up, be composed of, be formed, consist*

이 영어 책은 여덟 장으로 **구성되어 있습니다**.
This English book **consists** of eight chapters.

1118- 독특하다/dokteukhada [a.] *to be unique, unusual, distinctive, peculiar*

그 숙녀 분의 스타일은 매우 **독특합니다**.
The lady's style is very **unique**.

1119- 땀/ttam [n.] *sweat*

저희는 **땀**을 흘리며 일을 하고 있습니다.
We are working in a **sweat**.

1120- 사례/sarye [n.] *precedent, example, case*

그것은 이것을 설명하기에 완벽한 **사례**입니다.
It is the perfect **example** to describe this.

1121- 소개하다/sogaehada [v.] *to introduce*

당신에게 **소개해** 드리고 싶은 사람들이 많이 있습니다.
There are many people I would like to **introduce** you to.

1122- 잘되다/jaldoeda [v.] *to do well, prosper, turn out well, go well*

일이 **잘되고** 있다는 말을 당신으로부터 들으니 기쁘네요.
I am happy to hear from you that things are **going well**.

1123- 추진하다/chujinhada [v.] *to promote or propel an initiative, push ahead with, push forward with*

저희는 그 계획을 **추진할** 것입니다.
We will **push ahead with** the plan.

1124- 칠월/chirwol [n.] *July*

칠월에는 비가 많이 옵니다.
It rains a lot in **July**.

1125- 틀/teul [n.] *frame, framework, model, pattern, form*

알루미늄 **틀**은 가볍습니다.
The aluminum **frame** is lightweight.

1126- 평균/pyeonggyun [n.] *average, mean*

그는 **평균**적으로 하루에 아홉 시간 일을 합니다.
He works nine hours a day on the **average**.

1127- 훈련/hullyeon [n.] *training, drill, discipline, exercise*

군인들은 팔 주 간의 무기 **훈련**을 받을 것입니다.
The soldiers will receive eight weeks of weapons **training**.

1128- 흐름/heureum [n.] *flow, flowing, stream*

가스 **흐름**은 이 밸브로 조절할 수 있습니다.
The gas **flow** can be controlled by this valve.

1129- 십이월/sibiwol [n.] *December*

이제 **십이월**이 되었고 크리스마스도 다가오고 있습니다.
Now it is **December** and Christmas is coming.

1130- 쌓이다/ssaida [v.] *to pile up, be stacked, be heaped, build up*

일이 **쌓이기** 시작합니다.
Work is starting to **pile up**.

1131- 이익/iik [n.] *profit, gain, benefit, advantage, interest*

그는 그 사업으로부터 많은 **이익**을 얻었습니다.
He derived a lot of **profit** from the business.

1132- 쥐다/jwida [v.] *to clench, grasp, grab, hold, squeeze*

그녀는 그것을 손으로 **쥐고** 놓지 않았습니다.
She **held** it in her hand and did not let it go.

1133- 게다가/**gedaga** [adv.] *moreover, besides, further, in addition, furthermore*

게다가 운동을 하면 밤에 잠을 더 잘 자는 데 도움이 될 수 있습니다.
In **addition**, exercise can help you sleep better at night.

1134- 끓이다/**kkeurida** [v.] *to boil, to cause something to boil, heat, simmer*

그녀는 차를 마시려고 차 주전자에 물을 **끓였습니다**.
She **boiled** water in a tea kettle for tea.

1135- 논문/**nonmun** [n.] *essay, academic paper, thesis, dissertation, article*

저는 오늘밤에 집에서 **논문**을 마치려고 합니다.
I will finish the **paper** at home tonight.

1136- 멈추다/**meomchuda** [v.] *to stop, halt*

엘리베이터가 큰 소음을 내며 작동을 **멈췄습니다**.
The elevator **stopped** working with a loud noise.

1137- 사용되다/**sayongdoeda** [v.] *to be used*

원자력은 전력을 생산하는 데 **사용됩니다**.
Nuclear energy **is used** to produce electricity.

1138- 오랫동안/**oraetdongan** [adv.] *for a long time*

그는 **오랫동안** 계속해서 일을 했습니다.
He continued working **for a long time**.

1139- 위기/**wigi** [n.] *crisis*

최근 경제 **위기**에 대한 당신의 입장을 어떠한가요?
What is your position about the recent economic **crisis**?

1140- 정당/jeongdang [n.] *a political party, rightfulness, justness, legitimacy*

그들은 새로운 **정당**을 만들었습니다.
They formed a new **political party**.

1141- 종이/jongi [n.] *a paper*

이 **종이**를 스테이플러로 찍어주시겠어요?
Would you staple these **papers** together, please?

1142- 찾아가다/chajagada [v.] *to go to see or meet someone, visit*

그는 얼마동안 머무를 생각으로 그의 친구를 **찾아갔다**.
He **visited** his friend with a plan to stay a while.

1143- 폭력/pongnyeok [n.] *violence, violent acts*

그 교사는 자신의 학생들에게 **폭력**을 가했습니다.
The teacher committed **violent acts** towards his students.

1144- 혹시/hoksi [adv.] *by chance, by any chance, happen to*

혹시 이거 지하철에서 사지 않았나요?
Did you buy this on the subway **by any chance**?

1145- 늘다/neulda [v.] *to increase, improve, advance, grow, gain*

그는 몸무게가 십킬로그램 **늘었어요**.
He **gained** ten kilograms in weight.

1146- 양/yang [n.] *quantity, amount, volume*

거기에는 많은 **양**의 정보가 있었습니다.
There was a large **amount** of information.

1147- 절차/jeolcha [n.] *procedure, process, step, proceedings*

신청 **절차**에 대해서는 무엇이라고 언급되어 있나요?
What is stated about the application **process**?

1148- 진짜/jinjja [adv.] *really, actually, truly, indeed*

저는 **진짜** 그녀를 기분 나쁘게 할 의도가 없었어요.
I **really** did not mean to offend her.

1149- 공기/gonggi [n.] *air, atmosphere*

공기와 물은 천연 자원입니다.
Air and water are natural resources.

1150- 닿다/data [v.] *to touch, reach*

번개는 사람들에게 위험할 수 있습니다. 왜냐하면 그것은 수천 킬로미터 멀리 떨어진 사람들에게까지 **닿을** 수 있기 때문입니다.
Lightening can be dangerous to people, because it can **reach** them from thousands of kilometers away.

1151- 속하다/sokhada [v.] *to be part of, be a member of, belong to, be affiliated to*

저희는 축구 클럽에 **속해 있고** 일주일에 한 번 만납니다.
We **belong to** a soccer club and meet once a week.

1152- 올림픽/ollimpik [n.] *the Olympics, the Olympic Games*

4년마다 많은 사람들이 텔레비전에서 **올림픽**을 시청합니다.
A lot of people watch **the Olympics** on television every four years.

1153- 외/oe [n.] *apart from this, except, but for,*

용무 **외** 출입할 수 없습니다.
No admittance **except** on business.

1154- 제공하다/jegonghada [v.] *to provide, furnish, offer*

그 호텔은 손님들에게 낮이나 밤이나 언제든지 자동 모닝콜 서비스를 **제공했습니다**.

The hotel **provided** guests an automatic wakeup call anytime day or night.

1155- 증가하다/jeunggahada [v.] *to increase, add*

그 도시의 인구는 오십만 명에서 백만 명으로 **증가했습니다**.

The population of the city has **increased** from five hundred thousand to one million.

1156- 기대/gidae [n.] *expectation, hope, anticipation*

그의 연설은 제 **기대**에 미치지 못했어요.

His speech did not come up to my **expectation**.

1157- 떡/tteok [n.] *a rice cake*

그 **떡**에는 콩가루가 묻어 있었습니다.
The **rice cakes** were covered with bean flour.

1158- 식물/singmul [n.] *a plant*

그 **식물**은 죽어가고 있고 물을 필요로 합니다.
The **plant** is dying and needs water.

1159- 옛/yet [determiner.] *old, bygone*

저는 저의 **옛** 친구를 거의 알아보지 못했습니다.
I could scarcely recognize my **old** friend.

1160- 외치다/oechida [v.] *to shout, cry out, proclaim, yell, scream*

그녀는 저에게 도와 달라고 **외쳤습니다**.
She **cried out** to me for help.

1161- 적어도/jeogeodo [adv.] *at least*

그녀는 매일 밤 **적어도** 두 시간씩 공부했습니다.

She used to study **at least** two hours every night.

1162- 편하다/pyeonhada [a.] *to be easygoing, comfortable, convenient, relaxed*

일등석 좌석들은 넓고 **편합니다.**

The first-class seats are wide and **comfortable.**

1163- 권리/gwolli [n.] *right, privilege*

그는 재산에 대한 **권리**를 주장했습니다.

He claimed a **right** to the property.

1164- 끝내다/kkeunnaeda [v.] *to finish, end, close, complete, wind up*

당신은 보고서를 언제 **끝낼** 것인가요?

When will you **finish** your report?

1165- 대답/daedap [n.] *answer, response, reply*

그녀가 문을 두드렸으나 **대답**이 전혀 없었습니다.

She knocked at the door but there was no **response.**

1166- 시작/sijak [n.] *start, beginning*

저는 영화의 **시작** 부분을 놓치고 싶지 않아요.

I do not want to miss the **beginning** of a movie.

1167- 어려움/eoryeoum [n.] *difficulty, trouble, problem, hardship*

그 환자들 중 일부는 고기를 먹는 일에 **어려움**을 겪었습니다.

Some of those patients had **difficulty** eating meat.

1168- 일주일/iljuil [n.] *a week, seven days*

그녀는 **일주일**에 사 일을 운동합니다.
She exercises four days **a week**.

1169- 자원/jawon [n.] *resource*

땅도 천연 **자원**입니다.
Land is also a natural **resource**.

1170- 춤/chum [n.] *dance, dancing*

그들의 **춤**은 정말 예술 작품이었어요.
Their **dancing** was really a work of art.

1171- 넘기다/neomgida [v.] *to carry over, hand over, turn over, pass, hand in*

세관 직원들이 그 남자를 경찰에 **넘겼습니다**.
Customs officials **turned** the man **over** to the police.

1172- 물체/mulche [n.] *object*

이 현미경은 **물체**를 이백 배로 확대합니다.
This microscope magnifies an **object** two hundred times.

1173- 분명히/bunmyeonghi [adv.] *certainly, obviously, clearly, distinctly, plainly*

이것은 **분명히** 그것과 다릅니다.
This is **certainly** different from that.

1174- 안타깝다/antakkapda [a.] *to be unfortunate, to be poor, to be a pity*

거의 끝나가는데 지금 포기하다니 **안타깝다**.
It would **be a pity** to give up now. It's almost over.

1175- 시위/siwi [n.] *demonstration, protest, demo*

대규모 **시위**로 인해 나라가 혼란에 빠졌습니다.
Mass **demonstrations** threw the nation into disorder.

1176- 아무것/amugeot [n.] *anything, something*

아무것도 알고 싶지 않나요?
Don't you want to know **anything**?

1177- 온/on [determiner] *all, entire, whole*

온 집안이 난장판입니다.
The **whole** house is a mess.

1178- 젖다/jeotda [v.] *to become wet, indulge in, get damp, get moist, get drenched*

제 옷은 **젖어서** 제 몸에 달라붙습니다.
My clothes are **wet** and cling to my body.

1179- 제외하다/jeoehada [v.] *to exclude, leave out, count out, rule out*

그들은 그 사항을 회의 일정에서 **제외했습니다**.
They **excluded** the item from the agenda of the conference.

1180- 최대/choedae [n.] *the greatest, the largest, the biggest, maximum*

그 회사는 세계 **최대** 보험 회사입니다.
The company is the world's **largest** insurance company.

1181- 평소/pyeongso [n.] *the ordinary, ordinary conditions, usual day*

다른 직원들을 돕는 것이 그녀의 **평소** 행동과 어울리는 특징입니다.
Helping the other members is in character with her **usual** actions.

1182- 견해/gyeonhae [n.] *opinion, interpretation, view, opinion, point of view*

제 **견해**는 당신의 것과 정확하게 일치합니다.
My **views** coincide exactly with yours.

1183- 깨끗하다/kkaekkeuthada [a.] *to be clean, be spotless*

그의 집은 항상 정리가 되어 있고 **깨끗합니다**.
His house is always neat and **clean**.

1184- 농사/nongsa [n.] *agriculture, farming*

올해는 **농사**하기에 좋은 해입니다.
This is a good year for **farming**.

1185- 더구나/deoguna [v.] *also, furthermore, besides, moreover, in addition*

더구나 저희 모두는 사생활에 대한 권리를 가지고 있습니다.
Furthermore, we all have a right to privacy.

1186- 안정/anjeong [n.] *stability, stabilization, equilibrium*

그것은 당신의 마음의 **안정**을 유지하는데 도움이 될 것입니다.
It will help you to preserve the **equilibrium** of your mind.

1187- 어둠/eodum [n.] *the dark, darkness*

그 아이를 **어둠** 속에 혼자 두면 안 됩니다.
You should not leave the child alone in **the dark**.

1188- 어둡다/eodupda [a.] *to be dark, be gloomy, be dusky, is dim*

실내 조명이 너무 **어둡습니다**.
The interior lighting is too **dim**.

1189- 어쨌든/eojjaetdeun [adv.] *anyway, after all, regardless, anyhow, in any case*

그 음악은 매우 별로였지만, 저는 **어쨌든** 재밌는 시간을 가졌어요.
The music was pretty bad, but I had fun **anyway**.

1190- 주택/jutaek [n.] *residential building, house, housing, home*

일월에는 어느 지역에서 가장 많은 **주택**이 팔렸나요?
Which area sold the most **homes** in January?

1191- 고장/gojang [n.] *breakdown, trouble, failure, out of order*

엘리베이터가 갑자기 **고장**났습니다.
The elevator had a sudden **breakdown**.

1192- 관련하다/gwallyeonhada [v.] *to be connected, be related, be in a relationship, be associated, be involved*

두 경우는 서로 **관련되어 있습니다**.
The two cases **are connected** with each other.

1193- 눈길/nungil [n.] *gaze, eye, attention, the object of one's gaze*

내 **눈길**을 사로잡는 소녀가 있었다.
There was a girl who caught my **eye**.

1194- 물어보다/mureoboda [v.] *to ask, inquire, question*

지난 번에 제가 그에게 **물어보려고** 했어요.
I tried to **ask** him the other day.

1195- 미안하다/mianhada [a.] *to be ashamed of oneself, be sorry*

제가 너무 바빠서 당신을 도와줄 수 없어서 **미안합니다**.
I **am sorry** that I can't help you because I am too busy.

1196- 밀다/**milda** [v.] *to push*

그 남자가 문을 **밀고** 있습니다.

The man is **pushing** a door.

1197- 스트레스/**seuteureseu** [n.] *stress*

그는 일과 관련된 **스트레스**를 많이 받고 있습니다.

He is under a lot of work-related **stress**.

1198- 주어지다/**jueojida** [n.] *to be provided, be given, be allowed*

주어진 공란에 질문에 대한 답을 하시기 바랍니다.

Please answer questions in the space **provided**.

1199- 고려하다/**goryeohada** [v.] *to consider, reflect on, think, take account of*

당신의 아이에게 무엇이 최선인지에 대해 **고려해** 보시기 바랍니다.

Please **consider** what would be best for your child.

1200- 과일/**gwail** [n.] *fruit*

과일에는 많은 비타민이 있습니다.

There are many vitamins in **fruit**.

1201- 널리/**neolli** [adv.] *widely, magnanimously, generously, extensively*

가스는 요리를 할 때 **널리** 사용됩니다.

Gas is **widely** used for cooking.

1202- 농촌/**nongchon** [n.] *rural hamlet, farm town, farm village, farming area*

요즘 **농촌**에는 일손이 부족합니다.

Farming villages are shorthanded these days.

1203- 올라오다/ollaoda [v.] *to come up, ascend, be set on the table*

올라와서 몇 마디 해 주시겠어요?
Would you like to **come up** and say a few words?

1204- 챙기다/chaenggida [v.] *to collect, pack, set in order, take care of, look after*

그들은 캠핑 여행을 떠나기 위해 장비를 **챙겼습니다**.
They **packed** equipment for their camping trip.

1205- 고르다/goreuda [v.] *to pick, select, choose*

읽기에 가장 좋은 책을 **골라야** 합니다.
You need to **select** the best book for reading.

1206- 벌어지다/beoreojida [v.] *to occur, take place, happen, arise*

그녀는 어떤 일이 **벌어질** 것이라고 예상할까요?
What does she predict will **happen**?

1207- 소재/sojae [n.] *material, component, stuff, subject matter, content, location, presence of a thing at a place*

저 스웨터들은 최고의 **소재**로 직접 손으로 만든 것입니다.
Those sweaters are handmade from the best **materials**.

1208- 전망/jeonmang [n.] *prospect, physical view, future outlook, forecast*

내년 사업 **전망**이 밝습니다.
The business **outlook** for next year is bright.

1209- 포기하다/pogihada [v.] *to give up, abandon*

그는 부상 때문에 경기를 **포기했습니다**.
He **abandoned** the game because of an injury.

1210- 형성되다/hyeongseongdoeda [v.] *to be formed, be shaped, be built*

그 산들은 이 억 년보다 더 오래 전에 **형성되었습니다**.
The hills **were formed** more than two hundred million years ago.

1211- 고치다/gochida [v.] *to fix, correct, mend, repair, cure, heal*

그 남자가 자전거를 **고치고** 있습니다.
The man is **fixing** the bike.

1212- 그림자/geurimja [n.] *shadow, shady image*

그림자처럼 제가 당신 곁에 있을 것을 맹세합니다.
I swear I will be by your side like a **shadow**.

1213- 다하다/dahada [v.] *to complete, finish, be finished, be used up, run out, be exhausted, die, end, come to an end*

어떤 인기 제품도 언젠가는 그 수명이 **다하게** 된다.
The life of any hit product will **come to an end** someday.

1214- 마침내/machimnae [adv.] *finally, in the end, at last*

긴 토론 끝에 그들은 **마침내** 결말을 내릴 수 있었습니다.
After a long discussion, they **finally** could abide the issue.

1215- 비교하다/bigyohada [v.] *to compare, make a comparison*

그녀는 물건을 살 때 눈으로 가격을 꼼꼼하게 **비교합니다**.
When she buys things, she compares the prices meticulously with her eyes.

1216- 시월/siwol [n.] *October*

시월치고는 평소와 다르게 덥습니다.

It is unusually hot for **October.**

1217- 커지다/keojida [v.] *to become large or larger, expand, grow bigger*

저희 동네는 나날이 **커지고** 있어요.
Our neighborhood is **becoming larger** day after day.

1218- 한쪽/hanjjok [n.] *one side, one direction*

그 탑은 **한쪽**으로 비스듬하게 있습니다.
The tower leans on **one side.**

1219- 검사/geomsa [n.] *examination, inspection, test, check*

혈액 **검사** 결과는 다음 주에 나올 것입니다.
The blood **test** results will come out next week.

1220- 결론/gyeollon [n.] *conclusion*

저는 때때로 성급하게 **결론**을 내리는 경향이 있습니다.
I tend to jump to **conclusions** at times.

1221- 들이다/deurida [v.] *to let in, spend, expend, adopt*

저는 그것에 많은 시간을 **들입니다**.
I **spend** a lot of time on it.

1222-맡기다/matgida [v.] *to entrust someone with something, leave, deposit, assign*

저는 그 결정을 당신의 선택 사항에 **맡길게요**.
I will **leave** the decision to your option.

1223- 박물관/bangmulgwan [n.] *museum*

박물관이 가장 늦게 문을 닫는 날은 언제인가요?
On which days does the **museum** close the latest?

1224- 소문/somun [n.] *rumor, gossip*

저는 **소문**에 신경을 쓰지 않으려고 노력해요.

I try not to pay attention to **rumors**.

1225- 싣다/sitda [v.] *to load, carry, put*

그들은 장비를 버스에 **실었습니다**.

They **loaded** their gear on a bus.

1226- 쌓다/ssata [v.] *to stack up, pile up, build, heap*

그 여성은 선반 위에 종이를 **쌓고** 있습니다.

The woman is **piling** the papers on the shelf.

1227- 어서/eoseo [adv.] *quickly, promptly*

어서 대답해 주세요.

Please answer **promptly**.

1228- 자녀/janyeo [n.] *children, sons and daughters, offspring*

이 규칙은 자녀뿐만 아니라 부모에게도 적용이 됩니다.

This rule applies to parents as well as **children**.

1229- 제목/jemok [n.] *title of a book or other work, name*

저는 그 영화 **제목**을 기억할 수 없어요.

I can't remember the film **title**.

1230- 짓/jit [n.] *physical act or movement, (doing) a thing*

저는 그런 **짓**을 결코 다시는 하지 않을 것을 맹세합니다.

I swear I will never again do such **a thing**.

1231- 판결/pangyeol [n.] *judgment, verdict, juridical*

decision, decision of the court

그가 무죄라는 것이 법원의 **판결**입니다.
The **judgment** of the court is that he is not guilty.

1232- 팔월/parwol [n.] *August*

한국에서는 두 번째 학기가 **팔월**에 시작되나요?
Does the second semester start in **August** in Korea?

1233- 하얗다/hayata [a.] *to be white, pale*

밀가루는 눈처럼 **하얗습니다**.
Flour is as **white** as snow.

1234- 희망/huimang [n.] *hope, wish, desire*

그 약은 그녀의 마지막 **희망**입니다.
The medicine is her last **hope**.

1235- 가방/gabang [n.] *bag, briefcase, sack*

저는 도서관에 **가방**을 놔뒀어요.
I left my **bag** behind in the library.

1236- 군대/gundae [n.] *army, the military, the forces, troops*

군대는 명령에 따라 움직입니다.
The **army** moves at the word of command.

1237- 그만큼/geumankeum [a.] *to that extent, that much, so many, as many or much*

하루 빠지게 되면 **그만큼** 손해가 됩니다.
A day's absence means **so much** loss.

1238- 비로소/biroso [adv.] *for the first time, only after, at*

last

저는 암이 얼마나 무서운지를 **비로소** 알게 되었습니다.

I realized **for the first time** how dreadful cancer is.

1239- 상대방/sangdaebang [n.] *partner in conversation or other interaction*

상대방의 기분을 파악하는 게 중요합니다.

The important thing is to assess **the other person**'s mood.

1240- 서구/seogu [n.] *Western Europe, the West*

대부분의 **서구** 국가들에서는 겨울 방학이 매우 짧습니다.

In most **Western** countries, winter breaks are very short.

1241- 소유/soyu [n.] *possession, ownership*

그 집은 그의 **소유**입니다.

The house is in the **possession** of him.

1242- 시골/sigol [n.] *countryside, the country, rural area*

그는 도시에서 멀리 떨어진 **시골**에 살고 있습니다.

He lives in the remote **country** from the city.

1243- 실수/silsu [n.] *mistake, error*

이 **실수**로 우리의 모든 노력이 무산되었습니다.

This **error** undid all our efforts.

1244- 잘못되다/jalmotdoeda [v.] *to go wrong, go awry*

무엇인가가 잘못되었음을 저는 알았습니다.

I was aware that something **went wrong**.

1245- 치료/chiryo [n.] *treatment for a disease or injury, cure, therapy, remedy*

라듐은 암 **치료**에 사용됩니다.

Radium is used in cancer **treatments**.

1246- 폭/pok [n.] *breadth, width, range*

한국은 기온의 변동 **폭**이 큰 나라입니다.
Korea is a country with a wide **range** of temperature.

1247- 내밀다/naemilda [v.] *to push out, thrust out, hand out, stretch out, stick out*

팔을 차창 밖으로 **내밀지** 마세요.
Do not **stick** your arm **out** of the car window.

1248- 부문/bumun [n.] *category, classification, field of study or endeavor, sector*

그는 현재 일곱 개 **부문**에서 정상의 자리에 있습니다.
He now stands atop in seven **categories**.

1249- 시리즈/sirijeu [n.] *series*

이 영화 **시리즈**의 세 번째 편이 이번 여름에 개봉되었습니다.
The third film of the **series** was released this summer.

1250- 임신/imsin [v.] *pregnancy*

피임을 통해 여성은 원치 않는 **임신**을 피할 수 있습니다.
By using birth control, women can avoid unwanted **pregnancy**.

1251- 잡히다/japhida [v.] *to be caught, be seized, be grabbed*

그는 절도 현장에서 **잡혔습니다**.
He **was caught** in the act of stealing.

1252- 규정/gyujeong [n.] *provision, rule, code, regulation*

그 건물은 안전 **규정**을 준수하지 않았습니다.
The building did not conform to safety **regulations**.

1253- 그램/geuraem [n.] *gram (unit)*

그것은 **그램**당 천 원에 팔리고 있습니다.
It is sold at one thousand won a **gram**.

1254- 밭/bat [n.] *field, dry land for crops, farm*

그들은 **밭**에 밀의 씨를 뿌렸습니다.
They seeded their **fields** with wheat.

1255- 분석하다/bunseokhada [v.] *to analyze*

저희는 실패의 원인을 **분석했습니다**.
We **analyzed** the causes of failure.

1256- 식구/sikgu [n.] *mouth to feed, family member, family*

저희 **식구**는 저녁 여섯 시에 저녁을 먹습니다.
My **family** eats dinner at six p.m.

1257- 아예/aye [adv.] *altogether, entirely, from the beginning, throughout, from the very first, never, (not) at all*

그녀는 그를 **아예** 믿지 않습니다.
She does not believe him **at all**.

1258- 울리다/ullida [v.] *to sound, ring, make a sound*

전화가 다섯 번 **울렸습니다**.
The phone **rang** five times.

1259- 작용하다/jagyonghada [v.] *to act on, affect, act*

고무는 전기 절연체로 **작용합니다**.
Rubber **acts** as an electric insulator.

1260- 확실하다/hwaksilhada [a.] *to be certain, be definite,* *be confident, be sure*

그 후보가 당선될 것은 **확실합니다**.

The candidate is **sure** to win.

1261- 개선/**gaeseon** [n.] *reform, improvement*

위원회의 보고서는 저희가 **개선** 작업을 하는 데 있어서 도움을 줄 것입니다.

The committee's report will help us in the work of **reform**.

1262- 그릇/**geureut** [n.] *bowl, container, vessel, basin, dish, plate*

그 **그릇**에 우유를 넣고 섞습니다.

Pour the milk into the **bowl** and mix.

1263- 글자/**geulja** [n.] *letter, type, character of a writing system*

그는 간판의 **글자**를 바꾸고 있습니다.

He is changing the **letters** on the sign.

1264- 바람직하다/**baramjikhada** [a.] *to be appropriate, be of a desirable character, be desirable*

공공장소에서는 금연하는 것이 **바람직합니다**.

It **is desirable** not to smoke in public places.

1265- 연구하다/**yeonguhada** [v.] *to conduct research, study*

그 의사는 인체의 구조를 **연구했습니다**.

The doctor **studied** the structure of the human body.

1266- 착하다/**chakhada** [a.] *to be good-natured, be good, be nice, be kind*

그의 인성은 기본적으로 **착합니다**.

His personality is basically **good**.

1267- 라디오**/radio** [n.] *radio*

당신은 **라디오**를 매일 듣나요?

Do you listen to the **radio** everyday?

1268- 부동산**/budongsan** [n.] *real estate, property*

그녀는 자신이 가지고 있는 돈 전부를 **부동산**에 투자할 것입니다.

She will invest all of her money in **real estate.**

1269- 신화**/sinhwa** [n.] *myth, legend, mythology*

제우스는 그리스 **신화**에서 최고신이다.

Zeus is the king of the gods in Greek **mythology.**

1270- 직업**/jigeop** [n.] *job, work, occupation, career, vocation, profession*

여행 가이드로서의 **직업**에 당신은 만족하나요?

Are you satisfied with your **job** as a tour guide?

1271- 거두다**/geoduda** [v.] *to harvest, gather, collect, earn, reap*

당신은 뿌린 것을 **거두게** 될 것입니다.

You will **reap** what you have sown.

1272- 방학**/banghak** [n.] *school vacation, school holiday*

이번 **방학** 때 뭐 할 거예요?

What will you do this **vacation**?

1273- 범위**/beomwi** [n.] *field, scope, range, limit, scale, bounds, the border of such a scope or range*

그것의 길이 **범위**는 일 미터에서 이 미터입니다.

Its length **range** is from one meter to two meters.

1274- 조상/josang [n.] *deceased ancestor or ancestors, forefathers*

우리 **조상들**은 더운 날씨에 더위를 식히려고 부채를 사용했습니다.

Our **ancestors** used fans as a relief from the hot weather.

1275- 철학/cheolhak [n.] *philosophy*

데카르트는 근대 **철학**의 시조였습니다.

Descartes was the founder of modern **philosophy**.

1276- 검다/geomda [a.] *to be black, be dark*

그는 **검은** 모자를 쓰고 있습니다.

He is wearing a **black** hat.

1277- 너희/neohui [n.] *(plural, referring to the group of friends or lower-status people) you, your*

너희 둘 때문에 엄마가 화가 나셨어.

Mom got angry because of the two of **you**.

1278- 대형/daehyeong [n.] *large, on a large scale, big*

그는 대서양을 운항하는 **대형** 선박에서 일을 하고 있습니다.

He is working on **big** transatlantic boats.

1279- 따다/ttada [v.] *to separate, pick out, win as a prize, get, receive*

그녀는 올림픽에서 금메달을 **땄습니다**.

She **won** a gold medal in the Olympics.

1280- 문제점/munjejeom [n.] *problem, drawback, problematic point, controversial point*

사소한 **문제점**들이 있긴 하지만 전반적인 상황은 괜찮습니다.

The overall situation is good, despite a few minor **problems**.

1281- 불가능하다/bulganeunghada [a.] *to be impossible*

비행기에서 탈출하는 일은 **불가능합니다**.
It **is impossible** to escape from the plane.

1282- 구경하다/gugyeonghada [v.] *watch, see, look on, sightsee*

사람들이 싸움을 **구경하려고** 주변으로 모였다.
People gathered around to **watch** the fight.

1283- 충격/gidarida [n.] *blow, impact, shock*

법원의 판결은 모든 사람들에게 **충격**이었습니다.
The court's decision was a **shock** to everybody.

1284- 퍼지다/peojida [v.] *to spread outwards, diffuse, circulate*

그 소식은 마을에 빠르게 **퍼졌습니다**.
The news **spread** quickly through the town.

1285- 금방/geumbang [adv.] *soon, shortly, just now, just*

금방 돌아올게요.
I will be back **soon**.

1286- 남쪽/namjjok [n.] *south*

그는 **남쪽**으로 차를 운전했습니다.
He drove his car down **south**.

1287- 누르다/nureuda [v.] *to press, oppress, suppress, push*

그녀는 벨이 울리도록 버튼을 **눌렀습니다**.
She **pressed** the button to ring the bell.

1288- 미술/misul [n.] *art*

그의 부모님은 그가 **미술**에 관심을 갖도록 격려했습니다.
His parents encouraged him to have an interest in **art**.

1289- 백성/baekseong [n.] *the populace, the common people, subjects, the public*

왕은 **백성들**에게 전쟁을 준비하도록 재촉했습니다.
The king urged his **people** to prepare for war.

1290- 상당히/sangdanghi [adv.] *suitably, to an appropriate degree, considerably, quite, rather, fairly*

물가는 일월 최고점에서 **상당히** 하락하였습니다.
Prices declined **considerably** from the high peak of January.

1291- 색깔/saekkkal [n.] *color*

저는 두 번째 디자인의 **색깔**이 더 마음에 들어요.
I prefer the **color** in the second design.

1292- 요리/yori [n.] *cooking, cuisine*

수천년 동안 사람들은 **요리**를 할 때 올리브유를 사용해 왔어요.
Olive oil has been used for **cooking** for thousands of years.

1293- 유명하다/yumyeonghada [a.] *to be famous*

이 장소는 경치로 유명합니다.
This place **is famous** for its scenery.

1294- 꽤/kkwae [adv.] *rather, fairly, pretty, to a more than ordinary degree*

그날은 날씨가 **꽤** 추웠어요.
It was **rather** chilly that day.

1295- 외국인/oegugin [n.] *foreigner*

서울에는 많은 **외국인들**이 있습니다.

There are lots of **foreigners** in Seoul.

1296- 한참/hancham [n.] *a while, quite a while, a long time*

저는 산에 갔다 온 지 **한참** 됐습니다.

I have not been to the mountains in **a long time**.

1297- 군사/gunsa [n.] *soldier, military affairs*

군사들은 그들의 장군의 명예를 위해 싸웠습니다.

The **soldiers** fought for the name of their general's sake.

1298- 끊다/kkeunta [v.] *to cut, sever, shut off, pause, stop, break off*

그는 건강을 위해 담배를 **끊었습니다**.

He **stopped** smoking for his health.

\

1299- 무너지다/neomeogada [v.] *to collapse, tilt, cross over, pass, fall*

그 벽이 **무너졌을** 때 몇몇 사람들이 갇혔습니다.

Some people were trapped when the walls were **collapsed**.

1300- 담기다/damgida [v.] *to be put in, go into, be included in, be filled, be bottled, be contained*

그 이론에 대한 설명은 다섯 권의 책에 **담겨 있습니다**.

The explanations of the theory **are contained** in five books.

1301- 마당/madang [n.] *yard, garden, plaza, courtyard, state of afairs or condition*

마당 주위에는 담장이 있습니다.

There is a fence around the **yard**.

1302- 부인/buin [n.] *(honorific) (another person's) wife, denial, disaffirmation*

부인과 아이들도 데려오셔도 됩니다.
You can bring your **wife** and children, too.

1303- 서두르다/seodureuda [v.] *to hurry, rush, hasten*

시간이 많기 때문에 **서두르지** 않아도 됩니다.
You do not have to **hurry** because there is plenty of time.

1304- 지적하다/jijeokhada [v.] *point out, indicate*

그들은 온라인 게임은 위험할 수 있다고 **지적합니다**.
They **point out** that online games can be dangerous.

1305- 짝/jjak [n.] *pair, partner, mate*

옆에 있는 당신의 **짝**과 같이 하는 것은 좋은 방법입니다.
It is a good way to study with your **partner** next to you.

1306- 참으로/chameuro [adv.] *truly, indeed, really, very*

그 소식을 들으니 **참으로** 기쁘네요.
I am **really** pleased to hear the news.

1307- 충분하다/chungbunhada [a.] *to be sufficient, be adequate, be enough*

이 음식은 네 사람을 대접하기에 **충분할** 것입니다.
This food will **be enough** for four servings.

1308- 기쁘다/gippeuda [a.] *to be happy, be glad, be pleased, be delighted*

우리가 그것을 완수해서 **기쁘네요**.
I **am glad** we have done it.

1309- 뛰다/ttwida [v.] *to run, jump, leap, skip, dash, hop, bounce*

당신은 얼마나 빠르게 **뛸** 수 있나요?
How fast can you **run**?

1310- 숙제/sukje [n.] *homework, assignment*

저희는 **숙제**를 제 시간에 제출해야 합니다.
We must hand in our **assignments** on time.

1311- 앞두다/apduda [v.] *to have something ahead, look toward, have something ahead, be about to*

그 가게는 오픈을 **앞두고 있습니다**.
The store **is about to** open.

1312- 예산/yesan [n.] *budget, budgeting*

장기 **예산** 적자는 큰 문제가 됩니다.
Long term **budget** deficits are a big problem.

1313- 온갖/ongat [determiner.] *all, every, all kinds of*

그는 **온갖** 비방을 당했습니다.
He suffered **all kinds of** slanders.

1314- 우려/uryeo [n.] *concern, worry, fear*

간호사들은 병원 재정 지원 삭감에 대하여 **우려**했습니다.
The nurses felt **concerned** about cuts in hospital funds.

1315- 우산/usan [n.] *umbrella*

비가 오기 시작했는데 제 **우산**을 사무실에 두고 왔네요.
It has started raining and I left my **umbrella** at the office.

1316- 기쁨/gippeum [n.] *joy, happiness, pleasure, delight*

전쟁이 끝나게 되었을 때 온 나라 전역에는 **기쁨**이 넘쳤습니다. .

When the war ended, there was **joy** throughout the nation.

1317- 깊이/**gipi** [n.] *depth*

이 연못의 **깊이**는 약 팔 미터 정도입니다.
The **depth** of this pond is about eight meters.

1318- 꾸미다/**kkumida** [v.] *to adorn, decorate, fabricate*

예산 범위 안에서 그 집을 **꾸밀** 수 있습니다.
You can **decorate** the house within the budget.

1319- 늘리다/**neullida** [v.] *to expand, increase, add to, extend, enlarge, augment*

그 회사는 영업 사원을 열 명에서 열다섯 명으로 **늘렸습니다**.
The company **expanded** its sales force from ten to fifteen representatives.

1320- 무릎/**mureup** [n.] *knee, lap*

어제 그녀는 **무릎**을 다쳤습니다.
She hurt her **knees** yesterday.

1321- 발견되다/**balgyeondoeda** [v.] *to be discovered, be found*

아직 문제 해결의 단서가 **발견되지** 않았습니다.
A clue has not **been found** to solve the problem yet.

1322- 보호하다/**bohohada** [v.] *to protect, safeguard*

사법 제도의 목적은 국민의 권리를 **보호하는** 것입니다.
The purpose of the court system is to **protect** the rights of the people.

1323- 시스템/**siseutem** [n.] *system*

안전 모드에서는 **시스템** 복원을 사용할 수 없습니다.

System restore is unavailable in safe mode.

1324- 지난달/jinandal [n.] *last month*

고지서는 모두 **지난달**에 납부했습니다.
All the bills were paid **last month**.

1325- 참여/chamyeo [n.] *participation*

가을 설문에는 보다 많은 분들의 **참여**를 기대합니다.
I hope to see even greater **participation** in our fall survey.

1326- 걸음/georeum [n.] *step, pace*

그가 버스 정류장에 있는 나무를 몇 **걸음** 지나쳐 가고 있었습니다.
He was a few **steps** past the tree at the bus stop.

1327- 겨우/gyeou [adv.] *barely, with difficulty, only, just,*

그들은 이제 **겨우** 중학생들입니다.
They are **only** in junior high school.

1328- 마르다/mareuda [v.] *to dry up, become thin, thirst, be thirsty*

그녀는 얼굴이 창백하고 **말라** 보여요.
She looks pale and **thin** in the face.

1329- 비교적/bigyojeok [adv.] *quite, more than ordinarily, relatively, comparatively*

요즘에는 그러한 경우가 **비교적** 적습니다.
Such cases are **comparatively** few nowadays.

1330- 애쓰다/aesseuda [v.] *to exert or strain oneself to reach a goal, endeavor, work hard, try*

그는 환경문제에 관한 정보를 알아내려고 **애쓰고 있습니다**.
He **is working hard** to find out information about

environmental problems.

1331- 올바르다/**olbareuda** [a.] *to be proper, be upright, be right, be correct, be accurate*

암호가 **올바른지** 확인하고 다시 시도하십시오.
Check that the password **is correct** and then try again.

1332- 책상/**chaeksang** [n.] *desk, writing table*

그 책은 **책상** 위에 있습니다.
The book is on the **desk**.

1333- 춥다/**chupda** [a.] *to be cold, be chilly, be freezing*

방 안이 너무 **춥습니다**.
It **is** too **cold** in the room.

1334- 흔하다/**heunhada** [a.] *to be frequent, be common, be ordinary, be commonplace*

영국에서는 비가 **흔합니다**.
Rain **is common** in England.

1335- 높아지다/**nopajida** [v.] *to be heightened, be raised, become higher*

실업률이 조금이라도 더 **높아지게** 되면 장관의 경제 정책은 시험대에 오르게 될 것입니다.
The minister's economic policy will be tested if the unemployment rate **goes** any **higher**.

1336- 늙다/**neukda** [v.] *to age, grow old*

근심과 병이 사람을 **늙게 합니다**.
Worry and illness **age** a man.

1337- 단위/danwi [n.] *unit, counter, measure*

칼로리는 음식에서 생산되는 에너지의 **단위**입니다.
A calorie is the **measure** of energy produced by food.

1338- 둘째/duljjae [num.] *second, next after the first*

이틀 간 진행될 예정이었던 세미나의 **둘째** 날 행사는 취소됐습니다.
The **second** day of the two-day seminar was canceled.

1339- 뛰어나다/ttwieonada [a.] *to excel, be outstanding, be excellent, be remarkable*

그는 형제 중에서 가장 **뛰어납니다**.
He **excels** beyond the rest of his brothers.

1340- 무겁다/mugeopda [a.] *to be heavy, be weighty*

달걀은 물보다 **무겁습니다**.
An egg **is heavier** than water.

1341- 상상/sangsang [n.] *imagination, speculation*

그는 **상상**을 통해 소설을 썼습니다.
He used his **imagination** to write the novel.

1342- 소득/sodeuk [n.] *income, earnings, profit, gain*

세금은 **소득**에 따라 구간이 일정하게 나뉩니다.
Tax is banded according to **income**.

1343- 수도/sudo [n.] *the capital of a country*

한국의 **수도**는 서울입니다.
The **capital** of South Korea is Seoul.

1344- 역/yeok [n.] *station, stop*

기차가 **역**에 있습니다.

A train is in the **station**.

1345- 인식하다/insikhada [v.] *to recognize, understand, appreciate*

정부는 이것이 문제라는 것을 이제서야 **인식하기** 시작했습니다.
Governments are now starting to **recognize** that this is an issue.

1346- 침대/chimdae [n.] *bed (furniture)*

이 방에는 **침대** 하나와 테이블 하나, 그리고 의자 두 개가 있다.
There are a **bed**, a table, and two chairs in this room.

1347- 권/gwon [counter] *volume, book, copy*

당신은 책 다섯 **권** 모두 다 읽었나요?
Did you finish reading all of the five **books**?

1348- 수요/suyo [n.] *(economics) demand*

공급이 **수요**를 충족할 수 없습니다.
The supply cannot meet the **demand**.

1349- 스타/seuta [n.] *star (person)*

그 유명한 영화 **스타**는 자기 자서전을 썼습니다.
The famous film **star** wrote her autobiography.

1350- 시계/sigye [n.] *clock, watch*

이 **시계**는 하루에 이십 분 늦어집니다.
This **watch** loses twenty minutes a day.

1351- 입술/ipsul [n.] *lips*

추워서 그의 **입술**이 자줏빛으로 바뀌었습니다.
His **lips** turned purple with the cold.

1352- 잎/ip [n.] *leaf, foliage*

나뭇가지에 **잎**이 많이 달려 있습니다.
The branches are full of **leaves**.

1353- 중간/junggan [n.] *the middle, medium, center*

그것은 당신의 왼쪽 블록 **중간**에 있습니다.
It is in the **middle** of the block on your left.

1354- 지도자/jidoja [n.] *leader*

능력 있는 **지도자**들을 선택하는 것은 가장 중요한 일입니다.
The selection of able **leaders** is the most important thing.

1355- 천천히/cheoncheonhi [adv.] *slowly*

교통 사정이 안 좋지만, 저는 **천천히** 앞으로 움직이는 중입니다.
The traffic is bad, but I am moving ahead **slowly**.

1356- 구성하다/guseonghada [v.] *to constitute, configure, construct a plot*

귀하는 개인 정보 옵션을 **구성했습니다**.
You **have configured** your privacy options.

1357- 대체로/daechero [adv.] *on the whole, generally, mostly, overall*

이 지역의 기후는 **대체로** 따뜻합니다.
The climate in this area is **generally** warm.

1358- 때리다/ttaerida [v.] *to hit, beat, strike*

나는 너무 많이 화가 나서 그의 얼굴을 **때렸다**.
I was so mad that I **hit** him in the face.

1359- 몹시/mopsi [adv.] *exceedingly, to the greatest*

possible extent, very, really, extremely, badly

저는 새 차를 **몹시** 갖고 싶습니다.
I **badly** want a new car.

1360- 문득/mundeuk [adv.] *suddenly, all of a sudden*

문득 지난 날들이 생각납니다.
Suddenly I am reminded of the old days.

1361- 스포츠/seupocheu [n.] *sports*

야구는 아주 흥미가 있는 **스포츠**입니다.
Baseball is a very interesting **sport**.

1362- 위원장/wiwonjang [n.] *the chairman or chairwoman of a committee*

그가 위원회 **위원장**으로 선출되었습니다.
He was elected as **chairman** of the committee.

1363- 저기/jeogi [pron.] *over there, that place, there*

몇 시인지 **저기** 저 사람한테 물어 보세요.
Ask that person **over there** what time it is.

1364- 특별하다/teukbyeolhada [a.] *to be special, be exceptional*

손으로 쓴 편지는 더욱 **특별합니다**.
The handwritten letters **are** more **special**.

1365- 가까이/gakkai [adv.] *closely, close together, nearby, near*

저는 작년에 해안 **가까이** 살았어요.
I lived **near** the shore last year.

1366- 낫다/**natda** [a.] *to be better*

저는 어제보다 훨씬 기분이 **나아요**.

I am feeling much **better** than yesterday.

1367- 넘어서다/**neomeoseoda** [v.] *to cross over, pass through, outrun, exceed*

수요가 공급을 **넘어설** 때 가격이 오릅니다.

Prices rise when demand **exceeds** supply.

1368- 볶다/**bokda** [v.] *to parch (food), annoy (someone), fry, roast, stir-fry*

기름을 조금 넣고 고기를 **볶으세요**.

Stir-fry the meat in a small amount of oil.

1369- 생산하다/**saengsanhada** [v.] *to produce*

저희는 부품들을 조립해서 완제품을 **생산합니다**.

We assemble the parts and **produce** the complete products.

1370- 언젠가/**eonjenga** [adv.] *at some time, at any time, sometime, some time ago*

저는 **언젠가** 그 거리에 방문해 보고 싶어요.

I hope to visit that street **sometime**.

1371- 예술가/**yesulga** [n.] *artist*

어떤 돈 많은 여성이 한 젊은 **예술가**의 후원자였습니다.

A rich woman was a benefactor to a young **artist**.

1372- 의도/**uido** [n.] *intention, intent, plan*

당신의 **의도**를 저에게 숨기지 마세요.

Do not conceal your **intentions** from me.

1373- 저지르다/**jeojireuda** [v.] *to commit*

그는 범죄를 **저질렀습니다**.

He **committed** a crime.

1374- 줄어들다/**jureodeulda** [v.] *to diminish, decrease, lessen, shrink, dwindle*

일부 보고서에 따르면, 그 도시를 찾는 관광객들의 수가 해마다 **줄어들고** 있다고 합니다.

According to some reports, the number of tourists visiting the city annually has been **decreasing**.

1375- 가만히/**gamanhi** [adv.] *still, not moving, quietly, just as it is, motionlessly*

그는 고통을 **가만히** 참습니다.

He holds **still** for his pain.

1376- 교회/**gyohoe** [n.] *church*

이 건물은 모양이 마치 **교회**처럼 생겼습니다.

This building looks something like a **church**.

1377- 대개/**daegae** [adv.] *for the most part, largely, generally, usually, mostly*

커피, 차, 탄산 음료에는 **대개** 카페인이 들어 있습니다.

Coffee, tea and soft drinks **usually** contain caffeine.

1378- 한때/**hanttae** [adv.] *at one time, once, for a time, temporarily, for a while*

나의 가장 친한 친구는 **한때** 나의 적이었다.

My best friend was **once** my enemy.

1379- 화/**hwa** [n.] *fire, anger, rage, wrath*

나는 그녀의 **화**를 가라앉혀 보려고 했다.

I tried to soothe her **anger.**

1380- 흙/heuk [n.] *earth, soil, dirt, ground*

씨를 살짝 **흙**으로 덮어 주세요.
Cover the seeds with a thin layer of **soil.**

1381- 가난하다/gananhada [a.] *to be poor*

그는 그토록 일을 하는 데도 **가난합니다**.
He **is poor** in spite of all his labors.

1382- 고객/gogaek [n.] *customer, guest, patron, client*

이 가게는 **고객**을 위해 배달 서비스를 제공합니다.
This shop offers delivery service for **customers.**

1383- 과학자/gwahakja [n.] *scientist*

과학자들은 자료를 수집한 다음에 그 의미에 대해 연구를 합니다.
Scientists gather data, then study it for its meaning.

1384- 관광/gwan-gwang [n.] *tourism, sightseeing*

관광은 그 나라 경제의 주요 부분입니다.
Tourism is a key sector in the country's economy.

1385- 수술/susul [n.] *surgery, operation*

이 **수술**을 받기 열두 시간 전부터는 아무 것도 드시지 마십시오.
You must fast for twelve hours before this **surgery.**

1386- 식품/sikpum [n.] *groceries, food*

그녀는 집으로 가는 길에 **식품**을 조금 구입했습니다.
She bought some **food** on her way home.

1387- 연기/yeongi [n.] *smoke*

방 안이 **연기**로 가득 차 있습니다.
The room is clouded with **smoke**.

1388- 일월/irwol [n.] *January*

저는 작년 **일월**부터 여기에서 일하고 있어요.
I have been working here since last **January**.

1389- 첫째/cheotjjae [num.] *first (ordinal number), the oldest*

첫째 열은 항상 표시되어야 합니다.
The **first** column must always remain visible.

1390- 회원/hoewon [n.] *member*

이 클럽은 백 명의 **회원들**로 구성되어 있습니다.
This club is composed of one hundred **members**.

1391- 도서관/doseogwan [n.] *library*

저희는 **도서관** 대출 서비스를 얼마 동안 이용할 수 있나요?
How long can we use the lending service of the **library**?

1392- 들려오다/deullyeoooda [v.] *to be bruited about, have come to hearing, reach one's ears*

그것이 우연히 저에게 **들려왔습니다**.
It **came to** my **ears** by chance.

1393- 조금씩/jogeumssik [adv.] *incrementally, bit by bit, gradually, little by little*

개미는 그 과자를 **조금씩** 갉아 먹었습니다.
The ants ate up the cookie **bit by bit**.

1394- 조미료/jomiryo [n.] *seasoning, condiment*

겨자는 **조미료**로 쓰입니다.

Mustard is used as a **seasoning**.

1395- 풀리다/pullida [v.] *to be untied*

매듭이 **풀렸습니다**.

The knot **was untied**.

1396- 강력하다/gangnyeokhada [a.] *to be strong, be powerful, have great potential*

달이 근지점에 있을 때 조수는 더욱 **강력합니다**.

When the moon is at perigee, the tides are even **stronger**.

1397- 들여다보다/deuryeodaboda [v.] *to look into, look in on, peep*

그녀는 거울을 **들여다보고** 있습니다.

She is **looking in** the mirror.

1398- 마늘/maneul [n.] *garlic*

올리브 오일, 식초, **마늘**, 소금, 후추를 그릇에 넣고 섞으세요.

Combine the oil, vinegar, **garlic**, salt and pepper in a bowl.

1399- 선물/seonmul [n.] *gift, present*

그의 결혼 **선물**로 뭐가 좋을까요?

What would be a good wedding **present** for him?

1400- 습관/seupgwan [n.] *habit*

아침에 늦잠을 자는 것은 저의 나쁜 **습관들** 중 하나였습니다.

Sleeping late in the morning was one of my bad **habits**.

1401- 위험/wiheom [n.] *danger, risk, hazard*

그 거리에서는 아이들이 **위험**에 노출되어 있습니다.

Children are exposed to the **danger** on the street.

1402- 지하/jiha [n.] *below ground, basement*

그것은 **지하** 삼 층에 위치해 있습니다.

It is located three stories **below ground**.

1403- 활용하다/hwaryonghada [v.] *to apply, make use of, exploit, utilize*

그 기업은 가장 현대적인 기술을 **활용합니다**.

The company **makes use of** the most modern technologies.

1404- 가꾸다/gakkuda [v.] *to cultivate, decorate, raise, cultivate, grow*

정원에서 토마토를 **가꾸는** 건 어떤가요?

How about **growing** a tomato plant in the garden?

1405- 고민/gomin [n.] *agony, anguish, worry, trouble*

그녀는 **고민**이 있을 때마다 자신의 엄마에게 전화를 합니다.

Whenever she is in **trouble**, she calls her mother.

1406- 떠올리다/tteoollida [v.] *to make someone think of something, bring to mind, cause to appear, recall, recollect*

그녀의 말 때문에 저는 이전의 제 실수를 **떠올렸습니다**.

Because of her saying, I **brought** my former mistake **to mind**.

1407- 법률/beomnyul [n.] *law, act of parliament, legislation*

헌법은 다른 모든 **법률**보다 우선입니다.

The constitution takes precedence over all other **laws**.

1408- 상처/sangcheo [n.] *injury, scar, wound*

아직도 그녀의 얼굴에 **상처**가 남아 있습니다.

There are still **scars** remaining on her face.

1409- 좁다/jopda [a.] *to be narrow, be small*

이 문은 높이에 비해 **좁습니다**.

This door **is narrow** in proportion to its height.

1410- 지하철/jihacheol [n.] *subway*

저는 버스에서 **지하철**로 환승할 거예요.

I am going to transfer from the bus to the **subway**.

1411- 집다/jipda [v.] *to pick up, pinpoint*

연필 좀 **집어** 줄래요?

Would you **pick up** the pencil for me, please?

1412- 화면/hwamyeon [n.] *screen, monitor*

그들은 컴퓨터 **화면**을 보고 있습니다.

They are looking at a computer **screen**.

1413- 생겨나다/saenggyeonada [v.] *to emerge, be generated, occur*

낮과 밤은 지구가 축을 따라 자전하면서 **생겨납니다**.

Days and nights **occur** as the Earth rotates on its axis.

1414- 주부/jubu [n.] *housewife*

그녀는 전업 **주부**로 지내는 게 만족스럽다고 말합니다.

She says she is happy being a full-time **housewife**.

1415- 진리/jilli [n.] *truth*

그는 계속해서 **진리**를 찾아 헤맸습니다.

He kept on searching after the **truth**.

1416- 태양/taeyang [n.] *the Sun*

태양의 지름은 지구 지름의 109 배입니다.

The diameter of **the Sun** is 109 times the Earth's diameter.

1417- 틀림없다/teullimeopda [a.] *to be precisely correct, be obvious, be certain, be sure*

이 상태대로라면 콘서트의 성공은 **틀림없습니다**.
At this rate, the concert **is sure** to be a success.

1418- 프로/peuro [n.] *(TV) program, (TV) show*

저는 지난 주말에 아주 재미있는 **프로**를 봤어요.
I watched a very interesting **show** last weekend.

1419- 피다/pida [v.] *to bloom*

봄에는 꽃이 **펴요**.
In Spring, flowers **bloom**.

1420- 공급/gonggeup [n.] *supply, provision*

석유 **공급**이 줄었습니다.
The **supply** of oil has diminished.

1421- 도로/doro [n.] *road, thoroughfare*

도로 공사는 언제 시작되나요?
When will the **road** works begin?

1422- 동료/dongnyo [n.] *associate, colleague, coworker, comrade*

동료들의 도움이 없이는 당신은 성공할 수 없을 것입니다.
Without the support of **coworkers**, you will not succeed.

1423- 지다/jida [v.] *to carry on one's back, bear, undertake, be defeated, lose, be beaten*

저희 팀은 게임에서 **졌습니다**.
Our team **lost** the game.

1424- 채우다/chaeuda [v.] *to fill, fulfill, satisfy, cause to be filled, pack, stuff*

그는 차에 휘발유를 가득 **채웠습니다**.
He **filled** a car up with petrol.

1425- 균형/gyunhyeong [n.] *equilibrium, balance*

스트레스로 인해 몸의 **균형** 상태가 깨질 수 있습니다.
The body's state of **equilibrium** can be disturbed by stress.

1426- 부족/bujok [n.] *insufficiency, inadequacy, shortage, lack, deficiency, tribe*

사업 실패의 원인은 자본의 **부족**입니다.
The leading cause of business failure is a **lack** of capital.

1427- 사무실/samusil [n.] *office*

사무실은 육 층에 있습니다.
The **office** is on the sixth floor.

1428- 이월/iwol [n.] *February*

음력 설날은 일월 말이나 **이월** 초 정도가 됩니다.
The Lunar New Year falls on late January or early **February**.

1429- 일요일/iryoil [n.] *Sunday*

그는 **일요일**에는 항상 집에 있습니다.
He is always at home on **Sundays**.

1430- 지켜보다/jikyeoboda [v.] *to watch, keep an eye on, observe, look after*

그 부모들은 자신들의 아이들을 **지켜보고** 있습니다.
The parents are **watching** their children.

1431- 개성/gaeseong [n.] *individuality, distinction, personality*

그녀는 **개성**이 매우 강합니다.

She has a very strong **personality**.

1432- 더하다/deohada [v.] *to add, increase*

제가 몇 마디 말을 **더하겠습니다**.

Let me **add** a few words.

1433- 무너지다/muneojida [v.] *to collapse, crumble, decay*

산사태로 집 세 채가 **무너지고** 매몰되었습니다.

Three houses **collapsed** and were buried under a landslide.

1434- 일어서다/ireoseoda [v.] *to stand up, take place, arise*

그 여자는 군중 너머를 보려고 **일어섰습니다**.

She **stood up** in order to see over the crowd.

1435- 죄/joe [n.] *sin, fault, wrongdoing, criminal offense, misdeed, crime*

그 남자는 자신의 **죄**를 인정했습니다.

The man admitted to his **crime**.

1436- 총장/chongjang [n.] *president of a university, the head of any large organization*

이 대학교의 초대 **총장**은 김 박사님이셨습니다.

Dr. Kim was the first **president** of this university.

1437- 핵심/haeksim [n.] *something which is central or of key importance, core, the point, the heart*

그것이 바로 문제의 **핵심**입니다.

That is the very **core** of a matter.

1438- 후반/huban [n.] *the latter or second half*

그런 다음에 그들은 **후반**에 한 골을 허용했습니다.

Then they allowed one goal in **the second half**.

1439- 단순히/dansunhi [adv.] *simply, straightforwardly, just*

저는 **단순히** 그것을 아름다움을 위해 사용했습니다.

I **simply** used it for its beauty.

1440- 달려가다/dallyeogada [v.] *to go in a hurry, rush, go running, dash, run*

그 길을 따라 **달려가다** 보면, 그녀를 만날 것입니다.

If you **run** along the street, you will meet her.

1441- 방문/bangmun [n.] *visit, visiting*

저희는 여러분의 **방문**을 기대합니다.

We look forward to your **visit**.

1442- 불만/bulman [n.] *dissatisfaction, discontent, complaint*

고객들의 **불만**이 가장 많았던 것은 어느 해인가요?

In which year did the number of customer **complaints** peak?

1443- 불편하다/bulpyeonhada [a.] *to be inconvenient, be uncomfortable*

좌석이 매우 **불편합니다**.

The seats are very **uncomfortable**.

1444- 실제/silje [adv.] *practically, in fact, actually*

그들은 저희가 **실제** 이렇게 한 것에 대해 놀랐습니다.

They were amazed that we **actually** did this.

1445- 종/jong [n.] *kind or type, species, bell, slave*

많은 특징들이 이 **종**을 다른 것들과 구별해 줍니다.

A number of features discriminate this **species** from others.

1446- 피/pi [n.] *blood*

피는 골수에서 만들어진다.

Blood is produced in the bone marrow.

1447- 강/gang [n.] *river*

이 길로 가면 **강**에 이른다.

This road leads to the **river**.

1448- 관객/gwangaek [n.] *member(s) of an audience, audience*

그 영화는 새해 첫 주말에 가장 많은 **관객**을 끌었습니다.

The movie drew the largest **audiences** over the New Years' weekend.

1449- 동작/dongjak [n.] *movement (of the body), action, motion, gesture*

이런 **동작**은 팔과 어깨에 운동이 됩니다.

These **movements** will exercise your arms and shoulders.

1450- 뜻하다/tteuthada [v.] *to mean, signify, mean to do, intend, imply*

그의 침묵은 그 정책에 반대함을 **뜻한다고** 해석되었습니다.

His silence was understood to **mean** that he was opposed to the policy.

1451- 막/mak [adv.] *just, just now, at last, blindly, carelessly, wildly*

그들은 한 시간 전에 **막** 끝냈어요.

They **just** finished an hour ago.

1452- 밀리미터/**millimiteo** [n.] *millimeter*

혈압은 수은 **밀리미터**로 측정됩니다.
Blood pressure is measured in **millimeters** of mercury.

1453- 비싸다/**bissada** [a.] *to be expensive, be costly, be pricey*

다이아몬드 반지는 매우 **비쌉니다**.
This diamond ring is very **expensive**.

1454- 숫자/**sutja** [n.] *numeral, numbers, quantity, figure*

큰 **숫자**에서 작은 **숫자**를 빼세요.
Subtract the smaller **number** from the larger **number**.

1455- 열/**yeol** [n.] *ten, fever, heat*

저는 **열**을 내릴 만한 약이 필요합니다.
I need something to bring down the **fever**.

1456- 왼쪽/**oenjjok** [n.] *left side, left*

그것은 **왼쪽**의 두 번째 건물입니다.
It is the second building on the **left**.

1457- 중세/**jungse** [n.] *Middle Ages, the medieval era, medieval times*

중세 시대는 약 천 년 동안 지속되었습니다.
The **Middle Ages** lasted for about one thousand years.

1458- 택시/**taeksi** [n.] *taxi, cab*

택시를 불러 주세요.
Please, call a **taxi** for me.

1459- 계산/**gyesan** [n.] *calculation, reckoning, pay*

제가 잘못 **계산**했나요?
Did I make any errors in my **calculation**?

1460- 꼬리/kkori [n.] *tail*

그 강아지는 **꼬리**를 앞뒤로 흔들었습니다.
The dog wagged its **tail** back and forth.

1461- 놀랍다/nollapda [a.] *to be surprising, be amazing, be astonishing, be astounding*

그의 예술 작품은 **놀랍습니다**.
His art work **is amazing**.

1462- 양식/yangsik [n.] *form, mode, style, pattern, format, style*

이 보고서를 그 **양식**과 일치시켜 주세요.
Please confirm this report to the **form**.

1463- 예전/yejeon [n.] *the old days, the old times, the past, long ago*

저희 현재 환경은 **예전**보다 훨씬 나쁩니다.
Our circumstances now are far worse than in **the past**.

1464- 전기/jeongi [n.] *electricity, power*

이번 달 **전기** 요금은 정말 많이 나왔어요.
The **electricity** bill is really high this month.

1465- 주식/jusik [n.] *stock, share, staple food*

주식을 얼마나 파실 생각이죠?
How many **shares** do you intend to sell?

1466- 틀리다/teullida [v.] *to be wrong, be incorrect, be mistaken*

그의 생각은 재미있지만 논리적으로는 **틀립니다**.
His thought is funny, but it **is** logically **wrong**.

1467- 끊임없이/kkeunimeopsi [adv.] *continuously, ceaselessly*

이 텔레비전 프로그램은 나를 **끊임없이** 웃게 만든다.
This television program makes me laugh **continuously**.

1468- 모델/model [n.] *model*

그녀는 젊은 사람들의 롤 **모델**입니다.
She is a role **model** for young people.

1469- 붓다/butda [v.] *to pour, swell up, puff up*

그녀는 유리잔에 액체를 **붓고** 있습니다.
She is **pouring** liquid into a glass.

1470- 상식/sangsik [n.] *common knowledge, common sense*

당신의 행동은 **상식**과 일치하지 않습니다.
Your actions are not in accordance with **common sense**.

1471- 상표/sangpyo [n.] *trademark, brand*

그 회사만이 그 **상표**를 사용할 수 있습니다.
Only that company can use the **trademark**.

1472- 시원하다/siwonhada [a.] *to be cool, be refreshing*

그늘은 매우 **시원합니다**.
It **is** quite **cool** in the shade.

1473- 아니하다/anihada [a.] *to not be the case, to not be*

당신은 행복하지 **아니한가요**?
Are you **not** happy?

1474- 의식하다/uisikhada [v.] *to be aware, be conscious,*

be mindful

저는 무엇인가가 빠졌다는 것을 **의식하고 있었습니다**.

I **was conscious** that something was missing.

1475- 궁금하다/gunggeumhada [a.] *to be curious, be ravenous, wonder*

그들에게 무슨 일이 일어났는지 **궁금합니다**.

I **wonder** what happened to them.

1476- 둘러싸다/dulleossada [v.] *to surround, encircle, enclose, besiege*

그의 집을 경찰이 **둘러쌌습니다**.

His house was **besieged** by the police.

1477- 딱/ttak [a.] *exactly, perfectly, precisely, just, suddenly, only*

가사가 현실에 **딱** 들어맞습니다.

The words **exactly** fit the reality.

1478- 민주화/minjuhwa [n.] *democratization*

저희는 이제 **민주화**를 위해서 싸울 것입니다.

We will now fight for **democratization**.

1479- 보도/bodo [n.] *sidewalk, pavement*

사람들이 **보도**를 걸어가고 있습니다.

The people are walking down the **sidewalk**.

1480- 살피다/salpida [v.] *to look closely, observe, look*

길을 건너기 전에 양쪽 길을 주의 깊게 **살피도록 하세요**.

Look both ways carefully before crossing the street.

1481- 않다/anta [v.] _not to do something_

그는 학교에서 공부를 하지 **않습니다**.
He **does not** study at the school.

1482- 약하다/yakhada [a.] _to be weak_

저 다리는 무거운 차량들이 다니기에는 너무 **약합니다**.
That bridge **is** too **weak** for heavy traffic.

1483- 잘못하다/jalmothada [v.] _to err, make a mistake, do something incorrectly, make an error_

그는 계산을 **잘못했어요**.
He **made an error** in calculation.

1484- 잡지/japji [n.] _magazine, journal, periodical_

새 **잡지**가 다음 주에 발행됩니다.
A new **magazine** will be out next week.

1485- 거부하다/geobuhada [v.] _to refuse, veto, reject_

그는 그 명령에 따르기를 **거부했습니다**.
He **refused** to obey the order.

1486- 공무원/gongmuwon [n.] _public official, civil servant, public servant, official_

감시 **공무원들**이 그것들을 확인할 것입니다.
Conservation **officers** will be checking them.

1487- 그만두다/geumanduda [v.] _to quit, stop, cease, resign, give up_

저희 언니는 2년 전에 피아노 치는 것을 **그만두었습니다**.
My sister **stopped** playing the piano two years ago.

1488- 반갑다/bangapda [a.] *to be glad, be happy, be pleasant, be welcome*

이렇게 오랜만에 다시 만나게 되어서 정말 **반가워요**.
I **am** really **glad** to see you again after all these years.

1489- 운명/unmyeong [n.] *destiny, fate, fortune*

그는 실패를 **운명** 탓으로 돌립니다.
He ascribes his failure to **fate**.

1490- 재정/jaejeong [n.] *finance, financial condition, financial affairs*

지금 당장은 그 회사의 **재정** 상태가 좋지 않습니다.
The company is low on **finances** right now.

1491- 차라리/charari [a.] *preferably, rather*

저는 친구를 잃느니 **차라리** 돈을 잃겠어요.
I would **rather** lose money than a friend.

1492- 학자/hakja [n.] *scholar*

이 문제는 **학자들** 간에 장기간 토론의 주제가 될 것입니다.
This issue is one that **scholars** will debate for a long time.

1493- 다녀오다/danyeooda [v.] *to return, come back, be back, go and come back, go and get back*

금방 **다녀올게요**.
I will **be back** very soon.

1494- 대규모/daegyumo [n.] *largeness in scale, large-scale,*

대규모 환경을 관리하는 것은 어려울 수 있습니다.
Managing **large-scale** environments can be difficult.

1495- 민간/**mingan** [n.] *private, non-governmental*

그들은 **민간** 하청업체에서 관리합니다.

They are managed by a **private** contractor.

1496- 법원/**beobwon** [n.] *court*

법원의 판결은 모든 사람들에게 충격이었습니다.

The **court**'s decision was a shock to everybody.

1497- 비디오/**bidio** [n.] *video*

요즘 아이들은 **비디오** 게임에 중독되어 있어요.

Nowadays children are addicted to **video** games.

1498- 사실상/**sasilsang** [adv.] *in fact, in reality, actually, as a matter of fact*

그 이론은 **사실상** 기반이 없는 것 같습니다.

The theory seems to have no basis **in fact**.

1499- 아끼다/**akkida** [v.] *to cherish, save, conserve, economize*

돈을 **아끼기** 위해 할 수 있는 간단한 것들이 있습니다.

There are simple things you can do to **save** money.

1500- 이쪽/**ijjok** [pron.] *this side, our side, this way*

제 차의 **이쪽**을 보세요.

Look at **this side** of my car.

1501- 지대/**jidae** [n.] *region, area, zone, belt*

이 식물은 고산 **지대**에서 자랍니다.

This plant grows in alpine **regions**.

1502- 판단하다/**pandanhada** [v.] *to adjudge, determine,*

judge

사람을 겉모습을 보고 **판단해서는** 안 됩니다.
You should not **judge** people by the way they look.

1503- 행복하다/haengbokhada [a.] *to be happy*

저희 가족은 항상 **행복합니다**.
Our family **is** always **happy**.

1504- 굽다/gupda [v.] *to bake, broil, roast, grill, toast*

저희는 생선을 불에 **구웠습니다**.
We **broiled** the fish over a fire.

1505- 기름/gireum [n.] *oil, fat, grease, gas*

기름과 물은 섞이지 않습니다.
Oil and water do not blend.

1506- 실천하다/silcheonhada [v.] *to implement, carry out, practice*

저희는 배운 것을 **실천해야** 합니다.
We should **practice** what we learned.

1507- 쏟아지다/ssodajida [v.] *to splash out, be spilled, be poured, pour*

모래가 자루에서 **쏟아져** 나오고 있습니다.
Sand is **pouring** from the bags.

1508- 연습/yeonseup [n.] *practice, exercise, drill, training*

어학 습득의 방법은 다만 **연습**에 있을 뿐입니다.
Practice is the only way of mastering a language.

1509- 오른쪽/**oreunjjok** [n.] *right-hand, the right side*

오른쪽으로 약간 움직여 주세요.
Please, move a little to **the right**.

1510- 용어/**yongeo** [n.] *technical term or phrase, terminology, word, term, language*

그 의사는 제가 모르는 전문적인 **용어**를 많이 사용했습니다.
The doctor used a lot of technical **terms** I do not know.

1511- 익히다/**ikhida** [v.] *to become habituated, ripen, cook, master, become proficient, familiarize oneself*

그녀는 사전의 도움을 받아 외국어를 **익혔습니다**.
She **mastered** a foreign language by the aid of a dictionary.

1512- 지도/**jido** [n.] *map, guidance, leadership, instruction, coaching*

어느 길로 가야 하는지 이 **지도**를 보고 가르쳐 주세요.
Please show me on this **map** which road I should follow.

1513- 지위/**jiwi** [n.] *position, status, rank, level, standing*

그는 사회적 **지위**에 크게 관심을 두고 있지 않습니다.
He does not care much about social **standing**.

1514- 풍부하다/**pungbuhada** [a.] *to be rich, be plentiful, be abundant, be ample*

그 나라에는 천연 자원이 **풍부합니다**.
The country **is rich** in natural resources.

1515- 화장실/**hwajangsil** [n.] *bathroom, restroom, toilet, washroom*

여자 **화장실** 열쇠 좀 주세요.
I need the key to the women's **restroom**, please.

1516- 기억하다/gieokhada [v.] *to remember*

그곳에 몇 사람이나 올 거라고 그녀가 말했는지 당신은 **기억하나요**?
Do you **remember** how many people she said would be there?

1517- 식량/singnyang [n.] *food, provisions*

그녀는 그들에게 많은 **식량**을 공급할 수 있습니다.
She can provide them with a lot of **food**.

1518- 실험/silheom [n.] *experiment, implementation, test*

우리는 이 **실험**에 쓸 한 컵의 물이 필요합니다.
We need a cup of water for this **experiment**.

1519- 용기/yonggi [n.] *fearlessness, courage, bravery, container*

용기는 그가 그 게임에서 이길 수 있도록 도움을 주었습니다.
Courage helped him to win the game.

1520- 토론/toron [n.] *debate, controversy, discussion*

토론 끝에 다툼이 시작되었습니다.
A quarrel started at the end of the **discussion**.

1521- 고급/gogeup [n.] *seniority, high rank, top-notch, luxury, deluxe*

고급 택시는 다른 택시보다 훨씬 더 좋은 서비스를 제공합니다.
Deluxe taxis offer much better service than other taxis.

1522- 고생/gosaeng [n.] *suffering, hardship, trouble, hard work*

당신은 마침내 **고생**에 대한 대가를 받은 것 같네요.
It sounds like your **hard work** is finally paying off.

1523- 밟다/bapda [v.] *to step, tread, trample*

그녀는 실수로 고양이 꼬리 끝을 **밟았습니다**.
She **stepped** on the end of a cat's tail by mistake.

1524- 상당하다/sangdanghada [a.] *to be remarkable, be considerable*

그는 법률에 대한 지식이 **상당합니다**.
He has **considerable** acquaintance with the law.

1525- 섞다/seokda [v.] *to mix, blend*

서로 다른 종류의 술을 **섞는** 것은 좋지 않습니다.
It is not good to **mix** different kinds of liquor.

1526- 수석/suseok [n.] *premiere, head, top*

그녀는 법 과목 수업에서 **수석**을 했습니다.
She was at the **top** of her law class.

1527- 없애다/eopsaeda [v.] *to eliminate, kill, get rid of, remove, erase*

그녀는 얼룩을 **없애려고** 했습니다.
She tried to **remove** the stains.

1528- 이뤄지다/irwojida [v.] *to be attained, be fulfilled, be made up of, be formed*

그것은 서로 결합된 작은 분자들의 조합으로 **이뤄진** 거대한
분자이다.
It is a giant molecule **formed** from an arrangement of smaller connected molecules.

1529- 적절하다/jeokjeolhada [a.] *to be suited, be appropriate, be proper*

그 옷들이 학교에 입고 가기에 **적절합니다**.
Those clothes **are appropriate** for school wear.

1530- 정상/jeongsang [n.] *peak, apex, top, summit*

산 **정상**으로 가는 길은 쉽지 않습니다.
The ways to the **top** of the mountain are not easy.

1531- 주말/jumal [n.] *weekend*

이번 **주말**에 뭐할 거예요?
What are you doing this **weekend**?

1532- 지혜/jihye [n.] *wisdom*

책은 **지혜**의 원천입니다.
Books are the spring of **wisdom**.

1533- 참새/chamsae [n.] *sparrow*

집 밖에서는 **참새**와 귀뚜라미들이 울고 있었습니다.
The **sparrow** and crickets were chirping outside the house.

1534- 화장품/hwajangpum [n.] *cosmetics, makeup*

그녀는 고가의 수입 **화장품**만 씁니다.
She only uses high-priced, imported **cosmetics**.

1535- 굵다/gukda [a.] *to be thick, be bold, be big*

그 담쟁이덩굴의 줄기가 **굵습니다**.
The ivy stem **is thick**.

1536- 깨끗이/kkaekkeusi [adv.] *clean, in a clean fashion*

당신은 매일 아침 이를 **깨끗이** 닦아야 합니다.
You need to brush your teeth **clean** every morning.

1537- 낡다/nakda [a.] *to be old, be worn out*

그의 옷은 구식인데다가 **낡았어요**.
Those clothes **are** old-fashioned and **worn**.

1538- 내년/naenyeon [n.] *next year*

그 계약은 **내년**에 만료되는 것으로 설정되어 있습니다.

That contract is set to expire **next year**.

1539- 농산물/nongsanmul [n.] *agricultural product, farm produce*

올해 **농산물**의 양이 증가했습니다.

The number of **agricultural products** has increased this year.

1540- 대학생/daehaksaeng [n.] *college student, undergraduate*

저의 형은 **대학생**입니다.

My older brother is a **college student**.

1541- 방문하다/bangmunhada [v.] *to visit*

휴가 기간 동안 그들은 박물관을 **방문했습니다**.

During the vacation, they **visited** a museum.

1542- 붉다/bukda [a.] *to be red*

이 차는 장미처럼 **붉어요**.

This car is as **red** as a rose.

1543- 순서/sunseo [n.] *order, sequence, turn, procedure*

그것들은 알파벳 **순서**로 나열되어 있습니다.

They are listed in alphabetical **order**.

1544- 연구소/yeonguso [n.] *research institute, laboratory*

이 **연구소**는 첨단 장비를 갖추고 있습니다.

This **research institute** has state-of-theart equipment.

1545- 위대하다/widaehada [a.] *to be great, be remarkable*

그녀는 언젠가 **위대한** 음악가가 될 것입니다.

She will be a **great** musician some day.

1546- 이사/isa [n.] *moving (from one residence to another), director of a company, trustee of a corporation*

저희 **이사**님이 오전 열한 시에 위원회를 소집했어요.
Our **director** convened the committee members at eleven in the morning.

1547- 지배하다/jibaehada [v.] *to rule, control, govern, dominate*

소수의 기업들이 세계 경제를 **지배하고 있습니다**.
A small number of companies **control** the world economy.

1548- 틈/teum [n.] *crack, gap, spare time*

그 **틈**으로 기름이 흘러나오고 있었습니다.
Oil was flowing out through the **crack**.

1549- 거대하다/geodaehada [a.] *to be huge, be massive, be gigantic, be enormous*

그 잠재적 이윤은 **거대합니다**.
The potential benefits **are huge**.

1550- 닫다/datda [v.] *to close, shut*

들어올 때 문을 **닫아** 주세요.
Please, **close** the door when you come in.

1551- 드물다/deumulda [a.] *to be rare, be unusual, be uncommon, be exceptional*

저것은 요즘 보기에 **드문** 광경입니다.
That is a **rare** sight these days.

1552- 들르다/deulleuda [v.] *to stop by, come by*

떠나기 전에 **들러 주세요**.
Please **stop by** before you leave.

1553- 매달리다/**maedallida** [v.] *to be hung from, dangle, cleave to, hang on to, be suspended*

그 바구니가 울타리에 **매달려** 있습니다.
The basket **hangs** from the fence.

1554- 생일/**saengil** [n.] *birthday*

당신의 **생일**은 언제인가요?
When is your **birthday**?

1555- 섬/**seom** [n.] *island, islet*

비행기는 갑자기 작은 **섬**에 착륙했다.
The airplane suddenly landed on a small **island**.

1556- 이하/**iha** [n.] *the following, hereinafter, below*

올해 벼농사는 평균 **이하로** 예상됩니다.
This year's rice crop is estimated to be **below** the average.

1557- 참석하다/**chamseokhada** [v.] *to attend, be present*

당신은 어제 회의에 **참석했나요**?
Did you **attend** the meeting yesterday?

1558- 토대/**todae** [n.] *foundation, groundwork*

이 집은 굳건한 **토대** 위에 지어져 있습니다.
This house is built on a firm **foundation**

1559- 해결/**haegyeol** [n.] *resolution, settlement, solution, solving*

그 정책은 인구 문제 **해결**에 크게 이바지할 것입니다.
The policy will do much for **solving** the population problem.

1560- 행복/**haengbok** [n.] *happiness, good fortune*

새해에 평안하시고 **행복**하시길 바랍니다.
May peace and **happiness** be yours in the New Year.

1561- 걸어가다/georeogada [v.] *to walk, go on foot*

학생들이 거리를 **걸어가고** 있습니다.

The students are **walking** in the street.

1562- 근로자/geulloja [n.] *laborer, worker*

저희는 그 부서에서 일할 **근로자**를 좀 더 채용해야 합니다.

We need to hire some more **workers** for the department.

1563- 목숨/moksum [n.] *life*

그 어머니는 자신의 **목숨**을 걸고 자신의 아이를 구했습니다.

The mother rescued her child at the hazard of her own **life**.

1564- 백화점/baekhwajeom [n.] *department store*

그녀는 그의 넥타이를 사기 위해 **백화점**을 둘러봤습니다.

She looked around the **department store** to buy his tie.

1565- 변화하다/byeonhwahada [v.] *to change*

비즈니스 환경은 빠르게 **변화하고** 있습니다.

The business environment is **changing** rapidly.

1566- 여론/yeoron [n.] *public opinion*

이 설문 조사는 믿을 만한 **여론**의 척도라고 간주되고 있습니다.

This survey is considered to be a reliable barometer of **public opinion**.

1567- 의복/uibok [n.] *clothing, dress, garment*

가난한 사람들에게 식량과 **의복**이 제공될 예정입니다.

Food and **clothing** will be dispensed to the poor.

1568- 출발하다/chulbalhada [v.] *to depart, start, set off*

급행 열차는 정시에 부산을 **출발했습니다**.

The express train **departed** from Busan on time.

1569- 결정되다/gyeoljeongdoeda [v.] *to be decided, be settled, be fixed*

계획이 최종적으로 **결정되었습니다**.
The plan **was** finally **settled**.

1570- 고양이/goyangi [n.] *cat*

많은 사람들이 **고양이**를 애완동물로 키우는 것을 좋아합니다.
Many people love having **cats** as pets.

1571- 공격/gonggyeok [n.] *attack, assault, offense*

그들의 지속적인 **공격**은 적의 방어를 무너뜨렸습니다.
Their steady **attack** struck down the enemy's guard.

1572- 물가/mulga [n.] *price of a commodity*

물가는 환율에 따라 변동 가능합니다.
Prices are variable according to the rate of exchange.

1573- 민주주의/minjujuui [n.] *democracy*

다수결의 원칙은 **민주주의**의 중심 제도입니다.
Majority rule is the central system of **democracy**.

1574- 중학교/junghakgyo [n.] *middle school, junior high school*

그녀는 **중학교** 때 저의 제일 친한 친구입니다.
She is my best friend from **junior high school**.

1575- 킬로미터/killomiteo [n.] *kilometer*

마일을 **킬로미터**로 바꾸는 것은 쉽지 않습니다.
It is not easy to convert miles into **kilometers**.

1576- 파도/pado [n.] *a wave of water or emotion, a*

powerful societal trend

파도는 대개 바람에 의해 만들어집니다.
Waves are mostly made by the wind.

1577- 흰색/huinsaek [n.] *the color white*

벽은 **흰색**으로 칠해야 합니다.
You need to paint the walls **white**.

1578- 가수/gasu [n.] *a singer, vocalist*

그녀는 **가수**가 되고 싶어 합니다.
She wants to be a **singer**.

1579- 방송국/bangsongguk [n.] *broadcaster, broadcasting station, station*

그 라디오 **방송국**은 오전 다섯 시에 방송을 시작합니다.
The radio **station** signs on at five a.m.

1580- 빛나다/binnada [v.] *to shine, sparkle, twinkle, gleam*

그녀의 얼굴은 행복으로 **빛나고 있습니다**.
Her face **is shining** with happiness.

1581- 숨다/sumda [v.] *to hide, disappear, conceal oneself*

숨지 말고 자신을 보여주세요.
Do not **hide** and show yourself.

1582- 압력/amnyeok [n.] *pressure*

그 댐이 **압력** 때문에 터져 버릴지도 모릅니다.
The dam might burst under the **pressure**.

1583- 예금/yegeum [n.] *deposit, saving*

저의 은행 **예금**은 현재 백만 원에 이릅니다.

My **savings** in the bank now are nearly one million won.

1584- 예상되다/yesangdoeda [v.] *to be predicted, be anticipated, be expected*

공사는 십일 월 말까지 지속될 것으로 **예상됩니다**.
Construction **is expected** to last through the end of November.

1585- 물다/mulda [v.] *to bite, gnaw*

그 강아지를 약 올리면 당신을 **물** 수도 있어요.
The dog could **bite** you if you tease her.

1586- 선진국/seonjinguk [n.] *developed country, advanced countries*

그 나라는 **선진국**으로 분류됩니다.
The country is classified as a **developed country**.

1587- 재판/jaepan [n.] *trial*

검사는 그 남자에게 잘못이 있음을 발견하고 **재판**에 회부했습니다.
The prosecutor found the man guilty and put him on **trial**.

1588- 제자/jeja [n.] *disciple, pupil, student, follower*

그는 그의 가르침을 배우고 싶어하는 **제자들** 중 한 사람이었습니다.
He was one of the **disciples** who wanted to learn his teaching.

1589- 창문/changmun [n.] *window*

도둑이 **창문**을 통해 들어온 것 같습니다.
It seems that the thief came in through the **window**.

1590- 치즈/chijeu [n.] *cheese*

그 지역은 **치즈**의 생산지로 유명합니다.
The region is famous as a source of **cheese**.

1591- 구역/guyeok [n.] *area, zone, precinct*

여기는 견인 **구역**이어서 여기에 당신 차를 두고 가지 않는 것이 좋을 것입니다.

This is a tow away **zone**, so you better not leave your car here.

1592- 반대하다/bandaehada [v.] *to oppose*

저는 아무도 당신의 의견에 **반대하지** 않을 것이라고 생각합니다.

I think nobody will **oppose** your opinion.

1593- 소비/sobi [n.] *consumption, spending*

에너지 **소비**는 매년 증가하고 있습니다.

Energy **consumption** is increasing every year.

1594- 심장/simjang [n.] *heart (an organ)*

제 **심장**이 뛰는 소리가 들리나요?

Can you hear my **heart** beating?

1595- 진실/jinsil [n.] *the truth*

사람들이 무엇이라고 말하든지 상관없이 제가 말하는 것이 **진실**입니다.

No matter what people say, my saying is **the truth**.

1596- 협력/hyeomnyeok [n.] *collaboration, cooperation*

그들은 **협력** 증진을 위해 모임을 가졌습니다.

They had a meeting to promote **cooperation**.

1597- 가스/gaseu [n.] *gas, natural gas, poison gas*

저희는 **가스**를 사용할 때 주의를 기울여야 합니다.

We must be careful when we use **gas**.

1598- 구멍/gumeong [n.] *hole, aperture, opening, pit*

쥐가 판자를 갉아서 **구멍**을 냈습니다.
Rats gnawed a **hole** into a board.

1599- 만화/manhwa [n.] *comics, cartoon*

그녀는 매일 아침 신문에 있는 **만화**를 봅니다.
She reads the **comics** in the newspaper every morning.

1600- 먹이다/meogida [v.] *to feed, cause to eat*

하루에 몇 번씩 고양이에게 먹이를 **먹여야** 하나요?
How many times a day should I **feed** the cat?

1601- 무시하다/musihada [v.] *to ignore, disdain, disregard, neglect*

그는 부모님의 조언을 **무시했습니다**.
He **ignored** his parents' advice.

1602- 우유/uyu [n.] *milk*

그녀는 점심에 **우유** 한 잔을 마셨습니다.
She drank a glass of **milk** at lunch.

1603- 차갑다/chagapda [a.] *(of an object) to be cold (to the touch), be icy, be frosty, be chilly, be freezing, be cold-hearted*

바닥이 얼음처럼 **차갑네요**.
The floor **is** as **cold** as ice.

1604- 태아/taea [n.] *fetus, embryo*

태아는 삼 개월이 지난 시점에 지문이 생기기 시작합니다.
A **fetus** develops fingerprints at the age of three months.

1605- 관찰하다/gwanchalhada [v.] *to observe, view, watch*

그 박사는 그 동물을 삼 년 동안 **관찰했습니다**.

The doctor had **observed** the animal for three years.

1606- 날개/nalgae [n.] *wing*

독수리는 날기 전에 **날개를** 펼쳤습니다.

The eagle expanded its **wings** before flying.

1607- 드디어/deudieo [adv.] *finally, at last*

수 년 동안의 노력 끝에 그녀는 **드디어** 공무원 시험에 합격하였습니다.

After years of effort, she **finally** passed the civil service exam.

1608- 성공하다/seonggonghada [v.] *to succeed, achieve*

사업에서 **성공하려면** 자신감이 있어야 해요.

To **succeed** in business, you must be confident.

1609- 소나무/sonamu [n.] *pine, pine tree*

길에서 조금 떨어진 곳에 큰 **소나무가** 서 있습니다.

There stands a big **pine tree** a little way off the road.

1610- 운영하다/unyeonghada [v.] *to operate, run*

그녀는 자신의 회사를 좀 더 조직적으로 **운영하려고** 더 많은 직원을 고용했습니다.

She hired more employees to **operate** her company more systematically.

1611- 평가하다/pyeonggahada [v.] *to evaluate, assess, estimate*

각 팀은 선수들의 능력을 **평가합니다**.

Every team **evaluates** players' abilities.

1612- 표/pyo [n.] *ticket, vote, ballot, table, diagram, graph, chart*

학생 **표**는 얼마인가요?

How much does the student **ticket** cost?

1613- 감추다/gamchuda [v.] *to conceal, keep secret, hide, cover*

제 남동생은 그 상자를 자기 침대 아래에 **감췄습니다**.

My younger brother **hid** the box under his bed.

1614- 머무르다/meomureuda [v.] *to stay, remain, pause on one's way, stop going*

얼마나 오랫동안 손님들이 호텔에 **머물** 수 있나요?

How long can guests **stay** at the hotel?

1615- 부위/buwi [n.] *region, site, location, position, place, part, spot, area*

그 **부위**를 부드럽게 마사지해 줄 수 있나요?

Would you massage the **area** gently?

1616- 비우다/biuda [v.] *to empty, drain, evacuate, vacate, move out*

통에서 물을 **비우세요**.

Please **empty** out the water from the bucket.

1617- 설치하다/seolchihada [v.] *to install, set up*

저희 집에 전화를 **설치하고** 싶습니다.

I would like to have a telephone **installed** in my house.

1618- 십일월/sibirwol [n.] *November*

그녀의 책은 **십일월**에 출간될 것입니다.

Her book will be published in **November**.

1619- 거울/geoul [n.] *mirror*

당신은 하루에 몇 번 **거울**을 들여다보나요?
How many times per day do you look in the **mirror**?

1620- 몇몇/myeonmyeot [determiner] *some, a few, several*

그 영화는 **몇몇** 극장에서 상영되고 있습니다.
The movie is playing at **several** theaters.

1621- 무기/mugi [n.] *weapon, arms*

그 **무기**는 피고의 집에서 발견되었다.
The **weapon** was found in the defendant's home.

1622- 안전/anjeon [n.] *safety, security*

그는 그녀의 **안전**을 걱정했습니다.
He was anxious for her **safety**.

1623- 양파/yangpa [n.] *onion*

그의 수프에 **양파**를 넣지 마세요.
Please do not put **onions** in his soup.

1624- 틀다/teulda [v.] *to turn, twist, wrench, thwart, turn on a machine that produces sound*

라디오를 **틀어** 주세요.
Please, **turn on** the radio.

1625- 형편/hyeongpyeon [n.] *circumstances, conditions, situation*

그는 지금 경제적으로 어려운 **형편**입니다.
He is in a tight financial **situation** now.

1626- 감다/gamda [v.] *to close one's eyes, wash oneself, bathe, wind around, coil*

눈을 **감아** 주세요.

Please **close** your eyes.

1627- 고추/gochu [n.] *the chili pepper*

그것은 일반 **고추**보다 천 배 더 맵습니다.

It is one thousand times stronger than a normal **chili pepper**.

1628- 규칙/gyuchik [n.] *rule, code, regulation*

당신은 **규칙**을 너무 많이 어겼습니다.

You have broken the **rules** too many times.

1629- 빵/ppang [n.] *bread, zero*

저희 어머니는 저에게 주려고 **빵** 한 조각에 땅콩 버터를 발랐습니다.

My mother put peanut butter on a slice of **bread** for me.

1630- 서서히/seoseohi [adv.] *gradually, slowly, steadily*

아빠가 난방기를 켰고 방이 **서서히** 따뜻해졌습니다.

My dad turned on the heater and the room **slowly** warmed up.

1631- 스승/seuseung [n.] *teacher, master, mentor, instructor*

저희는 매년 오월 십오일에 **스승**의 날을 기념합니다.

We celebrate **Teacher**'s Day on May fifteenth every year.

1632- 실시되다/silsidoeda [v.] *to take effect, go into effect, come into effect or operation, become effective*

그 부서에 대한 임금 인상은 일월 일일부터 **실시됩니다**.

The salary increase for the department **becomes effective** January first.

1633- 아마도/amado [adv.] *maybe, probably, perhaps*

저희는 **아마도** 몇 시간 정도 일찍 떠나야 할 것입니다.
We should **probably** leave a few hours early.

1634- 어제/eoje [n.] *yesterday*

저는 **어제** 몸이 아팠는데 오늘도 조금도 나아지지 않았습니다.
I was ill **yesterday** and do not feel any better today.

1635- 오직/ojik [adv.] *only, solely, alone, exclusively*

선생님은 그 학생들 중에서 **오직** 한 사람만 뽑아야 했습니다.
The teacher had to choose **only** one person among those students.

1636- 위험하다/wiheomhada [a.] *to be dangerous, be at risk, be risky*

높은 곳에서 뛰어내리는 것은 **위험합니다**.
Jumping off a high place **is dangerous**.

1637- 졸업하다/joreophada [v.] *to graduate*

그녀는 저보다 일 년 더 빠르게 **졸업했습니다**.
She **graduated** from the school one year ahead of me.

1638- 증거/jeunggeo [n.] *proof, evidence*

법정에서는 물적 **증거**를 필요로 합니다.
The court needs any material **evidence**.

1639- 초점/chojeom [n.] *focus, focal point*

저희는 이 토론의 **초점**을 바꿀 필요가 있습니다.
We need to shift the **focus** of this debate.

1640- 포함되다/pohamdoeda [v.] *to be included, come under, include*

그 침대 가격에는 배송비가 **포함되어** 있지 않습니다.
The price of the bed does not **include** the delivery charge.

1641- 호랑이/horangi [n.] *tiger*

세 마리의 **호랑이**가 그들의 눈 앞에서 어슬렁거리고 있었습니다.
Three **tigers** were prowling around in front of their eyes.

1642- 강화하다/ganghwahada [v.] *to strengthen, intensify, reinforce*

최근 몇 년 동안 그 나라는 천연 자원 수출을 제한하는 규정을 **강화해** 왔습니다.
In recent years, the country has **reinforced** regulations restricting the export of natural resources.

1643- 공포/gongpo [n.] *fear, terror, dread, fright, horror, panic*

기쁨이 그녀의 마음에서 모든 **공포**를 몰아냈다.
Joy chased all **fear** from her heart.

1644- 권위/gwonwi [n.] *power, prestige, authority*

그 아버지는 자기 자식들에 대해 전혀 **권위**를 갖고 있지 않습니다.
The father has no **authority** over his own children.

1645- 덜/deol [adv.] *less*

오늘은 어제보다 **덜** 춥습니다.
It is **less** cold today than yesterday.

1646- 둥글다/dunggeulda [a.] *to be round, be circular, be spherical*

지구는 평평하지 않고 **둥글다**.
The earth **is round**, not flat.

1647- 미루다/miruda [v.] *to postpone, delay, put off, put back, defer*

오늘 할 수 있는 일을 내일로 **미루지** 마세요.
Do not **put off** till tomorrow what you can do today.

1648- 부엌/bueok [n.] *kitchen*

저희 엄마는 **부엌**에서 요리를 하고 계세요.
My mom is cooking in the **kitchen**.

1649- 세금/segeum [n.] *tax, duty*

그들은 **세금** 인상이 경제 성장을 둔화시킨다고 주장하고 있습니다.
They argue that raising **taxes** does slow economic growth.

1650- 육체/yukche [n.] *body*

사람들이 말하기를 허약한 **육체**는 마음을 허약하게 만든다고
합니다.
They say a feeble **body** enfeebles the heart.

1651- 입구/ipgu [n.] *entrance, entry, entryway*

건물의 남측 **입구**로 들어오세요.
Please enter the south **entrance** of the building.

1652- 최소한/choesohan [adv.] *at least*

최소한 출발 시각 오십 분 전에 체크인해 주시기 바랍니다.
Please check in **at least** fifty minutes before departure time.

1653- 경험하다/gyeongheomhada [v.] *to experience*

그 이야기들은 여러분들이 실제로 **경험한** 것에 근거해야 합니다.
The stories should be based on what you actually **experienced**.

1654- 넘치다/neomchida [v.] *to overflow, run over, brim over, flood, flow out*

시장에는 비슷한 상품들로 **넘치고** 있습니다.
The market is **overflowing** with similar goods.

1655- 놓치다/notchida [v.] *to let something slip, let*

something go, miss, lose, waste

그는 어제 마지막 버스를 **놓쳤습니다**.

He **missed** the last bus yesterday.

1656- 돌아보다/**doraboda** [v.] *to look back, think back, reminisce, look around*

오늘 지난 해를 **돌아보도록** 해요.

Let us **look back** to the last year today.

1657- 또 다시/**ttodasi** [n.] *again, once more, once again, over again*

그가 **또 다시** 당신을 귀찮게 하면 그녀에게 말하도록 하세요.

Let her know if he bothers you **again**.

1658- 북쪽/**bukjjok** [n.] *north, northward*

대구는 부산의 **북쪽**에 있습니다.

Daegu is **north** of Busan.

1659- 불안하다/**buranhada** [a.] *to be uneasy, be anxious, be insecure, be unstable*

그 나라의 정치 상황은 매우 **불안합니다**.

The political situation in the country **is** very **unstable**.

1660- 쇠고기/**soegogi** [n.] *beef*

실례하겠습니다. **쇠고기**와 생선 중에서 어느 것을 드시겠습니까?

Excuse me, what would you like, **beef** or fish?

1661- 위반/**wiban** [n.] *violation, breach, infringement, infraction*

과속은 교통법 **위반**에 해당합니다.

Speeding is the **infraction** of the traffic laws.

1662- 주/ju [n.] *week, alcohol, state, province*

다음 **주** 아무 때나 편하신 때에 저희와 만나시면 됩니다.

We can meet at your convenience any time next **week**.

1663- 카드/kadeu [.] *card, plastic*

그녀는 신용 **카드**로 음식 값을 지불했어요.

She paid by credit **card** for the food.

1664- 평생/pyeongsaeng [n.] *one's entire life, lifetime*

당신은 **평생**에 있을까 말까 한 이 큰 기회를 절대 놓쳐서는 안
됩니다.

You must not miss this big chance of a **lifetime**.

1665- 관념/gwannyeom [n.] *idea, sense, concept, notion*

그는 시간에 대한 **관념**이 전혀 없어요.

He does not have any **concept** of time.

1666- 굉장히/goengjanghi [adv.] *very, greatly, so, extremely, immensely, really*

그녀는 그 영화를 **굉장히** 지루해했어요.

She was **extremely** bored of the movie.

1667- 단어/daneo [n.] *an individual word, vocabulary*

여러분들이 실제로 사용하는 **단어**는 십오 퍼센트보다 적은 비중을
차지합니다.

The actual **words** you use account for less than fifteen percent.

1668- 덮다/deopda [v.] *to cover, close, shut*

책을 **덮으시기** 바랍니다.

Please, **close** your book.

1669- 도와주다/**dowajuda** [v.] *to help, assist, aid, give (somebody) a hand*

제가 이 과제를 마칠 수 있도록 **도와줄** 수 있나요?

Can you **help** me finish this task?

1670- 배우/**baeu** [n.] *actor (person who performs in a theatrical play or film), actress, (movie) star*

우리 엄마는 내가 유명한 **배우**가 될 것이라고 격려해 주셨다.

My mother encouraged me to be a famous **actor**.

1671- 신발/**sinbal** [n.] *shoes, footwear, footgear*

그 여성 분이 **신발** 끈을 묶고 있습니다.

The woman is tying her **shoe**.

1672- 알/**al** [n.] *egg, roe, grain, bead, spawn*

어미 새는 둥지로 돌아와서 계속해서 **알**을 품었습니다.

The mother bird came back to her nest and continued to incubate the **eggs**.

1673- 여건/**yeogeon** [n.] *conditions*

어려운 **여건**으로 인해 그는 할 수 없이 사업을 그만두게 되었습니다.

Adverse **circumstances** compelled him to close his business.

1674- 오래전/**oraejeon** [adv.] *long ago, long before*

그것은 너무 **오래전** 일이어서 제가 무엇을 했는지 기억을 할 수 없을 것 같아요.

It was so **long ago** that I could not remember what I did.

1675- 계단/**gyedan** [n.] *stairs, staircase, stairway, step*

그 **계단**은 높고 가파릅니다.

The **stairs** are high and steep.

1676- 김치/**gimchi** [n.] *kimchi, a dish made with fermented, seasoned vegetables*

그들은 모든 식사 때마다 **김치**를 먹어요.
They eat **kimchi** at every meal.

1677- 끄덕이다/**kkeudeogida** [v.] *to nod, give a nod*

내 친구가 그녀에게 물어보았을 때, 그녀는 고개를 **끄덕였다**.
She **nodded** to my friend as he asked her.

1678- 낯설다/**natseolda** [a.] *to be strange, be unfamiliar*

매니저라는 직책은 아직 저에게 **낯설어요**.
The title of manager **is** still **strange** to me.

1679- 높이/**nopi** [n.] *height*

이 탑의 **높이**는 십일 미터 이상을 넘어갑니다.
This tower rises to a **height** of over eleven meters.

1680- 닮다/**damda** [v.] *to resemble, look like, take after*

당신은 당신 어머니를 많이 **닮았어요**.
You **look like** your mother a lot.

1681- 뼈/**ppyeo** [n.] *bone*

사람들은 **뼈**를 튼튼하게 하려면 칼슘이 필요합니다.
People need calcium to have strong **bones**.

1682- 성장하다/**seongjanghada** [v.] *to grow, grow up*

그것은 거의 모든 나라에서 지속적으로 **성장하고 있는** 산업입니다.
It continues to be a **growing** industry in nearly every country.

1683- 연결되다/**yeongyeoldoeda** [v.] *to be connected, be joined, be linked, lead, connect*

내년에 이 두 섬은 다리로 **연결될** 것입니다.
These two islands will **be connected** by a bridge next year.

1684- 장사/jangsa [n.] *business, trade, commerce, deal*

그가 스무살이 되었을 때 그의 아버지는 그가 **장사**를 시작하게 하셨다.

His father started him in **business** when he became twenty years old.

1685- 제한/jehan [n.] *limit, restriction, limitation, constraint*

여기에서는 **제한** 속도가 시간당 오십 킬로미터입니다.

The speed **limit** is fifty kilometers per hour here.

1686- 콩/kong [n.] *soybean, bean*

저희 아이들은 당근이나 **콩**을 좋아하지 않습니다.

Our kids do not like carrots or **beans**.

1687- 헤어지다/heeojida [v.] *to part from, separate from, divorce oneself from, break up, split up, be scattered, disperse*

그는 여자친구와 **헤어진** 후에 눈물 젖은 주말을 보내는 것처럼 보였습니다.

He looked like he spent the weekend crying, after **breaking up** with his girlfriend.

1688- 구입하다/guiphada [v.] *to purchase, buy*

당신은 그 제품을 언제 **구입했나요**?

When did you **buy** the product?

1689- 날다/nalda [v.] *to fly*

그 종이 비행기는 아주 멋지게 **난다**.

The paper airplane **flies** really splendidly.

1690- 선장/**seonjang** [n.] *captain (person in command of a ship)*

그 **선장**은 배를 해협 쪽으로 향하게 하려고 시도하고 있는 중입니다.

The **captain** is trying to head the ship for the channel.

1691- 설탕/**seoltang** [n.] *sugar*

그녀는 소량의 **설탕**을 물에 녹였습니다.

She dissolved some **sugar** in water.

1692- 순수하다/**sunsuhada** [a.] *to be pure, be unmixed, be genuine, be innocent*

그들의 사랑은 매우 **순수합니다**.

Their love **is** so **pure**.

1693- 스타일/**seutail** [n.] *style*

그는 자주 자신의 헤어 **스타일**을 바꿉니다.

He often varies his hair **style**.

1694- 시점/**sijeom** [n.] *time, point of view*

저희가 바라는 것은 이 **시점**에서 모든 당사자들이 협력을 했으면 하는 것입니다.

Our hope is that at this **time** all parties will cooperate.

1695- 싸다/**ssada** [a.] *to be cheap, be inexpensive, be low-priced*

저 가게에서 나오는 옷들은 **쌉니다**.

The clothes from that store are **cheap**.

1696- 거짓말/**geojinmal** [n.] *a lie, a false statement*

실제 기록이 없다면, 그것은 **거짓말**일 가능성이 있습니다.

If there is no actual record, it is likely to be **a lie**.

1697- 대단하다/daedanhada [a.] *to be great, be huge, be immense, be outstanding, be awesome*

그녀는 사업 처리하는 능력이 **대단합니다**.
She **is great** at dealing in business.

1698- 매우/daedanhi [adv.] *very (much), so (much), extremely, exceedingly*

저희 아버지는 항상 **매우** 열심히 일하십니다.
My father is always **very** hardworking.

1699- 세계관/segyegwan [n.] *worldview, a view of the world, world view*

당신이 받는 교육은 필연적으로 당신의 **세계관**을 형성하게 됩니다.
Your education is bound to shape your **world view**.

1700- 온통/ontong [n.] *all, wholly, entirely, altogether*

왜 바닥에 **온통** 물이 있나요?
Why is there water **all** over the floor?

1701- 의존하다/uijonhada [v.] *to depend (on something or someone), rely*

앞을 보지 못하는 사람들은 느낌에 많이 **의존합니다**.
Blind people **rely** a lot on touch.

1702- 자세히/jasehi [adv.] *in detail*

그것들에 대해 저에게 **자세히** 얘기해 주시겠어요?
Would you tell me about them **in detail**?

1703- 점심/jeomsim [n.] *lunch, luncheon, midday meal*

당신 회사의 **점심** 시간은 몇 시인가요?
What time is **lunch** at your company?

1704- 정확히/**jeonghwakhi** [adv.] *exactly, accurately, correctly, precisely*

저희는 언제 그 일이 일어났는지 **정확히** 알지 못합니다.
We do not know **exactly** when that happened.

1705- 지치다/**jichida** [a.] *to be exhausted, be tired, be weary, be bored of*

벌써 **지치셨나요**?
Are you already **tired**?

1706- 청년/**cheongnyeon** [n.] *youth, young man*

그 당시에 많은 **청년들**이 국가를 위해 자신들의 목숨을 희생했습니다.
Many **young men** laid down their lives for the country in those days.

1707- 혀/**hyeo** [n.] *tongue*

의사가 제 여동생에게 **혀**를 내밀어 보라고 말했습니다.
The doctor asked my younger sister to put out her **tongue**.

1708- 확대하다/**hwakdaehada** [v.] *to expand, enlarge, magnify, extend*

그 제안된 계획에 따르면 내년에 예산을 **확대할** 것으로 기대됩니다.
The proposed plan is expected to **expand** the budget next year.

1709- 후춧가루/**huchutgaru** [n.] *ground pepper, pepper grounds, black pepper*

후춧가루 좀 저에게 주시겠어요?
Would you pass me **the pepper**, please?

1710- 건설하다/**geonseolhada** [v.] *to build, construct*

그들은 주요 도로를 따라 자전거 전용 도로를 **건설할** 예정인가요?
Are they going to **build** a bicycle path along the main road?

1711- 경쟁력/gyeongjaengnyeok [n.] *competitiveness, competitive power*

부패는 국가 **경쟁력**에 심각한 타격을 줍니다.

Corruption deals a severe blow to national **competitiveness**.

1712- 신용/sinyong [n.] *credit, credibility, confidence, trust*

사람들은 **신용** 카드를 너무 많이 사용하는 경향이 있습니다.

People tend to overuse credit **cards**.

1713- 온몸/onmom [n.] *whole body, entire body*

저는 어제 운동을 너무 많이 했어요. 지금 **온몸**이 아파요.

I exercised too much yesterday and my **whole body** hurts now.

1714- 증상/jeungsang [n.] *symptom (of a disease)*

열은 감기의 **증상들** 중 하나입니다.

A fever is one of the **symptoms** of a cold.

1715- 칼/kal [n.] *knife, sword*

칼은 탁자 위에 있습니다.

The **knife** is on the table.

1716- 출연하다/churyeonhada [v.] *to appear (as on a stage or on TV), make an appearance*

제가 처음 텔레비전에 **출연했을** 때 너무 무서워서 완전히 얼어버렸습니다.

The first time I **appeared** on TV, I was scared stiff.

1717- 건너다/geonneoda [v.] *to cross (a river, ridge, etc.), be moved from one side to another*

거리에 있는 표지판은 사람들이 길을 **건널** 때 조심하도록 경고하고 있습니다.

The street sign cautions people to be careful when **crossing** the street.

1718- 깨다/kkaeda [v.] *to break, smash, shatter, crack, break a record, return to a sober state of mind, wake*

그녀는 그가 그녀의 꽃병을 **깼기** 때문에 화가 났습니다.
She was angry because he **broke** her vase.

1719- 낚시/naksi [n.] *fishing, angling, catching the fish*

그는 하이킹과 **낚시**를 많이 합니다.
He does a lot of hiking and **fishing**.

1720- 다가가다/dagagada [v.] *to approach, get close, go near, come up*

그들이 오기를 기다리지 마시고 먼저 **다가가시기** 바랍니다.
Please, do not wait for them to come, but **approach** them first.

1721- 뛰어들다/ttwieodeulda [v.] *to run, rush, plunge into, dive into, jump into*

그는 다리에서 강으로 **뛰어들었습니다**.
He **jumped** off a bridge into the river.

1722- 문자/munja [n.] *letter, character, alphabet*

비밀번호는 열다섯 개의 **문자**보다 더 길 수는 없습니다.
The password cannot be longer than fifteen **characters**.

1723- 슬프다/seulpeuda [a.] *to be sad, be sorrowful, be mournful, be grieved*

전쟁은 항상 비극적이고 **슬픕니다**.
War **is** always tragic and **sad**.

1724- 신부/sinbu [n.] *bride*

신부가 자신의 친구들에게 부케를 던졌습니다.
The **bride** threw the bouquet to her friends.

1725- 여겨지다/**yeogyeojida** [v.] *to be considered, be regarded, be believed*

그는 그 직책에 가장 잘 맞는 사람 중 하나로 **여겨집니다**.
He **is considered** one of the top choices for the job.

1726- 오징어/**ojingeo** [n.] *squid, cuttlefish*

대부분 모든 종류의 물개들은 물고기, 조개류, 그리고 **오징어**를 먹습니다.
Most types of seals eat fish, shellfish, and **squid**.

1727- 요금/**yogeum** [n.] *fee, charge, fare*

버스 **요금**이 얼마인가요?
How much is the bus **fare**?

1728- 용돈/**yongdon** [n.] *pocket money, allowance*

저희 어머니는 저에게 한 달에 십만 원을 **용돈**으로 주십니다.
My mother allows me one hundred thousand won a month for **pocket money**.

1729- 음료/**eumnyo** [n.] *drink, beverage*

회의 때 사용할 음식과 **음료**는 어떻게 하면 좋을까요?
What will we do about food and **drinks** for the meeting?

1730- 의자/**uija** [n.] *chair, sofa, stool*

탁자 주위에 **의자**가 없네요.
There is no **chair** around the table.

1731- 전해지다/**jeonhaejida** [v.] *to be told, be reported, be conveyed, be handed down, be passed down*

지진으로 인해 백 명이 넘는 사람들이 사망했다고 **전해지고 있습니다**.
It **is reported** that over one hundred people died in the earthquake.

1732- 카메라/**kamera** [n.] *camera (a device for taking still or moving pictures)*

요즘에 그들은 디지털 **카메라**만 사용해요.

These days they use digital **cameras** only.

1733- 통증/**tongjeung** [n.] *pain, ache, agony*

이 약은 **통증**을 완화하는 데 빠르게 작용합니다.

This medicine acts fast to relieve **pain**.

1734- 편리하다/**pyeollihada** [a.] *to be convenient, be handy, be easy*

공공 도서관은 정보를 찾는 데 **편리합니다**.

Public libraries **are handy** for finding information.

1735- 하천/**hacheon** [n.] *river, stream, brook*

호우로 인해 **하천**이 범람하였습니다.

The heavy rain caused **rivers** to overflow.

1736- 현금/**hyeongeum** [n.] *cash*

현금으로 계산하시겠어요, 아니면 신용 카드로 계산하시겠어요?

Will you pay in **cash** or by credit card?

1737- 거칠다/**geochilda** [a.] *to be rough, be coarse, be wild, be desolate*

이 탁자의 표면은 너무 **거칠어요**.

The surface of this table is so **rough**.

1738- 껍질/**kkeopjil** [n.] *skin (of fruit), rind, bark, peel, shell*

그들은 사람들이 사과를 항상 **껍질**이 있는 상태에서 먹어야 한다고 주장합니다.

They argue that people should always eat apples with the **skin** on.

1739- 남부/**nambu** [n.] *the south, southern part*

부산은 한국의 **남부**에 있습니다.

Busan is in **the south** of South Korea.

1740- 명령/**myeongnyeong** [n.] *order, command, instruction*

명령에 대해 복종하지 않는 것은 군대에서는 중대한 범죄에 해당합니다.

Disobedience of **orders** is a serious offense in the military.

1741- 무조건/**mujogeon** [adv.] *unconditionally*

저희 어머니는 저를 **무조건** 지원해 주십니다.

My mom **unconditionally** supports me.

1742- 선택/**seontaek** [n.] *selection, choice, option*

그 대학교는 강의 **선택**의 폭이 넓습니다.

The college offers a wide **choice** of courses.

1743- 역사가/**yeoksaga** [n.] *historian*

역사가가 고서를 탐구하고 있습니다.

A **historian** is delving into an ancient book.

1744- 연구자/**yeonguja** [n.] *researcher, investigator*

그 회사는 최고 수준의 **연구자들**을 고용했습니다.

The company hired a group of top-class **researchers**.

1745- 연기자/**yeongija** [n.] *actor, actress*

그는 매우 뛰어난 가수, 댄서, 그리고 **연기자**입니다.

He is a very good singer, dancer, and **actor**.

1746- 줄기/**julgi** [n.] *branch, trunk, stem, stalk, cane,* *ridge*

나팔꽃 **줄기**가 벽을 따라 나선형으로 감기면서 올라갔습니다.
A trunk of morning glory twisted up along the wall.

1747- 찾아내다/chajanaeda [v.] *to find, discover, locate*

드디어 그녀가 해결책을 **찾아냈습니다**.
Finally, she **found** a solution.

1748- 토요일/toyoil [n.] *Saturday*

이번 주 **토요일**에 무엇을 할 계획인가요?
What are you going to do this **Saturday**?

1749- 경찰관/gyeongchalgwan [n.] *policeman, police officer*

그 **경찰관**은 용의자의 뒤를 쫓아 갔습니다.
The **policeman** ran after the suspect.

1750- 권하다/gwonhada [v.] *to advise, suggest, recommend*

저는 그 일이 즉시 이루어져야 한다고 **권하고** 싶습니다.
I would like to **recommend** that the work should be done at once.

1751- 극장/geukjang [n.] *theater, movie theater, cinema*

그 영화는 몇몇 **극장**에서 상영되고 있습니다.
The movie is playing at several **theaters**.

1752- 신/sin [n.] *God, god*

신 앞에서는 모든 사람들이 평등합니다.
In the sight of **God** all men are equal.

1753- 실내/sillae [n.] *indoor, within a room, interior*

일부 현대 **실내** 디자인에는 거울과 금속재가 많이 사용됩니다.

Some modern **interior** design uses a lot of mirrors and metal.

1754- 쏟다/ssotda [v.] *to pour out, spill, devote*

그녀는 바닥 전체에 커피를 **쏟았습니다**.
She **spilled** the coffee all over the floor.

1755- 연결하다/yeongyeolhada [v.] *to connect, join, attach, link*

새로운 다리는 그 섬을 육지와 **연결할** 것입니다.
The new bridge will **link** the island to the mainland.

1756- 외교/oegyo [n.] *diplomacy*

현재의 상황은 그 나라가 **외교**에서 실패했음을 보여주고 있습니다.
The present situation shows that the country has failed at **diplomacy**.

1757- 주머니/jumeoni [n.] *bag, sack, pouch, pocket*

이 휴대폰은 **주머니**에 넣기에 편리합니다.
This phone is handy for the **pocket**.

1758- 계약/gyeyak [n.] *contract*

그들은 지난 달에 구속력 있는 **계약**을 체결했고 그 계약은 여전히 유효합니다.
They signed a binding **contract** last month and it is still valid.

1759- 나란히/naranhi [adv.] *side by side*

그 두 소녀는 **나란히** 서 있었습니다.
The two girls stood **side by side**.

1760- 부끄럽다/bukkeureopda [a.] *to be embarrassed, be*

shy, be shameful, be ashamed

그녀와 이야기를 나누고 싶지만, 전 너무나도 **부끄럽습니다**.

I would like to talk with her, but I **am** too **shy**.

1761- 성공/seonggong [n.] *success, hit*

그들은 **성공**하기 위해 밤낮으로 고군분투하고 있습니다.

They are struggling for **success** day and night.

1762- 알아듣다/aradeutda [v.] *to understand, follow, see, get, recognize, make out*

제가 의미하는 바를 **알아듣겠어요**?

Do you **understand** what I mean?

1763- 일행/ilhaeng [n.] *party, company, troupe*

저희 **일행**에는 단지 다섯 사람만 있습니다.

There are just five in our **party**.

1764- 지식인/jisigin [n.] *intellectual*

지식인들의 목소리가 그에게 어떤 영향을 미칠까요?

What effect will the voices of **intellectuals** have on him?

1765- 진지하다/jinjihada [a.] *to be sincere, be earnest, be serious, be sober*

그녀는 모든 일에 있어서 너무 **진지해요**.

She **is** too **serious** about everything.

1766- 호흡/hoheup [n.] *breath, breathing, respiration*

호흡은 보통 무의식적으로 이루어지는 활동입니다.

Breathing is usually an involuntary action.

1767- 흔들리다/heundeullida [v.] *to shake, waver,*

wobble, quake, sway, swing, rock

나무가 바람에 **흔들리고** 있습니다.

The trees are **shaking** in the wind.

1768- 기온/**gion** [n.] *air temperature, temperature*

온도계는 **기온**의 변화를 측정합니다.

The thermometer measures changes of **temperature**.

1769- 날아가다/**naragada** [v.] *to fly (away, off), be blown away, be gone, be lost*

우산이 하늘에서 **날아가고** 있습니다.

The umbrella is **flying** in the sky.

1770- 많아지다/**manajida** [v.] *to pile up, increase, get more*

요즘에 과체중인 어린이들의 수가 **많아지고** 있습니다.

These days the number of overweight children is **increasing**.

1771- 바위/**bawi** [n.] *rock, boulder, crag*

많은 양의 **바위**가 산 아래로 굴러 떨어졌습니다.

A lot of **rocks** fell down the mountain.

1772- 버릇/**beoreut** [n.] *habit (an action done on a regular basis), manners, bad behavior*

그 아버지는 자기 자녀의 **버릇**을 고치기 위해 노력했습니다.

The father tried to correct his child's **behavior**.

1773- 비판하다/**bipanhada** [v.] *to criticize*

많은 사람들이 새로운 정책을 **비판하고** 있습니다.

A number of people are **criticizing** the new policy.

1774- 빨갛다/ppalgata [a.] *to be deep red, be red*

대부분의 토마토는 익으면 **빨갛습니다**.

Most tomatoes **are red** when ripe.

1775- 세워지다/sewojida [v.] *to be founded, be constructed, be built, go up*

어디에 풍력 발전소가 **세워지고 있나요**?

Where **is** a wind power station being **built**?

1776- 일부러/ilbureo [adv.] *deliberately, intentionally, on purpose*

그녀는 **일부러** 그 정보를 언론에 흘렸습니다.

She **intentionally** leaked the information to the press.

1777- 절반/jeolban [n.] *half*

원하신다면, **절반** 가격에 그것을 구입할 수 있습니다.

If you want, you can buy it at **half** price.

1778- 접근하다/jeopgeunhada [v.] *to approach, come close, get close*

버스가 나무 쪽으로 **접근하고** 있습니다.

The bus is **approaching** the tree.

1779- 편안하다/pyeonanhada [a.] *to be comfortable, be relaxed, be easy, be calm*

저희 거실에 있는 소파는 부드럽고 **편안합니다**.

The couch in my living room is soft and **comfortable**.

1780- 풍경/punggyeong [n.] *landscape, scenery, scene, view, sight*

그 건물은 그곳 **풍경**과 잘 어울리지 않습니다.

The building does not blend in with the **landscape**.

1781- 확실히/hwaksilhi [adv.] *surely, certainly, definitely, unquestionably, for certain, for sure, without doubt*

당신은 **확실히** 알고 있나요, 아니면 단지 추측일 뿐인가요?

Do you know **for sure** or is it only conjecture?

1782- 흩어지다/heuteojida [v.] *to scatter, disperse*

그녀의 가족들은 전국 전역에 **흩어져** 있습니다.

Her family members are **scattered** across the country.

1783- 갈다/galda [v.] *change, replace*

제가 지금 에어 필터를 **갈까요?**

Do you want me to **change** the air filter now?

1784- 교류/gyoryu [n.] *exchange, interchange*

그 두 나라는 문화 **교류**를 하고 있습니다.

The two countries make cultural **exchanges**.

1785- 글쓰기/geulsseugi [n.] *writing*

그 방법은 **글쓰기** 연습에 쓰일 수 있습니다.

The method can be used for **writing** practice.

1786- 기후/gihu [n.] *climate (longterm atmospheric conditions)*

기후와 농작물 사이에는 서로 밀접한 관계가 있습니다.

There is close correlation between **climate** and crops.

1787- 대기업/daegieop [n.] *large company, conglomerate, major firm, big company, big enterprise*

제 친구들은 같은 **대기업**에 입사했어요.

My friends entered the same **big company**.

1788- 대응하다/**daeeunghada** [v.] *to correspond to, react, reply, respond*

저희 또한 그들에게 공격을 당하게 된다면 **대응할** 것이라고 위협해 왔습니다.

We also have intimidated to **respond** if we are attacked by them.

1789- 도구/**dogu** [n.] *instrument, tool, kit, implement, means*

이 **도구**는 다양한 용도로 사용됩니다.

This **tool** serves many purposes.

1790- 매력/**maeryeok** [n.] *charm, attractiveness, appeal, magnetism*

그녀는 굉장히 **매력**이 있는 숙녀입니다.

She is a lady with a lot of **charm**.

1791- 백/**baek** [number] *one hundred*

백 살까지 사는 사람은 거의 없습니다.

Few live to be one **hundred** years old.

1792- 보험/**boheom** [n.] *insurance*

이 **보험**의 보장내역은 무엇인가요?

What does this **insurance** cover?

1793- 부럽다/**bureopda** [a.] *to be enviable, be envious*

제가 새 차를 구입해서 제 친구들이 너무나도 **부러워해요**.

My friends **are** so **envious** because I have bought a new car.

1794- 섞이다/**seokkida** [v.] *to mix, be mixed, blend, mingle*

물은 다른 액체와 **섞일** 수 있습니다.

Water can be **mixed** with other liquids.

1795- 소/**so** [n.] *cow, bull, ox, cattle, smallness, small things*

그 농부가 **소**를 끌고 가고 있습니다.
The farmer is leading the **cattle**.

1796- 쏘다/**ssoda** [v.] *to shoot, fire a shot, treat, pay for someone's drink or meal*

군인들은 나라를 지키기 위해 대포를 **쐈습니다**.
The soldiers **fired** cannons to protect their country.

1797- 위치하다/**wichihada** [v.] *to be located, lie*

그의 집은 산에 **위치하고 있습니다**.
His house **is located** on the mountain.

1798- 달성하다/**irukhada** [v.] *to achieve, accomplish*

그 연구소는 과학에 있어서 놀라운 발전을 **달성했습니다**.
The research institute **achieved** a remarkable development in science.

1799- 이틀/**iteul** [n.] *two days*

그녀는 여기에 **이틀** 동안 머물 것입니다.
She will stay here for **two days**.

1800- 전달하다/**jeondalhada** [v.] *to convey, pass on, transmit, communicate, forward*

전 세계에 있는 사람들은 특정한 메시지를 **전달하기** 위해 몸짓이나 또는 제스처를 사용합니다.
People around the world use body movements or gestures to **convey** specific messages.

1801- 정말로/**jeongmallo** [adv.] *really, truly*

그녀가 **정말로** 너를 좋아한다면, 너를 이해하려고 노력할 거야.
If she **really** likes you, she will try to understand.

1802- 켜다/kyeoda [v.] *to turn something on, to light an oil lamp or candle, strike a match or lighter, to play the string instrument*

그가 집에 돌아왔을 때 먼저 텔레비전을 **켰습니다**.
When he came back home, he first **turned on** the television.

1803- 행동하다/haengdonghada [v.] *to behave, act, conduct*

책임감 있는 방식으로 **행동하는** 게 좋을 거예요.
You better **behave** in a responsible way.

1804- 형사/hyeongsa [n.] *detective, investigator, criminal case*

그 **형사**는 사건 현장을 주위 깊게 조사하였습니다.
The **detective** carefully surveyed the scene.

1805- 희곡/huigok [n.] *play, drama*

이 **희곡**은 일반적으로 셰익스피어의 작품으로 여겨집니다.
This **play** is generally ascribed to **Shakespeare**.

1806- 공항/gonghang [n.] *airport*

저를 인천 **공항**까지 태워다 줄 수 있나요?
Can you give me a ride to Incheon **airport**?

1807- 군인/gunin [n.] *soldier*

저 **군인들**은 군 부대 내에서 생활하고 있습니다.
Those **soldiers** are living inside a military compound.

1808- 그늘/geuneul [n.] *shade, shadow*

그 소년들은 **그늘** 안에 앉아 있습니다.
The boys are sitting in the **shade**.

1809- 급하다/geuphada [a.] *to be urgent, be pressing, be impetuous, be rash, be rapid*

그녀는 정말 똑똑하지만, 때때로 성격이 **급한** 경향이 있습니다.
She is so smart, but she tends to **be rash** at times.

1810- 달걀/dalgyal [n.] *a hen's egg*

그 가게는 **달걀**을 낱개로 팔아요.
That store sells **eggs** by the piece.

1811- 대중문화/daejungmunhwa [n.] *pop culture*

그들은 텔레비전 드라마와 같은 한국의 **대중문화**를 좋아합니다.
They like Korean **pop culture**, like TV dramas.

1812- 마련되다/maryeondoeda [v.] *to be prepared, be arranged*

이 공연은 어르신들을 위해서 **마련되었습니다**.
This performance **was arranged** for the elderly.

1813- 마루/maru [n.] *floor, floor's covering, especially for wood flooring, the top of a roof or mountain*

저희 아버지는 **마루**를 닦고 계십니다.
My dad is mopping the **floor**.

1814- 무게/muge [n.] *weight*

지붕이 눈의 **무게**로 인해서 무너져 내렸습니다.
The roof collapsed under the **weight** of the snow.

1815- 성적/seongjeok [n.] *achievements, accomplishments, (school) grade, (exam) result, mark, record*

대학교 다닐 때 학교 **성적**은 어땠나요?
How were your **grades** in college?

1816- 솔직히/soljikhi [adv.] *honestly, frankly, truthfully, plainly*

솔직히 저는 그 선물이 마음에 들지 않아요.
I do not like the present, **honestly**.

1817- 시도하다/sidohada [v.] *to try, attempt*

담배를 끊어 보려고 **시도해** 본 적이 있나요?
Have you **tried** to quit smoking?

1818- 아니요/aniyo [interjection] *no*

그녀가 저에게 이것을 좋아하냐고 물어본다면, 저는 '**아니요**'라고 말할 것입니다.
If she questions me whether I like this, I will say '**no**'.

1819- 인터넷/inteonet [n.] *internet (specific internet consisting of the global network of computers)*

인터넷은 사람들이 쇼핑을 하는 방식을 바꿔오고 있습니다.
The **Internet** has been changing the way people shop.

1820- 적용하다/jeogyonghada [v.] *to apply*

당신은 같은 과정을 그들에게 **적용할** 수 있습니다.
You can **apply** the same process to them.

1821- 참가하다/chamgahada [v.] *to take part, participate, engage, enter*

이제 그녀는 성인 대회에 **참가할** 수 있어요.
Now she can **take part** in senior competitions.

1822- 치마/chima [n.] *skirt*

저는 오늘 **치마**와 블라우스를 입을 거예요.
I will wear a **skirt** and a blouse today.

1823- 친척/chincheok [n.] *kin, kinsmen, relatives*

그녀에게는 유명한 영화 배우인 먼 **친척**이 있어요.
She has a distant **relative** who is a famous movie star.

1824- 호텔/hotel [n.] *hotel (establishment providing accommodation)*

저는 종로역 근처에 있는 **호텔**을 찾고 있어요.
I am looking for a **hotel** near the Jongro station.

1825- 경계/gyeonggye [n.] *boundary, border*

그 울타리는 저의 땅과 그의 땅의 **경계**를 표시하고 있습니다.
The fence marks the **boundary** between my land and his.

1826- 공식/gongsik [n.] *formula, formality, being formal*

이 **공식**은 원의 면적을 계산하는 데 사용됩니다.
This **formula** is used to calculate the area of a circle.

1827- 깎다/kkakda [v.] *to cut, shave, peel, sharpen, reduce, discount*

제 아들이 저에게 연필을 **깎아** 달라고 말했어요.
My son asked me to **sharpen** a pencil.

1828- 따라가다/ttaragada [v.] *to follow, go after, catch up*

저 건물 끝까지 이 길을 **따라가세요**.
Follow this road to the end of that building.

1829- 머물다/meomulda [v.] *to stay, visit*

얼마나 여기에 **머물** 거예요?
How long will you **stay** here?

1830- 명예/myeongye [n.] *honor, fame, credit*

명예를 잃는다면 무엇이 남겠습니까?
What is left when **honor** is lost?

1831- 뱃사람/baetsaram [n.] *sailor, seaman, crewman, fisherman*

바이킹은 힘이 센 **뱃사람**으로 잘 알려져 있습니다.
Vikings are well-known as strong **sailors**.

1832- 숙이다/sugida [v.] *to bend, bow (one's head), incline, stoop, duck*

저희는 선생님을 만나서 인사를 할 때 보통 고개를 **숙입니다**.
We usually **bow** when we meet and greet a teacher.

1833- 온도/ondo [n.] *temperature (a measure of cold or hot)*

방의 **온도**를 어떻게 조절하나요?
How do I control the room **temperature**?

1834- 이마/ima [n.] *forehead, brow*

그녀는 자신의 손등으로 **이마**를 닦았어요.
She wiped her **forehead** with the back of her hand.

1835- 지붕/jibung [n.] *roof*

그는 저기 **지붕** 색이 파란 삼층 건물에 살고 있습니다.
He lives in that three-story building with the blue **roof**.

1836- 지원하다/jiwonhada [v.] *to support, aid, apply for*

그녀의 아버지는 최대한으로 그녀를 **지원하였습니다**.
Her dad **supported** her as best as he could.

1837- 짙다/jitda [a.] *to be dense, thick (of a solution, composition), be deep, be dark (of a color), be high (of probability)*

오늘은 안개가 **짙습니다**.
Today, the fog **is thick**.

1838- 청소/cheongso [n.] *cleaning, sweeping*

저 부부는 요리와 **청소**를 두 사람이 같이 합니다.
That couple shares the cooking and the **cleaning**.

1839- 침묵/chimmuk [n.] *silence, reticence*

그는 그녀의 **침묵**을 거절로 해석했습니다.
He translated her **silence** as a refusal.

1840- 텍스트/tekseuteu [n.] *text (a written passage)*

보내고자 하는 메시지 **텍스트**를 입력하세요.
Enter the message **text** you want to send.

1841- 표면/pyomyeon [n.] *surface, face*

그 길의 **표면**이 거칠어요.
The **surface** of the road is rough.

1842- 걱정하다/geokjeonghada [v.] *to worry, be concerned*

그것에 대해 **걱정하지** 않으셔도 됩니다.
You do not have to **worry** about that.

1843- 구름/gureum [n.] *cloud*

하늘에 큰 **구름**이 보이나요?
Can you see a big **cloud** in the sky?

1844- 구석/guseok [n.] *corner, a remote place*

그녀의 방 **구석**에는 피아노가 있었습니다.
There was a piano in a **corner** of her room.

1845- 끄다/kkeuda [v.] *to extinguish, quench, douse a fire or light, turn off the electricity*

잠시만 텔레비전을 **꺼** 주세요.
Please, **turn off** the television for a while.

1846- 담당하다/**damdanghada** [v.] *to take charge, be in charge*

누가 광고를 **담당하나요**?

Who **is in charge** of advertising?

1847- 둥지/**dungji** [n.] *nest*

그 아이는 어제 나무에 올라가서 새 **둥지**를 발견했습니다.

The child climbed up a tree and found a bird's **nest** yesterday.

1848- 벗기다/**beotgida** [v.] *to take off, undress, peel, skin, strip*

포장재를 **벗기고** 열어 보세요.

Peel and open the package.

1849- 부대/**budae** [n.] *(military) unit, troops, corps*

그 **부대**는 소수 정예의 사람들로 운영되고 있습니다.

The **unit** operates with a few good people.

1850- 시청자/**sicheongja** [n.] *viewer*

얼마나 많은 **시청자들**이 그 프로그램을 시청하고 있나요?

How many **viewers** are watching the show?

1851- 엄격하다/**eomgyeokhada** [n.] *to be strict, be severe, be stern, be rigid, be rigorous*

기내 금연은 매우 **엄격합니다**.

The prohibition of smoking in the aircraft **is** very **strict**.

1852- 완벽하다/**wanbyeokhada** [a.] *to be perfect, be immaculate, flawless*

그 땅은 농사 짓기에 **완벽합니다**.

The land **is perfect** for farming.

1853- 완전하다/**wanjeonhada** [a.] *to be complete, be full, be perfect*

완전한 문장에는 마침표를 사용해야 합니다.
You need to use end punctuation for **complete** sentences.

1854- 학기/**hakgi** [n.] *semester, trimester, term, quarter*

이번 **학기**에 그녀는 영어 수업에서 사학점을 땄습니다.
She earned four credits in her English course this **semester**.

1855- 한동안/**handongan** [adv.] *for a while, for a long time, for some time*

저는 **한동안** 극장에 가지 않았어요.
I have not been to the movie theater **for a long time**.

1856- 계절/**gyejeol** [n.] *season (of the year)*

한국에서 겨울은 스키를 타기에 가장 좋은 **계절**입니다.
Winter is the best **season** for skiing in South Korea.

1857- 만지다/**manjida** [v.] *to handle, manage, touch, feel*

동물을 **만지지** 마세요.
Please do not **touch** the animals.

1858- 목사/**moksa** [n.] *pastor, minister, clergyman, priest*

그 **목사**는 이 교회를 삼십 년 동안 섬겼습니다.
The **pastor** has served this church for thirty years.

1859- 바늘/**baneul** [n.] *needle, pin, (clock) hand*

그녀는 단추를 바느질하기 위해 **바늘**과 실을 찾았습니다.
She looked for a **needle** and thread to sew the button.

1860- 버티다/**beotida** [v.] *to endure, withstand, bear,*

stand

이번 여름의 더위를 **버티는** 것이 저에게는 쉽지 않네요.
It is not easy for me to **stand** the heat of this summer.

1861- 비중/**bijung** [n.] *specific gravity, importance, weight*

이 문제에 더 많은 **비중**을 둘 필요가 있습니다.
This problem should be given more **weight**.

1862- 아이디어/**aidieo** [n.] *idea*

그의 **아이디어**는 항상 아주 현실적입니다.
His **ideas** are always very down to earth.

1863- 예컨대/**yekeondae** [adv.] *for example, for instance, such as*

예컨대, 기존의 시스템은 업데이트가 되어야 합니다.
For **instance**, the existing system has to be updated.

1864- 운동장/**undongjang** [n.] *schoolyard, stadium, field, playing field, playground, sports grounds*

많은 학생들이 **운동장**에서 놀고 있습니다.
Many students are playing on the **playground**.

1865- 접촉/**jeopchok** [n.] *contact, touch, connection, association, interaction*

그 바이러스는 신체 **접촉**을 통해 감염됩니다.
The virus is transmitted via physical **contact**.

1866- 짐/**jim** [n.] *load, burden, package, parcel, cargo, freight, luggage*

차에 **짐**을 실어 주세요.
Please, load up your **luggage** into the car.

1867- 풀/pul [n.] *grass, green, glue*

그 말은 **풀**을 먹고 있어요.

The horse is eating the **grass**.

1868- 해마다/haemada [adv.] *every year, annually, year after year, yearly*

그 날은 **해마다** 기념되고 있습니다.

The day is celebrated **every year**.

1869- 휴가/hyuga [n.] *vacation, holiday, leave, break*

저희 남편은 여름 **휴가**로 일주일의 시간을 갖습니다.

My husband has a week for summer **vacation**.

1870- 계곡/gyegok [n.] *valley*

계곡은 두 산 사이에 있는 낮은 지역입니다.

A **valley** is an area of low land between two mountains.

1871- 국회의원/gukhoeuiwon [n.] *member of congress, congressman, member of the National Assembly, lawmaker, member of Parliament*

그는 한때 **국회의원**으로 있었습니다.

He was once a **member of the National Assembly**.

1872- 다투다/datuda [v.] *to argue, fight, quarrel*

서로 **다투는** 일을 그만 하도록 합시다.

Let us make an end of **arguing** with each other.

1873- 솔직하다/soljikhada [a.] *to be honest, be frank, be direct, be straightforward*

저는 항상 그녀에게 **솔직해요**.

I **am** always **frank** with her.

1874- 요청하다/**yocheonghada** [v.] *to request, claim, ask*

수리를 **요청하고** 싶으시면, 이 번호로 연락해 주세요.
If you'd like to **ask** for a repair, call this number.

1875- 일치하다/**ilchihada** [v.] *to agree, resemble, coincide, correspond, be in concordance*

새로운 정책은 사람들이 원하는 것과 **일치합니다**.
The new policy **is in concordance** with what the people want.

1876- 젓다/**jeotda** [v.] *to stir, churn, row*

그들은 배를 **저어서** 바다를 건너고 있어요.
They are **rowing** a boat across the ocean.

1877- 축제/**chukje** [n.] *festival, carnival*

그 축제는 언제 열리죠?
When will the **festival** take place?

1878- 학습/**hakseup** [n.] *learning, study*

게임이 **학습**에 도움이 될까요?
Do games aid in **learning**?

1879- 개발되다/**gaebaldoeda** [v.] *to be developed*

그 기술은 최근에 **개발되었습니다**.
The technology **was developed** recently.

1880- 당연히/**dangyeonhi** [adv.] *naturally, of course*

당연히 항상 예외는 있습니다.
Of course, there are always some exceptions.

1881- 대비하다/**daebihada** [v.] *to prepare, provide for*

젊었을 때 은퇴 생활에 **대비해야** 합니다.
When you are young, you need to **prepare for** retirement.

1882- 동쪽/dongjjok [n.] *east*

바람은 **동쪽**에서 불고 있습니다.

The wind is blowing from the **east**.

1883- 떨리다/tteollida [v.] *to shake, tremble*

제 손이 너무 **떨려서** 글을 쓸 수 없었습니다.

My hand **trembled** so much that I could not write.

1884- 만남/mannam [n.] *meeting, encounter*

저희는 그것을 고전과 현대의 **만남**이라고 부를 수 있습니다.

We can call it a **meeting** of the classical and the modern.

1885- 미디어/midieo [n.] *media*

그들은 요즘에 소셜 **미디어**를 너무 자주 사용합니다.

They use social **media** too often these days.

1886- 복도/bokdo [n.] *corridor, hallway, passage*

이 **복도**는 홀로 통합니다.

This **corridor** opens into the hall.

1887- 쓰러지다/sseureojida [v.] *to fall, collapse*

나무가 땅에 **쓰러졌습니다**.

The tree **fell** to the ground.

1888- 영상/yeongsang [n.] *picture, image, video*

원하는 경우, 시작하기 전에 **영상**을 볼 수 있습니다.

If you want, you can view the **video** before you begin.

1889- 영혼/yeonghon [n.] *soul (the spirit or essence of a person)*

그는 돈 때문에 자신의 **영혼**을 팔았습니다.

He sold his **soul** for money.

1890- 운전사/**unjeonsa** [n.] *driver (person who drives a motorized vehicle, such as a car or a bus)*

버스 **운전사**가 아직 안 왔어요.
The bus **driver** is not here yet.

1891- 자랑스럽다/**jarangseureopda** [a.] *to be proud*

저희 어머니는 제가 한 일을 정말 **자랑스럽게 여겼습니다**.
My mother **was** really **proud** of what I did.

1892- 잠깐/**jamkkan** [adv.] *(for a) short time, for a moment, awhile, briefly*

잠깐 얘기를 나눌 수 있을까요?
Can I speak to you **a moment**?

1893- 적당하다/**jeokdanghada** [a.] *to be fit, be suitable, be adequate, be proper*

저 집은 두 사람이 살기에 **적당합니다**.
That house **is suitable** for two people.

1894- 적용되다/**jeogyongdoeda** [v.] *to apply*

이 법은 한국인과 외국인 모두에게 **적용됩니다**.
The law **applies** to both Koreans and foreigners.

1895- 진행하다/**jinhaenghada** [v.] *to progress, make progress*

그녀는 자신의 프로젝트를 **진행하고** 있습니다.
She is **proceeding** with her project.

1896- 차별/**chabyeol** [n.] *discrimination*

그들은 성**차별**에 대해서 이야기를 나누었습니다.
They discussed gender **discrimination**.

1897- 둘러보다/dulleoboda [v.] *to look around, take a glance around*

학부모님들이 학교를 **둘러볼** 기회가 있을 것입니다.
There will be a chance for parents to **look around** the school.

1898- 분노/bunno [n.] *rage, anger, indignation, fury*

그들의 **분노**는 파업으로 이어졌습니다.
Their **anger** led to strikes.

1899- 비교/bigyo [n.] *comparison*

돈을 절약하고 싶다면 **비교** 구매를 하는 것이 좋을 것입니다.
You had better do **comparison** shopping if you want to save your money.

1900- 소위/sowi [n.] *so-called*

그것은 **소위** 대박 할인이 될 수 있을 것입니다.
It is a **so-called** super discount.

1901- 열차/yeolcha [n.] *train*

이것은 서울행 **열차**인가요?
Is this the **train** for Seoul?

1902- 영원히/yeongwonhi [adv.] *forever, eternally*

그는 그녀와 **영원히** 함께하겠다고 약속했다
He promised to stay with her **forever**.

1903- 의무/uimu [n.] *duty, obligation*

그는 세금 납부를 그의 **의무**로 하고 있습니다.
He holds paying taxes as his **duty**.

1904- 잃어버리다/ireobeorida [v.] *to lose, no longer have*

in one's possession

제가 열쇠를 **잃어버렸기** 때문에 저희 엄마가 화가 났습니다.

My mom was angry because I **lost** the key.

1905- 잠들다/jamdeulda [v.] *to go to sleep, fall asleep, sleep*

차의 모든 창문이 닫혀진 채로 차에서 **잠들지** 않도록 주의하세요.

Be careful not to **fall asleep** in the car with all the windows shut.

1906- 조용하다/joyonghada [a.] *be silent, be quiet, be still, be calm*

모든 아이들이 밖에 있기 때문에 이제 **조용합니다**.

Now it **is quiet** because all the kids are outside.

1907- 즉시/jeuksi [adv.] *immediately, promptly, instantly, at once*

계약서에 따르면, 그들은 저에게 **즉시** 돈을 지불해야 합니다.

According to the contract, they have to pay me **immediately**.

1908- 탑/tap [n.] *a tower or similar tall structure, (Buddhism) a pagoda or such a monument that has evolved from the archaic stupa*

이 **탑**은 높이가 팔 미터 이상에 이릅니다.

This **tower** rises to a height of over eight meters.

1909- 귀엽다/gwiyeopda [a.] *to be cute, be charming, be adorable, be sweet*

아기의 통통한 볼은 너무 **귀여워요**.

The baby's round cheeks **are** so **cute**.

1910- 당황하다/danghwanghada [a.] *to be embarrassed, be flustered, be taken aback, be bewildered*

그녀는 너무 **당황해서** 무엇을 해야 할 지 잊어버렸습니다.

She **was** so **embarrassed** that she forgot what to do.

1911- 동일하다/dongilhada [a.] *to be the same, be identical, be equal*

저 영화의 제목은 원작의 책과 **동일합니다**.
The title of that movie **is the same** as that of the original book.

1912- 떨어뜨리다/tteoreotteurida [v.] *to drop*

그녀는 자신의 지갑을 **떨어뜨렸습니다**.
She **dropped** her purse.

1913- 똑같이/ttokgachi [adv.] *equally, evenly, impartially, alike, likewise, identically*

이 빵을 **똑같이** 나누도록 해요.
Let us share this bread **equally**.

1914- 밀가루/milgaru [n.] *(wheat) flour*

밀가루와 계란이 섞일 때까지 저어 주어야 합니다.
You should stir the **flour** and the eggs until blended.

1915- 바지/baji [n.] *pants, trousers*

저는 이 **바지**와 어울리는 셔츠가 필요해요.
I need a shirt to match these **pants**.

1916- 보고서/bogoseo [n.] *(written) report, paper*

보고서를 언제 끝낼 예정인가요?
When will you finish your **report**?

1917- 보관하다/bogwanhada [v.] *to keep*

그 약은 아이들의 손이 닿지 않는 곳에 **보관해야** 합니다.
You need to **keep** the medicine out of the reach of children.

1918- 부딪치다/**buditchida** [v.] *to strike, hit, bump into, collide with, face, crash*

차들이 길에서 서로 **부딪쳤습니다**.
The cars **collided with** each other on the road.

1919- 빨래/**ppallae** [n.] *laundry*

제가 **빨래**를 할게요.
I will do the **laundry**.

1920- 상하다/**sanghada** [v.] *to go bad (sour, rotten), get stale, get hurt, be offended, grow emaciated*

당신의 기분을 **상하게 해서** 너무나도 죄송합니다.
I am so sorry to **hurt** your feelings.

1921- 식용유/**sigyongnyu** [n.] *cooking oil*

이 조리법에서는 버터 대신에 **식용유**를 사용해도 됩니다.
You can substitute **cooking oil** for butter in this recipe.

1922- 싫어하다/**sireohada** [v.] *to hate, dislike, to not like*

그녀는 콘택트렌즈 끼는 것을 **싫어합니다**.
She does **not like** wearing contact lenses.

1923- 피곤하다/**pigonhada** [a.] *to be tired, be exhausted, be weary, be worn out*

그는 하루 종일 운전을 해서 **피곤합니다**.
He **is tired** from having driven all day.

1924- 한국어/**hangugeo** [n.] *the Korean language*

그녀는 **한국어**를 배우는 데 관심이 많습니다.
She is so interested in learning **the Korean language**.

1925- 근육/geunyuk [n.] *muscle*

팔을 굽히게 되면 **근육**이 수축됩니다.
When you bend your arms, your **muscles** contract.

1926- 사전/sajeon [n.] *dictionary, encyclopedia*

영어 **사전**은 A 자부터 시작합니다.
The English **dictionary** starts with the letter A.

1927- 산소/sanso [n.] *oxygen*

산소는 인간의 삶에 있어서 필수적입니다.
Oxygen is essential to human life.

1928- 석유/seogyu [n.] *oil, petroleum*

전쟁이 시작되자 **석유** 가격이 뛰어올랐습니다.
The price of **oil** jumped up when the war started.

1929- 소리치다/sorichida [v.] *to shout, call out, yell (utter a sudden and loud outcry)*

지나가는 사람들을 향해 **소리치고** 있는 저 남자는 자주 이상하게 행동을 합니다.
That man who is **shouting** at passing people often behaves oddly.

1930- 신선하다/sinseonhada [a.] *to be fresh*

이 상추는 신선합니다.
This lettuce **is fresh**.

1931- 안경/angyeong [n.] *glasses, spectacles*

그 여성 분은 **안경**을 쓰고 있습니다.
The woman is putting on her glasses.

1932- 약속하다/yaksokhada [v.] *to promise*

그는 제 손실에 대해 저에게 보상하겠다고 **약속했어요**.

He **promised** to compensate me for my loss.

1933- 연합/yeonhap [n.] *federation, coalition, alliance, union*

유럽 **연합**에 얼마나 많은 회원국이 있는지 알고 있나요?

Do you know how many member states are in the European **Union**?

1934- 조심하다/josimhada [v.] *to be careful, beware, watch*

가위를 사용할 때 **조심하세요**.

Be **careful** when you use the scissors.

1935- 질/jil [n.] *quality, nature, disposition, matter*

당신은 서비스 **질**에 대해 만족하시나요?

Are you content with the **quality** of the service?

1936- 찌르다/jjireuda [v.] *to prick, stab, pierce, poke, nudge*

그는 그녀의 옆구리를 **찔렀습니다**.

He **poked** her in the ribs.

1937- 총/chong [n.] *gun, rifle, machine gun*

그는 **총**에 실탄을 장전했습니다.

He loaded the cartridges into the **gun**.

1938- 취미/chwimi [n.] *hobby, interest, taste*

옛날 동전을 수집하는 것은 사람들이 많이 하는 **취미** 중 하나입니다.

Collecting old coins is a popular **hobby**.

1939- 품목/pummok [n.] *item, article*

당신은 그곳에서 면세 **품목**을 구입하실 수 있습니다.
You can buy duty-free **items** there.

1940- 확대되다/hwakdaedoeda [v.] *to be expanded, be magnified, be inflated, expand*

여성을 위한 취업 기회가 **확대되었습니다**.
Employment opportunities for women **have expanded**.

1941- 덥다/deopda [a.] *to be hot, be warm*

5월인데도 너무 **더운** 것 같아요.
I think it **is** too **hot** for May.

1942- 부작용/bujagyong [n.] *side effect*

이것의 **부작용**은 위험할 수 있습니다.
The **side effect** of this can be dangerous.

1943- 야구/yagu [n.] *baseball*

야구는 한국에서 아주 인기 있는 스포츠 중 하나입니다.
Baseball is a very popular sport in South Korea.

1944- 위협/wihyeop [n.] *threat, menace*

그녀는 그녀를 해고하겠다는 사장의 **위협**에 겁을 먹은 것 같습니다.
She seemed to be frightened by the boss's **threat** to fire her.

1945- 잠기다/jamgida [v.] *to sink, be submerged, be absorbed in, be flooded*

폭풍으로 인해 그 집들이 물에 **잠겼습니다**.
The houses **were sunk** under water by the storm.

1946- 주먹/jumeok [n.] *fist, blow, punch*

그는 **주먹**으로 탁자를 내려쳤습니다.

He struck down the table with his **fist**.

1947- 경고/gyeonggo [n.] *warning, caution*

그들은 **경고**에 주의를 기울이지 않았습니다.
They did not heed the **warning**.

1948- 공개하다/gonggaehada [v.] *to make something or someone noticeable to the public, make public, release, uncase*

주요 언론 매체는 그 이름을 **공개하지** 않았습니다.
The major news media did not **release** the name.

1949- 과목/gwamok [n.] *subject (at school), course*

수학은 제 아들이 가장 흥미를 느끼는 **과목**입니다.
Math is the most interesting **subject** to my son.

1950- 달아나다/daranada [v.] *to escape, flee, run away*

그 강도는 범죄 현장에서 **달아났습니다**.
The burglar **ran away** from the scene of the crime.

1951- 묶다/mukda [v.] *to tie up, bind, restrict, limit, constrain, pull together*

쓰레기 봉투를 **묶어** 주세요.
Please, **tie up** the garbage bag.

1952- 신다/sinda [v.] *to wear on one's feet, put on, slip on*

그녀는 그 신발을 **신었어요**.
She **wore** those shoes.

1953- 유교/yugyo [n.] *Confucianism*

유교는 한국 사람들의 삶에 영향을 미쳤습니다.

Confucianism influenced the lives of Korean people.

1954- 이불/ibul [n.] *duvet, blanket, covers, comforter, bedding*

이불이 부드럽고 푹신푹신해요.
The **bedding** is soft and fluffy.

1955- 이성/iseong [n.] *opposite sex, reason, logic, rationality, intellect*

그가 그러한 말을 했을 때 저는 **이성**을 잃었습니다.
I lost my **reason** when he said such a thing.

1956- 중요성/jungyoseong [n.] *importance, significance*

저희 아버지는 제가 열심히 일하는 것의 **중요성**을 배우기를 원했습니다.
My dad wanted me to learn the **importance** of working hard.

1957- 특별히/teukbyeolhi [adv.] *especially, in particular, specially*

그 비디오는 **특별히** 학교용으로 제작되었습니다.
The video was **specially** produced for school use.

1958- 품질/pumjil [n.] *quality (of a product)*

이 제품은 **품질** 면에서 최고입니다.
This product is the best in **quality**.

1959- 훔치다/humchida [v.] *to steal*

차를 **훔쳤던** 그 남자는 체포되었습니다.
The man who **stole** a car got arrested.

1960- 흔적/heunjeok [n.] *trace, evidence, vestige, tracks,*

sign

그 남자는 **흔적**도 없이 사라졌어요.
The man disappeared without a **trace**.

1961- 구분하다/gubunhada [v.] *to classify, sort, separate*

저희는 보통 쉼표를 사용해서 항목들을 **구분합니다**.
We usually use a comma to **separate** entries.

1962- 뇌/noe [n.] *brain*

신체 운동은 여러 측면에서 **뇌**를 돕습니다.
Physical exercise helps the **brain** in many ways.

1963- 봉투/bongtu [n.] *envelope (wrapper for mailing), bag, sack*

그는 편지를 **봉투**에 넣었습니다.
He inserted the letter into an **envelope**.

1964- 추억/chueok [n.] *recollection, reminiscence, memory, remembrance*

그녀는 어린 시절에 대한 **추억**에 잠겨 있습니다.
She is absorbed in **memory** of childhood.

1965- 하여튼/hayeoteun [adv.] *anyway, anyhow, in any case, at any rate*

하여튼 제가 곧 다시 연락드리겠습니다.
Anyway, I will call you back soon.

1966- 향기/hyanggi [n.] *fragrance, aroma, perfume, scent, redolence*

그 방은 장미 **향기**로 가득 차 있었습니다.
The room was filled with the **fragrance** of roses.

1967- 가늘다/ganeulda [a.] *to be thin, be slender, be fine*

그것은 길고 매우 **가늘어요**.

It is long and very **slender**.

1968- 근무하다/geunmuhada [v.] *to work (as a career for a person)*

그녀는 그 회사에서 십 년 동안 **근무했습니다**.

She **has worked** for ten years at the company.

1969- 넓히다/neolphida [v.] *to expand, widen, extend, broaden*

그들은 많은 교통량으로 인해 도로를 **넓히기로** 결정했습니다.

They decided to **widen** the road due to the heavy traffic.

1970- 매년/maenyeon [adv.] *every year, annually*

그 축제는 **매년** 이 시기에 열립니다.

The festival is held at this time **every year**.

1971- 손바닥/sonbadak [n.] *palm (inner, concave part of a hand)*

박수를 칠 때 손의 **손바닥**이 서로 부딪치게 됩니다.

When you clap, you hit the **palms** of your hands together.

1972- 장점/jangjeom [n.] *advantage, strength, merit, virtue, strong point*

그는 새로운 제품의 많은 **장점들**을 광고했습니다.

He advertised many **advantages** of the new product.

1973- 줍다/jupda [v.] *to gather up, pick up*

그녀는 저에게 길에서 지갑을 **주웠다고** 말했어요.

She told me that she **picked up** a wallet on the street.

1974- 킬로그램/killogeuraem [n.] *kilogram*

밀가루는 **킬로그램** 단위로 팝니다.
Flour is sold by the **kilogram**.

1975- 평범하다/pyeongbeomhada [a.] *to be average, be ordinary, be common, be mediocre, be normal*

그녀의 외모는 **평범합니다**.
She **is average** in appearance.

1976- 방금/banggeum [adv.] *just a moment ago, just now*

그는 **방금** 떠났어요.
He **just** left.

1977- 생선/saengseon [n.] *fish (as food)*

생선 가격은 더 비싸질 것입니다.
Prices for **fish** will be higher.

1978- 슬픔/seulpeum [n.] *sadness, sorrow, grief*

슬픔에 대한 유일한 치료제는 행동하는 것입니다.
The only cure for **grief** is action.

1979- 이튿날/iteunnal [n.] *next day, the following day*

제가 온라인으로 주문한 책이 **이튿날** 도착했습니다.
The book I ordered online arrived **the next day**.

1980- 제거하다/jegeohada [v.] *to exterminate, remove, eliminate*

여러분은 쉽게 연락처 정보를 추가하고 **제거할** 수 있습니다.
You can add and **remove** contact information easily.

1981- 줄다/julda [v.] *to decrease, shrink, diminish,*

lessen

최근에 지원자의 수가 **줄었습니다**.

The number of applicants **has decreased** recently.

1982- 지우다/**jiuda** [v.] *to erase, rub out, wipe away, make someone carry, load something up, charge (a person with a duty)*

저는 그 일을 기억에서 **지웠어요**.

I **erased** the event from my memory.

1983- 참기름/**chamgireum** [n.] *sesame oil*

참기름 없이는 이 요리의 맛을 완벽하게 만들 수 없습니다.

You cannot make this food perfect without **sesame oil**.

1984- 합치다/**hapchida** [v.] *to combine, merge, unite, join together*

두 약을 하나의 알약으로 **합쳤습니다**.

It **combined** two drugs in a single pill.

1985- 호기심/**hogisim** [n.] *curiosity*

그 아이는 **호기심**에 찬 눈으로 그것을 보았습니다.

The child eyed it with **curiosity**.

1986- 골목/**golmok** [n.] *alley, byway, backstreet, alleyway*

그 **골목**에는 그라피티가 많이 있습니다.

The **alleyway** has a lot of graffiti.

1987- 동화/**donghwa** [n.] *fairy tale, children's story*

그 이야기는 마치 **동화** 같네요.

The story sounds like a **fairy tale**.

1988- 두껍다/dukkeopda [a.] *to be thick*

그 얼음은 당신의 무게를 충분히 버틸 수 있을 정도로 **두껍습니다**.
The ice **is thick** enough to bear your weight.

1989- 모자라다/mojarada [v.] *to be short, be inadequate, be deficient, be insufficient*

그는 항상 돈이 **모자릅니다**.
He **is** always **short** of money.

1990- 상상하다/sangsanghada [v.] *to imagine*

그것은 제가 **상상했던** 것보다 훨씬 더 아름다웠습니다.
It was more beautiful than I had **imagined**.

1991- 생산력/saengsannyeok [n.] *productivity, productive capacity, production power*

그 정책은 **생산력** 증대를 위해 고안된 것입니다.
The policy is designed to boost **productivity**.

1992- 안전하다/anjeonhada [a.] *to be safe*

헬멧을 쓰는 것이 **안전합니다**.
It **is safe** to wear a helmet.

1993- 유학/yuhak [n.] *studying abroad, studying overseas*

유학에 관한 많은 인기 책들을 확인해 볼 수 있을 것입니다.
You can check many popular books about **studying abroad**.

1994- 장비/jangbi [n.] *equipment, gear, apparatus*

그 일을 하려면 저희는 무슨 **장비**가 필요할까요?
What **equipment** will we need for the job?

1995- 정치인/**jeongchiin** [n.] *politician, statesman*

저 **정치인**에게는 부유한 많은 후원자들이 있습니다.
That **politician** has many wealthy backers.

1996- 끓다/**kkeulta** [v.] *to boil*

차 주전자의 물이 **끓고** 있습니다.
The water in the teapot is **boiling**.

1997- 농담/**nongdam** [n.] *joke, jest*

그는 **농담**을 진담처럼 말합니다.
He tells a **joke** like a truth.

1998- 닭/**dak** [n.] *chicken, hen, rooster, cock, fowl*

이 **닭**은 매일 계란 하나를 낳습니다.
This **hen** lays an egg every day.

1999- 맥주/**maekju** [n.] *beer*

집에 가는 길에 잠시 들려서 **맥주**를 마십시다.
Let us stop for a **beer** on the way home.

2000- 모래/**morae** [n.] *sand*

사막의 **모래** 언덕은 바람에 의해 형성됩니다.
The **sand** dunes on the desert are formed by the wind.

CONCLUSION

And thus, we've finally reached the very end of this wonderful list of the *2000 Most Common Words in Korean*! Be glad - your vocabulary has been greatly increased. Just remember: don't be too harsh on yourself! Learning a language is a gradual process - you have to keep doing it. To be honest, Korean is one of the hardest languages to learn, so take your time. Once you feel comfortable with the basics of the Korean language, consider taking a trip to South Korea.

We are happy to have helped you with your practice of Korean and hope to see you again soon; we'll surely meet again in future books and learning materials.

So, take care and study hard, and don't forget the tips we gave you at the beginning if you want to become a Korean pro!

1. Repetition
2. Concentration
3. Application
4. Movement
5. Associations

With that said, we've covered every single thing. Now go out and learn some more Korean — you're already more than halfway there! I believe you can understand much more of K-drama, K-pop, etc.

PS: Keep an eye out for more books like this one; we're not done teaching you Korean! Head over to **www.LingoMastery.com** and read our free articles, sign up for our newsletter and check out our **YouTube channel**. We give away so much free stuff that will accelerate your Korean learning and you don't want to miss that!

If you liked the book, we would really appreciate a little review wherever you bought it.

THANKS FOR READING!

CPSIA information can be obtained
at www.ICGtesting.com
Printed in the USA
LVHW081336030920
664984LV00019B/1858